The Hills of Wales

Impressions, Explorations,
Recollections

The Hills of Wales

Impressions, Explorations, Recollections

from the notebooks and writings of
JIM PERRIN

Gomer

Published in 2016 by
Gomer Press, Llandysul, Ceredigion, SA44 4JL

ISBN 978 1 78562 146 8

A CIP record for this title is available from the British Library.

This book is published with the financial support of the
Welsh Books Council.

Printed and bound in Wales at
Gomer Press, Llandysul, Ceredigion
www.gomer.co.uk

For Conor Gregory

indefatigable stravaiger

I remember when my mother was seventy and I was looking forward to rather a gentle walk with her, she insisted that we ascend Arenig Fawr, which is a rough hill. She was always particularly enthusiastic about her hills. Both she and my father were very sound towards me when I was a child. When I complained of cold and hunger, as I must often have done at an early age, they would cajole me if need be. I remember the first time the hills became a pleasure rather than a pain for me was on the Bwlch y Rhiwgyr above Bontddu. As we arrived on top of the ridge, my father began to recite Keats's sonnet 'On first looking into Chapman's Homer', and there in front of us was that skyline of the Llŷn Peninsula over the water, stretching down to Ynys Enlli. There came a magic that day which the Welsh hills have never lost for me – I was under their spell.

Ioan Bowen Rees

Contents

Foreword   ix

Introduction   xiii

PART ONE:
The Northern March   1

PART TWO:
On High Hills   17

PART THREE:
West of Snowdon   71

PART FOUR:
Between Glaslyn and Dyfi   97

PART FIVE:
Around Dyffryn Tanat   169

PART SIX:
The Middle March   203

PART SEVEN:
Elenydd   216

PART EIGHT:
The Southern Ramparts   247

ENVOI:
Hill of the Angels   275

Suggested Further Reading   277

Foreword

When I was a young radio arts producer who dreamed every minute of becoming a writer, I vowed that should it ever happen for me I would live in London. Broadcasting House, an Art Deco ship sailing down Portland Place, has welcomed (and persuaded) talkers and writers of every kind and passport through its doors since they opened in 1932. We had great ghosts. Our smoking room was the disused basement studio where Dylan Thomas out-acted Richard Burton. MacNeice and Orwell had staff passes. But it was easier, quicker and cheaper to fly in a writer from, say, Venice, than it was to get one down from Snowdonia.

London-based 'creatives' thus held and still hold a decisive advantage before and during the ongoing era of cuts which followed the vengeance of the Hutton Enquiry (into the BBC's coverage of the Iraq war) in 2004. Hampstead or Brixton to the studio was and is no challenge at all. Hence my career-minded vow. Geography is destiny, said someone, and although this might not be true it may explain why Jim Perrin is a reader's writer, and writer's writer, and not yet really a listener's or a screen-watcher's writer. Alas for them.

But this is to the advantage of Perrin's great works and his very many devotees. Who can write well under the world's eyes? Suppose we stand on the slopes of Yr Wyddfa. The mountain is described with reference to Afghanistan, Faerieland, King Arthur and its climbing cliffs, arrayed, in fact, in all its natural and human history, art and awe in Perrin's majestic little volume *Snowdon: The Story of a Welsh Mountain*, which precedes the one you hold. Now. See? There! And there – you overlook the roosts of a hidden host of writers little seen or heard in the British broadcast media.

Go to Berlin, New York, Paris, Rotterdam, Hong Kong or Sarajevo and someone will tell you all about Jan Morris, Jay Griffiths, Jim Perrin, Niall Griffiths, Justin McGuinness, Gillian Clarke or some of many resounding others, of several generations. All Wales, but peculiarly North and Mid Wales (because South Wales to London is easy) enfolds and conceals some of the greatest and most distinctive producers of contemporary European literature. And this without our Irish sea-cousins' advantage of a genuine literary performance culture. Extraordinary and electrifying performances of the written word do take place in Wales, especially at our famous festivals and eisteddfodau (many readers will have seen some or all of the writers named and implied above at them) but song still takes precedence in the hills. We are at least a decade – or is it nine centuries? – behind Ireland's mastery of the local, live performance of writing, and so our literature exists in gossip, conversation, in jokes and on the page.

One funny thing is how Welsh these writers are, and how other-than-Welsh many sound on tape. Wales takes you in – if it is not already in you, which it generally is – and makes you hers. Accent, colour and creed be blowed. Dylan and R. S. Thomas sound even more English than me. (I inherited the classic BBC English/Received Pronunciation 'advantage' imposed by the English on the parents of the mighty Thomases and their children from my own post-colonial parents, one a Lloyd-Williams.) Jan 'Trefan Morys' Morris has a timeless British Imperial voice. Niall Griffiths sounds as Scouse as the Mersey. Jim Perrin has a soft, confiding tone such as you might hear under the hubbub of a good Manchester pub. A quiet Northwestern accent is one of the most seductive of our isles: I fell for a girl from Rochdale, and the only time I saw him speak, at Y Gelli, during a Hay Festival, I fell for Jim Perrin.

It was said of Chekov that the evident, obvious goodness of the man made you behave at your best and reach for more than your best in his company. I think this is true of all the great artists I have met. Perrin's presence, and perhaps his (very Northern) reputation for no backward steps and no prisoners taken, made me stumble up to him afterwards and stammer out something heartfelt and self-hating (I was in depression) about being a middle-class dilettante, and very sorry for it, and being his devoted fan. With few words he drained all the humbug and anxiety out of me, invited me on a walk which I will always wish I had been able to join, and sent me on my way elated. (I remember the way he walked. He lopes with a bounce like a boulder rolling over flat ground.)

This only matters because any of Perrin's books will do the same service for you, should you suffer blues. Read them in equanimity and you will be given delight, knowledge, company and the elevation only art and learning can bring. He is the most rigorous of scholars and the most fluent of stylists. Read him on nature. Read him on men. Read him on loss. Read him on love, on sex, on fatherhood, on the spirit world. Read him on women and read him on rock. Often you can do all this in a single one of his publications, and sometimes in a couple of hundred of his words for a newspaper.

I am fighting to resist mentioning this, Perrin's new book on the hills of Wales. The great treat awaiting you over the page has its proper introduction, from its author. Those hills, our hills, are the secret of Wales. I write this during the Brexit summer, with blood, money, politics, fanaticism and fear stomping abroad with even more than their usual fury, apparently. What stuff and what nonsense! In the hills we will remember this, another Jim Perrin publication year, as the time Wales delighted the television-watching world with an unexpected foray into a game we were not known to play. Travelling Europe in the aftermath I discovered that many of our football-loving continental brothers and sisters still do not know where to find us, which seems right and normal. But they do like us, very much. And for this and other Celtic and Anglo-Saxon reasons they like Britain too, in spite of everything London does (Llundain, Caer Lludd, named after a Welsh king, of course).

Life is hills and valleys, our mother taught us, as she raised us on the slopes of Pen Allt-mawr. Only let the hills be high, I learned to pray. Ours are not, really, or are they? Wales is a small coat made entirely of deep pockets. One attempt to record its sacred sites failed utterly when the compilers ascertained that every village and hamlet regarded every little feature of their small territories as sacred, and had stories about them too. The main point is worth making twice: our secret is in our hills, which belong to any who walk or think on them. You would have to cross them all and read the entire library of Aberystwyth in all its languages to grasp that secret fully, but as you will see now, Jim Perrin has done a deal of that joyous work for you. Hereafter it is set down.

Horatio Clare
Hardcastle Crags
August 2016

Introduction

This book is a companion volume to my *Snowdon: The Story of a Welsh Mountain* (Gomer, 2012), in which I sought to tell the story of Wales's finest mountain from historical, literary, folkloric and social perspectives. It's also the third in a set of themed essay collections, the first two being on travel and on climbing from 2002 and 2006 respectively. In those books I brought together, significantly juxtaposed and extensively re-written, all that seemed worthy of preservation from large bodies of my work on these subjects. The present volume, concerned with a lifetime's explorations on foot, rather than seeking to apply *Snowdon*'s more formal approach to a wide-ranging description of Welsh hill country, attempts instead to give an impressionist and subjective account of the hills of Wales, drawn from an archive produced over many decades and presented here in revised and re-drafted form. These, if you like, are sketches from the notebook or extracts from the journals, worked up into a fragmented narrative and commentary. I have devoted space again to Snowdon, but not much – for the detail on Wales's highest hill you must look to the other book. Nor would I make any claim for what follows as comprehensive gazetteer. It's no such thing. Plenty of perfectly worthy hills are missed out, or only mentioned in passing. If your favourites happen to be among these, don't take this as qualitative dismissal. I'd have been thrilled to write, for example, or to have included writings on, Pencaergybi, Carmel Head, Yr Eifl, Rhobell Fawr, Tarren Hendre, Gorllwyn, Hergest Ridge, Mynydd Mallaen, The Blorenge, or Beacon, Gwaunceste and Cilfaesty Hills, all of which have meaning, association and attraction for me; and I would have done, had a million words been at my disposal instead of a scant 80,000. Perhaps as recompense the *aficionado* will be pleased to encounter Craig yr Allor, Gyrn Moelfre, Cefn Gwyntog, Waunygriafolen, Whimble – and if not yet acquainted, thus come to know their characters and locations? If here and there I've been partisan about choice of base and route for ascent, may I plead that these have been incidental to my main purpose, which is to give the flavour, the atmosphere of hills among which I've spent the greater part of my life.

What I've opted for, then, are impressions, accounts of personal explorations, journeyings, sojournings, encounters, rather than the inventorizings of the guidebook approach. This is not a guidebook; plenty of far better examples of those are available than I could write (though I would hope in passing to give you plenty of detailed information about your hill-objectives). It is more in the nature of peripatetic literary celebration. Its companion volume on Snowdon drew some criticism for the lack of photographs and maps. Their absence, there and here, is to make a point. As with guidebooks, plenty of picture-books are available for those who like to leaf idly through such things until their size and weight induces fatigue and causes them to be put aside. This is a different kind of book, one for reading, its approach an older and more discursive one. The pedestrian writers I admire, from Thomas Pennant and William Hazlitt, George Borrow and Gerald Brenan, Walter Starkie and Augustus John to Thomas Firbank, Paddy Leigh Fermor and Patrick Monkhouse, would have recognized where I'm going and the means used for getting there. So too would the modern Welsh poets to whom I continually return – Parry-Williams, Williams Parry, Gwyn Thomas, Gwenallt, Kitchener Davies, Waldo Williams, Euros Bowen – all of whom give the lie to the recreational community's occasional misconception that the Welsh do not know their own hills. On maps, in no way is the present text a substitute for a map, and I'd thoroughly recommend having O.S. 1:25,000 sheets to hand to follow many of the itineraries described. They will add immeasurably to any enjoyment you may derive from the text. For my part, I'd as soon read a map as a book, its information being interpretable at so many levels.

Of my own connection with these hills, let me say briefly that it began in ragged childhood when I made my first solitary ventures out from the northern city where I grew up, and saw these hills where my refugee Huguenot ancestors had found work and safety centuries ago ranged along the western horizon. I found my way to them, discovered there a freedom all too few young people are afforded in our contemporary society, and a welcoming indigenous community too, infused with old knowledge of the land. The hills of Wales haunted my consciousness then, and they do so still, inexhaustibly, always offering new perspectives, moods and experiences. The ones given to me over six decades of – useful Scottish word! – *stravaiging* among them, I now share with you, the readers, in the hope that you will find something here to entice, sustain and delight. What has particularly absorbed me over many years has been the nature of change in this landscape. It is not now as I first knew it. Much has been lost or despoiled, particularly in that desperate decade of the 1980s when political ideologues let loose ravening demon hosts upon the land. So in a sense the writings collected here have an elegiac quality, and a further purpose as chronicle of record, of description of things as they were in a rapidly evolving society with ever greater demands upon the environments in which it lives. I'm reminded in writing this of George Sturt's questioning from the years before and after the Great War, expressed in books such as *Change in the Village* (1912) and *The Wheelwright's Shop* (1923). In a significant passage from the former, Sturt writes:

Out of all these circumstances – the pride of skill in handicrafts, the detailed understanding of the soil and its materials, the general effect of the well-known landscape, and the faint sense of something venerable in its associations ...there proceeded an influence which acted upon the village people as an unperceived guide to their conduct, so that they observed the seasons proper for their varied pursuits almost as if they were going through some ritual. Thus ... when, on an auspicious evening of spring, a man and wife went out far across the common to get rushes for the wife's hop-tying, of course it was a consideration of thrift that sent them off; but an idea of doing the right piece of country routine at the right time gave value to the little expedition. The moment, the evening, became enriched by suggestion of the seasons into which it fitted, and by memories of years gone by.

The crucial question implicitly posed here is one with which contemporary society still wrestles; and to which – despite increasing cultural signs of a yearning for the renewal of a close relationship with nature – we have yet to find an adequate answer: what measure of compensation can be found in contemporary life for the loss of connection with process and the natural cycle which was woven through the whole human life-fabric in a pre-industrial world, the disappearance of which has left us with a kind of psychic insubstantiality by comparison with those who, in the marvelling and resonant phrase of the American nature-writer Barry Lopez, 'radiate the authority of first-hand encounters'? As a child of the inner-city, reared by aged grandparents who had been transplanted there from the countryside and whose hearth-talk expressed and retained their sense of natural wonder and yearning for the green life, their beliefs in sympathetic magic and the shamanic presence of bird and beast, that connection with the natural cycle had become by the age of twelve an obsession with me. Even before then I was steeped in the work of Richard Jefferies and Henry Williamson, had copies of *Bevis* and *Tarka* on near-permanent loan from Rusholme library.

My grandparents having died and my parents being too preoccupied with marital strife to pay much attention to what I was doing, even before I was in my teens at every conceivable opportunity I walked out of the city – quite literally at first, having used my school bus-pass to get to the outskirts – and took to wandering. Wales then became my focus. I became expert at evading attention and the payment of fares on trains; I hitch-hiked, caught buses; most of all I walked – immense distances, to look back on which now amazes me. In tattered clothes and leaking boots, carrying an old army rucksack, a primus stove, porridge and a sleeping bag, I slept in haylofts and under hedges, in telephone boxes and bus shelters, among rocks, in ancient castles, beneath the trees of quiet copses. Sometimes I was taken into farmhouse kitchens, dried out, kindly interrogated, sent on my way with stories and directions, a belly full of tea and *llaeth enwyn*, bread and butter and cake, and often a bag of eggs and a slice of ham carved from the one hanging in the inglenook and wrapped in greaseproof paper for my supper, to cook out of the wind and rain under a boulder or behind some mountain wall. If fate dealt me a meagre hand in terms of home place, providence watched over me in the richness of these solitary travels and the opulence of experience they brought. I made my way throughout the hill-country of Wales, and came to know and love its people and culture at a time when it was still a place with an indigenous community of old tradition that I could recognize from the heart-talk of my grandparents.

Much of this texture has vanished now. What I encountered then was on a significant cusp. The land – a crucial concept that politicians so seldom grasp, as well as a physical reality – has been exploited and marred, its natural life depleted, its affective quality diminished. Yet the hills remain as vantage points, beacons of hope, and the efforts of those who shore up and preserve their physical texture can be so heartening, are so valuable in retaining what's left, the detail of which is anyway still subject to the transformational sorceries of weather and light. 'Allan ar y mynyddoedd,/ Ac yn y cymoedd amyneddgar,/ Hwy a wynebant yr estronwynt,/ A phob hin.' ('Out there on the mountains, and in the patient valleys, they face the alien wind and all weather.') In what follows, I have sought to celebrate the essential qualities of Welsh hill country, and to record the harm done to it and warn against the continuance of that assault. These hills are vital to the physical and spiritual health of a nation, and remain so, however we may abuse them, and by whatever means we seek to engage with them. Where government and capital connive to ruin wild beauty and misinform the populace of their intentions, only the passion of hill-loving communities can save and protect. May the younger outdoor generations become aware of all the manifold threats even from those who claim to be saviours of the planet, and continue the long traditions that best preserve the fabric of the land. It is so crucial now, and is in their hands.

It only remains to record my gratitude to all who have accompanied, instructed and guided me among the Welsh hills over so many years. Particular thanks, then, to Roger Alton, Shan Ashton, Keith Bowen, Bill Bowker, Mark Charlton, Mark Cocker, Bill and Penny Condry, David Cox, Bill Curtin, Cecil Davies, Monsignor James Dunn, Siân Melangell Dafydd, Paul and Nancy Evans, Kevin FitzGerald, Anthony Griffiths, Niall Griffiths, Mary Hill, John Angelo Jackson, Dewi Jones, Rebecca

Loncraine, Jack Longland, Isobel Macleod, Jane MacNamee, Cameron MacNeish, Sian Northey, Owen Wyn Owen, Ioan Bowen Rees, Bob Rickford, Evan Roberts ('Ifan Gelli'), John Ellis Roberts, Myfanwy Roberts, Sam Roberts, Showell Styles, Tony Shaw, Gwyn Thomas ('Yr Athro'), Amanda Townend, Jan Wolf and Ray Wood. Special thanks to Horatio Clare, most elegant and attentive of young miscellaneous prose writers in English, for his graceful and generous foreword. I also need to thank the editors – Cameron McNeish, Celia Locks, Emily Rodway and Anne-Marie Conway in particular – of various publications in which earlier versions of some of these pieces have appeared for their encouragement and permission to reproduce. My apologies to anyone I may, through inattention or growing forgetfulness, have omitted. For permission to use quotations, my thanks where appropriate to the copyright holders (the sources are acknowledged in the text, rather than in the habitually inauthentic contemporary padding device of the immense bibliography). Finally, the debt I owe to the scrupulousness and enthusiasm for this project of my editor at Gomer, Ceri Wyn Jones, is, as always, immense.

Llanystumdwy, Gorffennaf 2016

PART ONE

The Northern March

The first Welsh hills you encounter, coming into the country from north-west England as I invariably did in my early ventures, are those of Flintshire. I still retain a fondness for the low eminences – Hope and Halkyn Mountains – that look down on the Sands of Dee, and they always bring with them an odd poignancy in their sense of past exploitation. Also, they have a sense of long histories. Here, political and administrative borders never quite tally with the historical, leaving writers on landscape free to cross and reclaim as they will.

MOTHER MOUNTAIN

For one reason and another these last few weeks I've frequently found myself driving back to Wales from the flat lands of Cheshire, of The Wirral, of Merseyside. Whatever bleak foreground I've been passing through, time and again behind and above, spreading her comfortable, familiar shape along the western horizon, has been Moel Famau ('the Mother Mountain'), highest point of the Clwydian range and one of the most visited hills in Britain. Because I had not been up here for several years, having a couple of hours to spare recently and the need to get some exercise upon me, I drove up to the Bwlch Penbarras, parked at the top of the pass among the midweek afternoon throng, and set off northwards into a flaying wind along the broad path that winds up to the summit belvedere on the reconstructed remains of the Jubilee Tower ('... built in 1810 to commemorate the fiftieth year of the reign of George the Third... at one time [it] sported a spire nearly 200 feet high. This has mercifully crashed, but what remains is bad enough.' – Patrick Monkhouse). People of all ages, shapes and sizes ambled or panted up there too as I dawdled along, and sight of them all intent on this popular objective set my mind drifting around certain themes.

Foremost among them was the maintained and constructed quality of the path I was following, and I thought of all the labour that had gone into its creation. It reminded me of the furore years ago at the Snowdonia National Park's footpaths restoration scheme on Snowdon itself – of how members of the outdoor community had then inveighed against Park Authority 'vandalism', and paths that were 'reaching motorway proportions'. It seemed to me then, as it seems to me now, that some hills fall inevitably victim to their own popularity. The arguments adduced against minimizing environmental impact of visitor numbers and against defining and maintaining the popular lines of ascent are for the most part fuelled by rather an unpleasant elitism – a questioning of people's rights to be there – by which standards I'm quite sure I would have been judged inadequate at the outset of my own outdoor enthusiasm and involvement. They're closely related to, and as self-serving maybe and beside the point, as Dr Johnson's famous supposed maxim, 'That which is popular cannot be good' – a statement there is no evidence that he ever uttered. That which is popular can on occasion be very good indeed, and that it suffers by its popularity does not detract from its innate quality. Snowdon to my mind is the most majestic and interesting hill south of the Scottish border, and the equal of many to the north of it. But it's one of the mother mountains, and all that nurturing it accords to us has left it in need of some care and kind attention itself. Thus also with Moel Famau....

There is another factor, though, to be taken into account with Moel Famau, and one which brings me back to its presence in those journeyings of the first paragraph; it is visibility...

You can see Moel Famau from a great swathe of the flat lands of north-western England, rising there westerly against the sunset as the first rampart of Wales. So it has allure, and how can we gainsay any who succumb to that? We have all done so. My going into the outdoors, my journeyings there, came about not through having read about the hills so much as from having seen them – those same hills and moors, rimming the eastern bounds of Manchester, that Robert Roberts in his autobiographical slum classic, *A Ragged Schooling*, termed 'the ramparts of paradise' – on fine days at the end of every street or rearing above the houses to define the horizon in every one of that city's scuffed green spaces. It is not the subtle or the understated or the more quietly suggested that attracts us when we are young, but the obvious and the accessible, which is what the hills and moors of the Dark Peak and those of Wales rising westwardly beyond the Cheshire Plain were for me in my earliest teens. However well-known their ways might be, to everyone who goes there for the first time, the journeys among them are ones of exploration. I can remember now the thrill of walking out from Hayfield, Kinder Low in front of me, and arriving at the top of Jacob's Ladder with all that lovely configuration of landscape leading down into Edale. What did it matter that thousands had passed this way and worn down through the sparse soil to the flaking red strata beneath, so that the descent was all clattery and skittering discomfort?

However threadbare, it was then – and surely now from old memory would still be – beautiful to me. I remember it now, not having been that way for decades, in much the same way that I recall my grandmother, pillowy-bosomed in a faded print dress and apron, nurturing and kind. Let the passion come later – her soft care was enough for infancy, as gentling along an old hill bridle path was kind and nurturing for an outdoor infancy. And memorable, too, in the long retrospect. All the hills that invite – Kinder wrapping itself round my field of vision and disturbing with its craggy tors, its veiling mists and distances; remote Ben Alder plunging away eastwardly towards the long silvering of Loch Ericht – we come to them strong from the security of early and easeful attachments, in which Box Hill, Moel Famau, Jacob's Ladder will all have had their place.

For all that, necessarily we move on if we are not to stay infantilized in our experience of the outdoors. The made paths and supervised ways ultimately encourage only dependency, and no good parent would desire that for a child. Apron strings are no aids to exploration. Only in the freedom to make our own way, and our own mistakes, do we grow (small wonder then that hill-going increases in popularity as an adjunct to twenty-first century living). In the hills we discover not the solipsisms of what we are – which for all our society's stress on revealing them will anyway remain forever concealed until provoked by the contingent – but what's there, truly, in the external world, which is enduringly beautiful for all our marring of it; and also the continuing resonance, subtle and faraway, of what has been.

(1999)

TIME'S LANDSCAPES

These autumn days, when the leaves burn up with the ferocity of their own colour, put me in pensive mood. Thoreau had it that in each of us there is 'a need to witness our limits transgressed', and the mountains, the hills, the sea and their seasons and their weather – all our outdoor landscapes – are exquisitely tuned to provide that yearned-for dimension. But as well as the exterior I like too the anterior, often turn – and particularly at this time of year – to the human perspectives that stretch across time and landscape. I find them in their way as satisfying, as demanding of the engaged and moral imagination, as I have ever found the unalloyed elemental in those few places – American wilderness country, the Arctic, the *altiplano* of Bolivia, the Himalaya – where it is still to be found. When I surrender to that impulse to let land dwarf me, I am simply taking, through the agency of awe, the first daylight step towards extinction of the ego, towards the *'noche oscura'* of St. John of the Cross's most perfect lyric, which is the gateway to religious experience:

> En la noche dichosa,
> En secreto, que nadie me veia,
> Ni yo miraba cosa,
> Sin otra luz y guia,
> Sino la que en el corazon ardia.

> (Upon that lucky night
> In secrecy, inscrutable to sight,
> I went without discerning
> And with no other light
> Except for that which in my heart was burning.)

I can have no argument with that. It seems to me a crucial part, an underpinning, of the whole outdoor experience, and one through which, just possibly, we may come to treat each other, the world, even ourselves, better than we might in its absence. And I love its allied sense, the Wordsworthian 'serene and blessed mood/ In which the burthen of the mystery,/In which the heavy and the weary weight/Of all this unintelligible world/Is lifted'. It has its own rigour too, but still, there are times when I don't want its suspensions and stillnesses, when I would rather take my discernment with me than be 'without discerning', when I'm happy with the mystery and the unintelligible nature of the world and would rather puzzle over that than what might lie beyond it or at the heart of it – when I'm happier, in fact, poring over the pages maybe of W.G. Hoskins' *The Making of the English Landscape* than I would be in reciting the lines of even the greatest of the poet-mystics. I love the completed sense of people's work upon the land, remember so many days spent walking out of towns along disused railways or along canal towpaths, or wandering amongst abandoned, echoing quarries bitten into the flanks of Welsh mountains. I have a picture in my mind at this moment of a winter's day of my youth spent heading into the Cheshire countryside on the bank of the Macclesfield Canal, red sun rising over wintry hills, ice crazed into jagged patterns on the canal's surface. I like at times to see the mark of the human on the face of the land, respond to it every bit as eagerly as I do to what, since the late eighteenth century, we have been taught to look on as the sublime. The former gives you something to question, pictures to create in your mind, purposes to unravel, the jigsaw of history to piece together from the disparate elements of fact, feature, literature, place, imagination and mood.

There was a morning, for example, as the sun heaved and dragged itself free of mist and fume that sprawled grey and grimy all across the Cheshire Plain before illuminating these first hills of Wales where my home then lay, when I walked up on to Wat's Dyke. It's an earthwork, solid, seemingly simple, perhaps constructed in the eighth century and running from a point close to Basingwerk Abbey on the Dee Estuary to somewhere a little south of Oswestry. I say perhaps because there is no consensus of expert opinion about when it was built, or by whom, or even to what purpose. There's much conjecture around it, and folk belief too, which often raises its faint echo in these Welsh borderlands. The Devil, who is never far from the popular imagination along the Marches – unsurprisingly, given their history – ploughed it in a night, the story went. In its northern stretches, like the one on which I was walking, Wat's Dyke is considerably the more substantial and better-marked construction than its famous neighbour, Offa's Dyke (which runs parallel and a little to the west of it for some of its length farther to the south, but here in Flintshire is virtually absent). Thomas Pennant, the great eighteenth-century naturalist and antiquary, who was a native of Flintshire, has it that 'this work is little known, notwithstanding it is equal in depth, though not extent, to that of Offa'. Some of today's warring Dark Age experts think Wat's Dyke and Offa's Dyke are one and the same in Flintshire.

Thomas Churchyard, a copious but ineluctably minor sixteenth-century versifier (his most famous work is entitled *The Worthiness of Wales* – a subject which assigns all who tackle it to more or less welcome obscurity), put forward the most pleasing, but also unfortunately the least likely, explanation for the coexistence of the two dykes when he suggested that one was Welsh, one was Saxon, and that the space between was a sort of free trade area where both nations might move in perfect safety. If only human nature were so reasonable and pacific! What seems relatively certain amidst all this chaos of theorizing is that the dyke where I was walking this morning marked an attempt by the rulers of Mercia in the eighth century to mark out their territory. Land and difference! It's not a defensible earthwork, so its purpose seems more likely to have been political, and perhaps commercial. And form and purpose are what it felt apt to muse upon as I stood with my back against the crazed bark of an ancient oak tree far beyond its prime, but still not so old as the dyke itself. Beyond the litter of broken branches, the steep western revetment fell away into a ditch, shadowy and gorse-choked, rabbits scurrying there. A green frond of the dog rose trailed up from it into the light, its leaves saw-edged, thorns hooked and blanched, the hips hanging in branched and curving clusters, flapped open where birds had fed on them, a brilliant scarlet where they caught the light, brighter than those of the hawthorn, that crouched away from the wind, out of the low sunlight, its berries the colour of darkening blood.

That image and the dyke's meaning put me in mind of another resonant place, so on an impulse I drove down into Shropshire to search out The Berth, among that strange region of meres and drumlins and sodden meadows around Baschurch and Weston Lullingfields. It's a place that in its atmosphere is apt as the setting for tragedy, and the mood hangs round it even on so bright a morning as this. The fields were still dew-drenched, the grass frosted lightly in hedge shadow and along field margins as I approached the two glacial hillocks, with their earthwork fortifications and linking causeway. It took me time to find a way in, to get across to them. This is a site of great historical and I think human interest; yet at each point of approach there was threat, exclusion, the assertion of ownership, that stretched their small-scale prohibitions across a deserted landscape – barbed wire, locked gates, notices – the frozen paraphernalia of human ownership. They seemed appropriate for a place that has lines of poetry like these resonating around it:

> More common was blood on the field's face
> Than ploughing of fallow...

Beyond the modern defences that express their own aggressive fears, rising above marsh and lake, this brooding, imposing site. It seems probable – uncertainty hovers continually in the margins of Dark Age history – that this was the house, the fortress, of Cynddylan, a British chieftain of the early sixth century who died in fighting against the Saxons, and from whose demise stems the archetypal and perhaps the greatest lament in the whole Western poetic tradition – the cycles of poems known as *Canu Llywarch Hen* from the ninth century. The central image in them is of a sister, Heledd, left forlorn and lonely in her old age, weeping for the ruin of her brother's great hall:

> Ystafell Cynddylan ys tywyll heno,
> Heb tan, heb wely,
> Wylaf wers, tawaf wedyn.

> (The hall of Cynddylan is dark tonight,
> Without fire, without bed,
> I shall weep for a while, and then be silent.)

They come back to me, these lines, the image of this place, as the statement of something rooted in human nature, and dark. I watched the news last night, and on it talk of plans to put up a new Holocaust memorial in London, with architects to tender for it no doubt, and a competition to choose. The discussion circled round all twentieth-century atrocity, illustrated it with footage of Auschwitz, Rwanda, Serbia – all that pornography of desecration and despair on which the media love to dwell, all those desolate faces. Differently, it resonates in this place too:

> The hall of Cynddylan is dark tonight.

Maybe the erection of a memorial – often in isolation and at a remove – has less force, too much tokenism about it, than confrontation in the place itself with the sense of what has gone before. I think of Lot 301 in Új köztemető cemetery on the outskirts of Budapest, the heroic resolve of the people of

1956, the protesting children rounded up and executed when they came of age, and the quiet remembrancers who visit their burial place; I think of Chief Joseph and his tribe at the Big Hole battlefield in Montana, and the terrible way in which the configuration of that landscape tells at a glance its own story of corrupt usage and cowardly surprise; from my heart-country's history I think of Hyddgen in the fastnesses of Pumlumon, and Owain Glyndŵr's stand there. The sense of the anterior can so powerfully combine emotional pain of understanding, and the moral lessons it brings. These landscapes of time take into another dimension entirely that 'need to witness our limits transgressed' of which Thoreau wrote, and into a more painful and I think perhaps more important one too. With that thought I turned away from The Berth and all its troubled sense of history, walked back through fields the weak sun was freeing all too slowly from the lingering and marginal grip of frost, and returned to the place under the dyke, and a fire to keep the chills of autumn at bay.

(1999)

CLWYDIAN

It was just after six on an October morning when I left the car outside Prestatyn station and set off southwards up the High Street, fumbling around in my mind for the exact words of that Philip Larkin poem about the defaced railway poster: 'Come to sunny Prestatyn'. It wasn't sunny yet, and it took a large act of faith to believe that on this day it was going to be. My small dog, The Flea, was keeping very close to heel, nonplussed by this early turn of events, stoical at having been lured from her bed before the first hint of daylight. We were setting off to walk in stages through Wales.

So what were the prompts which brought about this – to her mind inexplicable – action? Well, there's a version of seasonal affective disorder, for a start. I get restless in the autumn, want to be stirring before the leaves burn on the fires. I wanted a journey and hadn't a lot of spare time in which to do it. But it struck me that the Offa's Dyke Path from Prestatyn to Llangollen would be a fine little trek to accomplish in a day. I'd been in the Eglwyseg valley the week before and longed to follow the lovely traversing path there between the woods and the white-tiered rocks. There were other prompts as well: a specialist I'd seen about a knee problem had told me it was wearing out and shouldn't I treat it with more respect, old chap, at my age, which had stung me to a string of unspoken expletives, and the resolution that I'd just get up, rage against the dying of the light and make it work again; also, I was well aware of this particular designated Long Distance Footpath's reputation as a glorified, glorious pub crawl, and The Flea likes pubs. She gets petted in them by solicitous barmaids, admired by old men whose pockets oddly produce biscuits (how many people's secret vice is to carry biscuits in their pockets?) She has water brought to her in little bowls and is talked about, which appeals to her vanity and makes her put on the winsome expression she wears to lure people close enough to nip, which is her favourite activity. So for her benefit, chiefly, I thought we would take a walk along the border.

I had an idea that these designated Long Distance Paths were walking's equivalent of climbing's most controversial issue of the day – bolt-protected routes. I imagined they were idiot-proof; that there were signposts and markers every fifty yards for the whole of this one's 168-mile length; that you would scarcely need to consult map or guide. And for the most part that's an accurate appraisal and you find the little acorn symbol scattered everywhere on stiles and posts and great baulks of timber –

reach one, cast about for the next, and on you go. But some good burgher of Prestatyn had obviously taken a fancy to one of these latter and pinched it for his fire and a good blaze it must have made, which perhaps warmed him up as much as the hill I climbed after missing the turning it once marked warmed me.

I knew after a couple of hundred yards that I'd gone wrong, and I didn't turn back because I was too idle to countenance the descent, because I was hot and bothered, because I was hoping that maybe I hadn't missed it after all, and because a noisy small Ford car with spoilers on its back which doubled its length had roared past and irritated me and ruined the gently stirring peace of the morning. So I ended up in a hamlet called Gwaen Ysgor at the arrival of daylight, being viewed suspiciously by those breakfasting behind windows and being assailed by a plethora of ferocious signs as I gave way and consulted the map to find a way back to the path. Do you know the feeling? Have you noticed also the phenomenon by which the closer you are to so-called civilization, the more barbaric and blood-curdling become the strictures expressed on signs against straying walkers? Dangerous dogs, prosecution, death by shooting or impalement all lie in wait for the errant rambler in the environs of Prestatyn or Beaconsfield or Killiney and would never be encountered around Aberdaron, Renvyle or Achiltibuie. Beware those places where the god of property rules seems to be the moral, and I mused on it painfully before regaining the authorized path by a post box which politely requested all walkers thereon to complete a form requesting name, address, date, duration and destination of journey before passing on.

The detour had cost me half an hour I suppose, and that oppression was matched by the dove-grey heavy cloud above contrasting with a sky the colour of robins' eggs over Snowdonia whence I'd come. I began to think this path's whole reason for existence lay in that matchless outline to the west, and it was a thought to which I kept returning throughout the day. For the moment, though, to set against that far skyline was the immediate perspective of a teasing serendipity through little jigging lanes and across field-paths which gave every impression of being virtually untrodden. Where it crossed the fine tilth of a ploughed and harrowed field, there was not a footmark; across a mushroomy, lush pasture not a blade of grass was bruised. Who walks the length of Offa's Dyke? The answer seems on this northernmost stretch to be few, and yet it is an impressive piece of route-finding through the sort of pleasantly nondescript countryside you find throughout England and hardly at all in Wales. The sense of careful negotiation, of respectfully reciprocal goodwill accumulates as you pass along, and acts as a tacit critical chorus against the times where it has been refused or denied – the mile outside the forestry of Coed Cwm, for example, where the speculators in timber have ruled against the public's pleasure and responsibility towards trees and consigned our feet to circuitous tarmac. How tawdry that attitude seems by contrast with the graceful new footbridge across the new section of expressway at Rhuallt, which you cross immediately after Coed Cwm, having passed some of the most savage dog signs (and dogs) along the whole route. I hate the vicarious savagery of a chained dog, bounding and restrained, its teeth expressing all its owner's animus towards those who encroach on what is his and his alone. And I was glad to be leaving it and the roar of the expressway behind as The Flea and I climbed over a gorse-blown, pretty little hill by the name of Moel Maenefa, on the far side of which a camping barn nestled under a huge electricity pylon and made me ruminate on the depression felt by some on finishing the walk being due to external factors like spending a night under that thing. Which was an apt thought to accompany me through the village of Sodom. How did any village ever come by that name? It wasn't unappealing, either, though the bottle dumps at the path-side and the abandoned hen-coop cars didn't invite you to look back. Not that I mind bottle dumps and scrap cars – you might not get them in the Lake District, but generally they're a part of the British countryside. Maybe we get too precious about such things and scold and thus estrange. I'm seditiously reminded of Swift taking his 'Country Walk' along the banks of Glandore Harbour and complaining all the while that he took no pleasure in the beauties of the scene, being preoccupied with not stepping in the human and animal ordure that lay all about. With this in mind, I wound down the hill to Bodfari, passing on the way a frail, tired-looking woman being towed up by a large Airedale who was, she informed me, called Digby, and boisterous, and when I commented on his good looks and obvious breeding she countered that he, like all dogs (even The Flea, who was baring her teeth from behind my legs, her critical look seemed to say), and unlike any of the human race, was beautiful. Thus I arrived at the door of the Downing Arms just as the landlady was opening it, who in her turn informed me that all dogs were banned from her premises but The Flea could come in for a bowl of water if she desired, and what would I like?

I had a pint of Guinness and took it into the beer garden by the river. All foot-travellers through Wales pass in the shade of George Borrow, so I amused myself by constructing an imaginary conversation resisting his aspersions against those who preferred this papist brew to good ale, and I'd passed on to some Borrovian etymological fancies around Sodom, Serendipity and Coed Efa which had me giggling into my glass before I realized the butcher was listening. He made no comment on the two voices to which he'd been listening. He came straight out with what was troubling him: 'That dog of yours could do with some meat.' The

Flea jumped off the bench at this, trotted across, leapt on to his lap and started to lick him under the chin. He was four feet ten inches in height, width, and neck measurement. He sat her Tom Thumb-style on a vast palm and walked over to his van, shooting back at me as he went: 'You're not one of those veggies, are you?' I was reduced to silence, but The Flea made up for both of us as she smacked her lips and crunched her teeth on the scraps and bones he'd given her, whilst the butcher wedged himself behind the steering wheel of his van and rolled out. Thus fortified – and in my case chastened – we made for the Clwydian hills.

It's a long step from Prestatyn to Bodfari, but the Clwydian Range is a walker's dream. 'The bracken hill at its best', declares Patrick Monkhouse, and you know exactly what he means the minute you set foot on these rounded, alluring heights. For twelve miles they swell and heave away southwards, dark with heather and glowing with the autumn fern. The northern end is curiously quiet and unvisited, farms lying silent and deserted under its flanks. On top of Penycloddiau, The Flea and I came across a dog fox stretched out on its back sunning itself, and a merlin scudded round the flank of Moel Arthur as we crossed it. The tops of this range hurry by, the walking as broad and easy as the hill shapes, the route so logical you merely follow your own momentum. From Moel Famau, with its squat stump of a memorial tower, on a clear day you can see from the Derbyshire Peak District to Snowdonia, from Cader Idris to the Lake District and the Shropshire Hills. Half the population of Merseyside crowds up here on fine Sundays, but today it was deserted and I raced on down over Foel Fenlli, with its vicious ascent from the Bwlch Penbarras, and on past Clwyd Gate and over Moel Llanfair with the sun westering behind Eryri and the knowledge of a dreary tract of countryside between Llandegla and World's End ahead – squelchy forestry, tussocky moor with grouse exploding away, and then the open road over from Minera in the twilight, bats flickering past, a half-moon rising over the long ridge of Berwyn and its glimmer on the yew-tree-sentried white rocks of Craig Arthur. If you walk through the fading of the light, it never really becomes dark until you hit the artificial illumination of the town. I descended into Borrow's old Llangollen in thick dusk, past the shop window sign that read 'Taxidermist – Closed for Renovation', pondering on the burden of getting back to my car through post-deregulation border country. The Flea sat on the kerb and looked her most appealing to solve the one problem. Two lifts and a bus and we were back in Prestatyn. I ached, and The Flea snored peacefully on my knee.

(1995)

PART TWO

On High Hills

The peaks of Eryri have been a magnet to visitors since the late eighteenth century. The use and abuse of them, their native character, their celebration and significance for recreation, have been literary themes for just as long. Here are a few of my responses over the years to the central heights of Eryri – to their magnificence, atmosphere, and treatment at the hands (and feet) of ever-increasing hordes of visitors.

TWO VISITS TO CARNEDD LLYWELYN

1: *The wild white dome.*

I remember being on the wild white dome of Carnedd Llywelyn – second-highest hill in Wales – one April afternoon. Wind had bitten into the crisp snow and etched sastrugi across its crystalline, untainted surface. Looking down the steepening slope to tiny Ffynnon Llyffant – at 850 metres the highest and most remote of Welsh lakes – I debated whether to unstrap the ice-axe from my sack, imagining the unstoppable slide, but indolence prevailed. The snow anyway was that firm texture where a firm kick produces a secure toe-hold.

I soon arrived at the summit – alone, no-one else on the hills, the sun westering but still high in the sky – and sat in the hollow cairn to eat an orange and ponder the mystery of why people quit the hills so long before nightfall. It was six o'clock. An occasional bank of cloud encroached from the east, rolled across the moor and quickly dispersed. A bitter, subdued wind streamed constantly from the north. Peaks and snowy ridges radiated out in every direction. Below me, to give added sense of height, was the cliff that Thomas Pennant in the eighteenth century referred to as 'the most horrid precipice that thought can conceive'. The three prime hours of the day in terms of visual splendour were still to come, and yet there was not another person in view. Perhaps people are frightened of these places, frightened of their solitude? Beyond the ice-crystalled walls of my shelter not a thing stirred but the wind. In a few short weeks the snow would have melted. Dotterel would be scurrying in small flocks among the clubmosses and shattered stones of this bleak tundra. But for the moment it was a primal place, turning in the slow wheel of the day down towards darkness and marking its descent with magic.

At this hour the mountains begin to grow in stature, levered up by the slant of the light. I made my way slowly towards Foel Grach, Yr Elen all bold monochromes of accentuated ridge and strata. At its back, Garnedd Elidir might have been the Dent Blanche. Ahead lay the five-mile ridge over Yr Aryg, Bera Bach and Drosgl down to Bethesda, and I wasn't going to hurry. These hills have an atmosphere unique to themselves. Even their detail – the frost-heaved surface, the scattered stone, the woolly profusion of moss and lichen – is different to that of any other part of Snowdonia. The place is spacious, little-visited, unspoilt. I drifted on to find shelter among rocks on the tor of Bera Bach. The sun was a deep, orangey red, hanging over Holy Island, which was separated from the mainland of Anglesey by a glint of sea. As the sun sank into a dark band across the horizon, the peaks to my left glowed briefly, then became colourless and phantasmal. There was a flat period of a few minutes, until suddenly the sky on the horizon lit up and distinct bands of colour resolved from what had previously been neutral and obscure. Above me the sky was a dark blue, lightening imperceptibly to an eggshell-blue arc in the west, which in its turn modulated into palest green and then a yellow streaked with dove-grey. Beneath this the bands were sharply defined: orange, a rosy mauve, muted purple and then charcoal grey above the glittering pewter strip that was the sea. As if to balance this light-show in the sky, the red moor grass all around was leaping into vivid life. This spectral phenomenon always startles me, and seems near-miraculous in its intimacy and close-at-handness, bringing in its evanescence an indelible sense of the mountain kingdom's power and glory, a sense which stayed with me as quiet exultation throughout the descent to stacked, steep terraces of Bethesda.

(1996)

2: *Where nothing new ever happens*

That ridge again! I saw it in morning light rising from a sea-fret that laced and billowed across Conwy Bay. It was gilded, patched with cloud-shadow, hazily blond, outstretched, those great high rounded domes of the Carneddau the solid base from which it grew. Something I knew about that high place in the warm bright of May, something old and certain that I wished to see again, something so heart-seizing. There's a Mary Oliver poem simply entitled 'Nature'. These lines are from it: '…another morning/in which nothing new/would ever happen,/which is the reason/we love it.' I drove up through Llanllechid, Rachub and Gerlan, parked at the bottom of Ciltwllan, idled up the tarmac to where it gave out by the gathering pens and took the path up Y Garth for Gyrn Wigau. There was a point beyond the ladder stile over the *ffridd* wall where the strata stood regular and exposed, the cleaved rocks ranged in rows like coursed masonry, like steps to the temple. I climb on, remembering.

In the fine old Welsh scholar Ifor Williams's 1959 collection of essays, *I Ddifyrru'r Amser* (*Passing the Time*) there comes one of my favourite passages on the hills of Wales. Here it is, in English translation:

> The clock struck the right number and off we went in a small, silent procession, leaving the houses and streets for the mountain and its darkness, and finding the start of the path past Garth. We walked like First Nation Americans, in single file…
>
> By now we were on the open mountain, with Gyrn Wigau to the left and aiming for the edge of Drosgl. I looked back and saw that by now many more shepherds and their dogs had joined us. Nobody spoke and nobody greeted the newcomers – all simply kept on walking. Then we saw a flaming torch far to the left in the region of Llanllechid and one of the group said, 'The Bryn Eithin lads are letting us know they're on their way.' Eventually we saw two men sitting down above our path – they had crossed Waun Cws Mai and come over to meet us, 'You go with the Bryn Eithin lad', said my uncle, 'He's going furthest of anyone, to the dip of the hill right behind the summit of Carnedd Llywelyn. I'm turning off now to where I have to be.' He left us, and I looked behind; the whole procession had disappeared, every shepherd and dog gone to reach his appointed place by first light, each one knowing where and when to go. And by break of day there would be a ring of men and dogs around the great mountain on its Arllechwedd side. As dawn came, and soon as you could tell which sheep were shorn, which unshorn, everybody was to walk forward and drive the fleeced ones into the pens along the Afon Wen under the ridge.
>
> But my task was to tail the son of Bryn Eithin and quiz him. Who had arranged for him to take that particular position given to him? He didn't know. He only knew this:

that the shepherd from Bryn Eithin, on the morning of gathering the Braich, was to be there at daybreak in that spot, according to old, old custom.

That there is nothing new in my being here – that all the long generations have preceded me – is part of the pleasure and the echoing delight of being in these hills. What I see now, they have seen before me. What I have come to see has pleased their eyes. I climb on, contemplating.

Lazily, where the path comes in from Waun Cws Mai, across which the true kiss of May is drawing out the black-budded stems, tight-furled, of the bog-cotton, I take the shepherding way that slips round Drosgl and again under the craggy tors of Bera Bach. Because what I am doing, where I am going – it feels like a lover's assignation. On the slope below graze a herd of the sturdy little wild ponies of the Carneddau, white blazes on their foreheads. A sentinel mare considers my approach, gives a shake of her long mane in acknowledgement of my presence before she canters to a safer distance from humankind. At the craggy tor – 'strange serrated rocks' as Pennant called them – of Bera Mawr two ravens – always a pair with these birds – chuckle truculently back and forth before diving among and scattering a flock of thirty or forty smaller birds that have ventured too near their lair. I watch. Are these what I have come to see?

Close at hand are sky-reflecting pools in the peat. On this great hill-gable of Eryri, the sense of space is a kind of ecstasy. I loved to come here in winter when the hills were deserted, paths obliterated by snow, the slopes wind-howled from the north, streamered with spindrift, spiked rocks and sastrugi sketching in a texture of such clear, fine austerity the mind is purged by it and brought to peace. I drift on, the day still fine, people in twos or threes lounging at ease on rocks here and there, delighting quietly in the tranquillity of the place. There is scarcely a breath of wind. A mile or two ahead, mist rolls in, patchy, obscuring and then disclosing the coming peaks. Around the other three quadrants of the compass, the eye travels for miles. Cader Idris and Pumlumon stand out to the south; the Clwydian hills delimit visibility to the east beyond dragon-crested Tal-y-fan; in the sea behind the Isle of Man hovers like a cloud and the Fylde Coast smudges the margins of vision. All the lesser hills of Snowdonia – Moelwynion, Cnicht, the 'Ridge of the Red Cairns' – skip among the greater ones like lambs. To the west gleams the long arm of the Llŷn Peninsula, with Ynys Enlli punctuating its end. I drift on, sit for a while outside the refuge shelter on Foel Grach, lean my back against the wall and satisfy my caffeine addiction. This here and now of a fine Welsh spring day, this is a kind of heaven.

Onward again, over the shattered stone barren and the brown clubmosses, over the same textures I've traversed in rapture from the Cairngorms to the high Arctic. I have so dawdled in the ascent that the people have left. At Carnedd Llywelyn in the summit shelter, nobody. Those who have formerly been here keep company in my mind instead. Thomas Pennant, at this place in 1781, revelled in the 'amazingly great' view; Hugh Derfel Hughes, author of the first guidebook to a British mountain, the *Llawlyfr Carnedd Llywelyn* of 1864, sat up here among the frost-rimed rocks and the January snow with the preacher Tanymarian, watching the mist roll in beneath them whilst discussing Darwin, geology and evolution with speculative excitement and eyes eager for the significance of detail. My good old friend Ioan Bowen Rees, former chief executive of Gwynedd, father of Gruff Rhys of Super Furry Animals, and best of all Welsh-language mountain writers, has been here too, and all the information he'd gleaned from long generations, all the gifts of instruction he bestowed on me before his too-early death, all the encouragement and the pleasure his company and his writing and his combative nature gave, I remember now with gratitude. From out of the shelter I walk a little way, to look down first on Ffynnon Llyffant and then on its precious counterpart to the west, Ffynnon Caseg. These are the springs of enchantment. I sit on the frost-shattered tundra, a low boulder against my back, and watch.

At last, what I have come to see. The small scurrying birds barely noticed before now resolve from perfect camouflage into movement and approach. I toss crumbs from my sandwich. One is by my feet now, unafraid. I study her. The thinnest crescent of moon sailing boat-like across the eastern sky is echoed in her bright semi-lunar breast-marking. Her shaded chestnut underparts are the tone of the mosses, her grey nape that of the lichens on the stones. She is a part, belongs in this place at this time – every year for as long as I have known these hills she has been here, and for all time beyond my passing she will visit here still. The dotterel!

They are nothing new. Yet they are so certain. They come from the world between, that we too seldom see, are the loved gift. Of nature. May you too receive it. May we never destroy it.

(2006)

'THE WELSH 3000S' – SLOWLY AND THE WRONG WAY

1: *The Strangest Summits*
Metrication presents the British hillgoer of a certain age with problems. There is the matter of the Munros, for example. I don't even know what the qualifying height in metres for inclusion in the Munros list is. The same holds true for the Corbetts and Felicitys and Daphnes and Marilyns, or whatever those other lesser lists call their summits. Not only do I not know, I don't

intend finding out. That 3,000-foot marker may be just as arbitrary as its metrical equivalent, but somehow it seems more elegant and logical. Also, I grew up with it and hence am loath to let it go. So let me state the ruling premise for what follows – it comes in imperial measure (if there were an available Welsh unit of height I'd probably use that, being opposed on principle to all forms of cultural imperialism; but there isn't, so feet it will have to be). What I'm writing about here is the classic high traverse of Eryri, which long usage allows us to refer to by the even older name of Snowdonia; and usage also tempts us to refer to the traverse as the Welsh 3000s, or the Fourteen Peaks. Though I gather these days there are fifteen or perhaps even sixteen of them for those who take fine distinctions seriously and like to collect. Who cares? Not me, that's for sure. But I do care passionately about this landscape, that's been my home base for most of my adult life. I first visited here in 1960 as a thirteen-year-old schoolboy. In August of the following year I first, through the course of a long summer's day, raced along the switchback route from Beddgelert to Abergwyngregyn that links its loftiest peaks.

I had an urge to go back, 'just to see', as the line from the song has it, 'if everything is still the same/In this land'. These days I'm past the stage 'when, like a roe, I bounded o'er the hills.' I like to dawdle along, observe, let my thoughts wander rather than drive my body along to some fixed objective. The conventional wisdom has it that you begin the Welsh Peaks from Snowdon. Instinct born of long knowledge tells me that's not the best approach. Start from the shore below them to the north and east, from Abergwyngregyn ('the river-mouth of the white shells') climb into the hills, then wheel around to the west with the whole of this mountainous, sea-surrounded country spreading out before you across receding blue horizons. Head west, young person! That way you'll catch at mood of landscape, at spirit of place; that way the peculiar spell of these hills will start to work upon you. So, prosaically, I alighted from the bus in Aber one bright morning, walked the half-mile down to where the river debouches on to the sand flats of Traeth Lafan, watched flocks of wading birds scud low across the flood of the tide, bathed my feet at the mingling of salt and fresh in gesture of commencing another journey, and set off towards the Carneddau.

We all have our favourite routes into the hills, as well as our favourite hill-groups. I love the Carneddau. Crusty old Showell Styles is certainly right when he wrote that there is something odd about them. By virtue of height, distance and loneliness they exist at a curious remove from the standard hill-going curriculum. Together the six 3,000-foot summits here comprise the largest land mass over that height south of the Cairngorms plateau. Like their northern counterpart they have something of the Arctic about them, something of a sense of earth yearning away into the abstractions of the barrenlands. That aesthetic or even metaphysical dimension is one you enter into stage by stage if you climb from sea level to Foel Fras by way of the Afon Goch.

There was a time when I'd have suggested reaching this north-easternmost of the Welsh 3000s by way of the Afon Anafon, but for me the valley of the latter was ruined in the 1980s when Welsh Water plc, as it then was, drove a road up it, causing wholesale damage to archaeological sites and destroying the atmosphere of a wild and special place in that profligate outpouring of public money countrywide that preceded the Conservative government of the time's scandalous privatization of the nation's utilities. The wound – psychological as much as physical – does not heal, and I can no longer bear to go that way. Instead, I prefer to straggle along with the crowds to the foot of Rhaeadr Fawr – the famous Aber Falls, probably the finest waterfall in Wales, the pulse of its rippling laciness in delectable contrast to black underlying rock.

There are crosses to bear if you come this way. A sagging span of power cables across the lower valley is loathsome, the valley-side plantations of Sitka spruce as alien in their own way. But compensations arrive as you enter the valley above the fall to scour them from your mind.

It is called Cwm yr Afon Goch ('Red River Valley') and Showell Styles reserves for it particular opprobrium: 'Only the bog-and-heather enthusiast will enjoy the upward slog behind the rim of Aber Falls. Two-and-a-half map-miles and a rise of 1,800 feet is all one can say about the obvious route up the true right bank of the Afon Goch, in a deep and featureless trough with no views to alleviate its toilsomeness.' I feel tempted to respond to that in the words of Christina Rossetti: 'Could we but look with seeing eyes,/This very spot might be Paradise.' To climb into Cwm yr Afon Goch, you leave the lower valley, with its alder and oak by the stream, its sharp, ammoniac scent of overgrazed pasture, its pathway-latticed heather-and-bracken hillsides, and ascend by a secretive little path that slants rockily right across the top of the falls – a *mauvais pas* here has seen frequent fatalities – to disgorge you into an upland glen of Scottish proportions, winding away into high hills. At first mountain ash and hawthorn, gorse and herb Robert at its upper limit grow from sheltered crevices or across rocks dappled with apple-green, black-outlined lichens to lend luxuriance to the scene. As the valley leads you on into its own solitude, the path fading into illegibility, you enter the zone of heather, in flower now, its faint, sweet scent hanging in the air. On the green levels by the stream are remains of settlements from the Bronze Age. All across these slopes, unexpectedly, you come across hut circles, stones re-aligned millennia ago by human hand to unsurmizable purpose. A yearling ewe, bright-fleeced, grazes unconcernedly on young bilberry shoots in one of them, looks up in brief surprise as I pass by. A sentinel buzzard peels off a rock outcrop, flaps heavily into slow orbit, collapses groundwards in a fluster of wings before rising again and heading away purposefully, a vole in its talons. Clouds trammel the sky to north and west and their shadows play peek-a-boo with feature and contour, suddenly passing to throw that rock, that strange runnel into vivid, gleaming perspective.

On Llwytmor I walk right up to one of the sturdy little wild ponies of the Carneddau, a white blaze on her forehead, a shake of her mousy long straggle of mane given in acknowledgement of my presence before she canters away to a safe distance. From Bera Mawr opposite, on the long ridge out of Bethesda that is the other sublime approach to these hills, two ravens rise to playful flight. Is all this texture of wild land, that so eases us along our way and gives such pleasure or even joy, really unworthy of our notice? Is blind dismissal really 'all one can say'? The whaleback ridge leads up to Foel Fras at last, Llandudno looking disconsonantly close and the wakes of tiny boats flecking the blue of the sea. At the Ordnance Survey pillar on Foel Fras, a group of young people from an outdoor centre stood chattering around in a landscape-occluding circle, before trailing off in order, leader to the fore, in quest of their day's destination. There was scarcely a breath of wind. Mist drifted in idly, obscuring and then disclosing the coming peaks. Under the canopy of cloud to the west gleamed the long arm of the Llŷn Peninsula, with Ynys Enlli punctuating its end. This was heaven.

It's heaven with a main thoroughfare these days, patched and paved across the moor through the labours of National Trust voluntary workers, leading by way of Foel Grach with its refuge hut, to Carnedd Llywelyn. On top of Snowdon today there would be hundreds of people. Here there's a bare half-dozen, myself included. In the summit shelter, proprietorial, looking inward with the view blanked out for them, sat a party of four.

Two young men and two young women clad in the gaudiest gear were avidly discussing intimate minutiae from television's latest snoop-show. A lone bespectacled man in his mid-twenties perhaps, clad in old country clothing and with a shabby rucksack on his back, wandered around the plateau, peering down into the valleys and along the ridges, quiet, wide-eyed, shining with wonder. The mist was closing in fast. I made my dutiful detour to the elegant outlier of Yr Elen, then plodded along the ridge above Ysgolion Duon, ribs of rock gleaming ahead in Cwm Tryfan. Around the pert little peak of Tryfan itself white cloud like teased-out cotton wool was bleached by sunlight. Beneath me Ffynnon Lloer ('The Moon Spring') was leaden and shadowed. By the time I reached Pen yr Ole Wen the sunlight was entirely gone and a great bank of dark cloud had moved in. The pleasant way down this mountain is by its gentle east ridge, and as I came off it to the *ffridd* wall in the Nant y Benglog the first heavy drops of rain were blotching the pale rock, and had turned into Welsh downpour by the time I reached the road.

2: *Holiday Hills*

I have to say that, ladders apart – and beyond those, various artificial and mechanical means all more or less terrifying – there is nothing quite so efficient for gaining height as a staircase. Or so I found myself thinking as I plodded up from the A5 into the shadow of Tryfan late one morning, bound for its North Ridge. Right up from the road and along beneath the damp and heathery cliff known to climbers as the 'Back of the Milestone', there were steps. Maybe I'm dementing faster than I think, or maybe it was some time since I last came this way, but I didn't remember them. They were solid stone steps, too, built of the rock that lay around, and whoever had built them had integrated them as well into that environment as the medieval builders of the so-called 'Roman Steps' in the Rhinogydd thirty miles to the south had done with their workmanship. Still, as a hillwalker I'm duty bound to object to man-made intrusions into the wild environment, however necessary they may be at times as means to preserving the fabric of that environment. So I used them to climb out of the shade and into the sun on what is by far the best line of ascent for a walker of the most exciting British hill-summit outside Skye.

In the days of Owen Glynne Jones and the Abraham Brothers of Keswick, at the close of the century before last, the North Ridge of Tryfan and its natural continuation on a day's circuit out of Ogwen, the Bristly Ridge of Glyder Fach, were deemed to be rock-climbs, albeit easy ones. If you have the inclination, you can still make them thus. Or not as the case may be, for on these broad spurs there are always easier options to be taken. This makes it a particularly unfrustrating line of ascent when you find yourself behind a large party of overweight, slow-moving, paunchy and jovial devotees such as this mountain attracts in droves. Where the side-effects of their other long devotion – to the bottle – is productive of mountain bottlenecks, you simply find an alternative line of ascent and slip quietly round them, leaving them to carouse over their problems. You think I exaggerate? I do not. Perhaps it's that unexhausting proximity to the road, or the ease of that stepped approach. In the course of an hour-and-a-half of sidling up this glorious feature I counted eighty-three other scramblers, of whom the minority I would have judged to have weighed under sixteen stone. They were everywhere, picnicking on well-upholstered heather ledges, egging each other on to attempt ever-more-gymnastic problems, turning the mountain into a regular academy of jollity.

But could the mountain bear such weight of traffic? Well, the mountain, in truth, is a remarkably solid one. Its rock, outcropping ubiquitously, may be productive of thin, sour, acid black soil entirely devoid of the flowers that for me are one of the joys of mountain-going; but it is beautifully silvery and firm, its texture (except where a century's traffic has imparted a fine sheen to it) satisfyingly rough, its holds numerous and comforting to the grip. No wonder that generation upon generation of hill-goers have extended their allegiance from walking to climbing on this very peak. It suggests to you that to climb is as easy and natural a thing as the act of walking itself. It is, to come back to the image with which we started, like an eccentrically-devised and twisting staircase that leads you up to the most remarkable of Welsh mountain summits – the twin tall columns of Adam and Eve that look like watching giants when you first see the peak's impressive East Face from along the Nant y Benglog.

These have been a focus for hill-activity for centuries. In the last decade of the eighteenth century the Reverend William Bingley, a plump young Oxford curate, came up here with his guide, the Reverend Peter Bayley Williams, rector of Llanrug, who recounted to him how 'a female of an adjoining parish' was famous for having often made the leap from Adam to Eve. Not everyone who climbs Tryfan today dares to do that. The monoliths are ten feet high, the gap between them not much more than a long stride; but on the side away from the summit plateau the rocks of the East Face plunge downwards for hundreds of feet. If you slipped in that direction, you'd bounce a long way. When I was presenting a television series on the Welsh in 1992, I had to make this leap over and over again in tandem with a cameramen, who was doing it whilst filming me. He had astonishing sangfroid, but then, I was on the outside...

Enough of Tryfan – everybody knows it, everybody loves it, and so they should. But on a hot day in August, it can bear a closer resemblance to the beach at Rhyl than any other mountain top I know. I rattled away down the South Ridge to Bwlch Tryfan, and there ran into the goats. One of several herds that spectacularly inhabit the Welsh mountains, they belong by a tradition to the Williams family of Gwern y Gof Uchaf in the valley below. Feral now, they were probably released into the hills as the fashion for wearing wigs faded in the eighteenth century and their hair was no longer saleable for that purpose. These days, they keep to their little flocks and ornament the scene, magnificent-horned and flowing-coated, able to gain access to even the most remote and perilous of cliff-ledges. The farmers regard them with some benevolence, since they graze those places and hence keep the sheep from straying there and needing rescue. They seemed disinclined to negotiate with me for a substitute for my own thinning hair, and disappeared away over the rocks at my approach, bent on scrounging food from the summiteers. I took the path that slanted across scree from the *bwlch* and brought me to the toe of the Bristly Ridge.

This and the North Ridge of Tryfan are so often paired that we tend to think of them as a single entity. They're quite distinct in character, and the Bristly Ridge, though much the shorter, is the steeper, airier and more exciting of the two. Its rock is very rough, the holds magnificent all over it, but in places it rears up dramatically. The crowds had evaporated by this point. A couple from Liverpool with a tiny son of six or seven were occupied in hauling him or throwing him up or across its gaps and gendarmes. A lean man raced past. In too short a time the arête – for it is that – gave out on to the broad flat ridge of the Glyderau.

This is truly a barren and desolate landscape, its rock splintered and bare, sheaves and splintered stooks of it stacked all around like the arrows of geological time. As I wandered over to the little rocky tor that's the summit, glancing over as I did so to the Cantilever and seeing in my mind Moses Griffiths' wonderfully precise engraving of Thomas Pennant standing on its end, a young couple approached, asked if I'd just come up the Bristly Ridge. We talked. They'd come up the gruelling scree to the side. I told them the ridge was easier, and it is physically, so long as consideration's given to route-choice and you have some head for heights. I advised them to use their judgement, watch the weather, and treat scrambling guides with circumspection because some of the routes they recommend are death traps. 'You must think us wusses,' the man said. He had a frank, pleasant, open face. 'Not at all,' I replied, 'I just think the better route would give you a more memorable experience.' 'He's a pilot,' the young woman told me proudly. 'She's my fiancée,' he explained, beaming. I left them there, hand in hand, bringing a glow to the place.

By Castell y Gwynt a hat-wearing man was seated among rocks with a paintbox and palette to hand: 'Aha,' I addressed him, 'a British eccentric! May I take your photograph?' He complied, a little testily, told me how few painters come up here. From the information he gave out, and because I knew and liked his painting, I deduced who he was: 'You must be David Woodford?'

We talked on about evocation of mood, about the presence fractionally below the surface of death and desolation in this landscape. He gave me a very long, intelligent and detailed account of a new transport initiative that our more-than-usually asinine and nepotistic National Park Planning Authority was intending to foist on residents and visitors to the Park alike; we concurred in vitriolic denunciation of management culture and its hill-application. I told him of a sign I'd spotted recently down by Ogwen that said: 'You may access the Carnedd Mountains from here'. Before I knew it half-an-hour had passed and the sun was wheeling westwards. I wished him improving light and hurried on, playing as I went an entertaining and satisfying little game to which Cameron McNeish, the Scottish hill-writer, had introduced me. It's called wreck-a-cairn and involves judicious application of trekking poles to supernumerary examples of the latter. Across the whole summit gable of the Glyderau there are plenty of those, so I was well occupied. After a little while there came a shout from behind, and a red-faced gentleman with a prominent vein ticking in his temple rushed down towards me: 'May I ask why you are knocking the top stones off these cairns?' he enquired. 'Because I consider them an unnecessary despoliation of a prime landscape and their bizarre proliferation here a needless intrusion; because I believe their presence fosters a carelessness in navigation that could prove hazardous; and…'

Before I could go further he launched in again, temple vein throbbing by now: 'I live just down there, I'm in the mountain rescue team, and I'm telling you that those few inches you're destroying may be a matter of life and death in winter when all that's showing through the snow are the top stones…'

Restraining an urge to laugh, I glanced round, surveyed large mounds of stones two or three yards apart in every direction. 'Personally,' I responded coolly, 'I rather hold to Tilman's view that "every herring should hang by its own tail". The dependency you propose I find rather alarming coming from a member of a rescue team. Besides, as you'll be aware if you've come up here often in winter, the snow seldom lies deep on the plateau, and for the most part is scoured away into the Nameless Cwm, so…'

He interrupted again: 'I shall report you to the National Park wardens…'

'Please do,' I countered, 'some of them are good friends of mine, and I'm sure they'd be very interested in looking up what bye-laws forbid the destruction of unnecessary cairns.'

He glared at me, the vein in his temple a writhing worm, his complexion the colour of ripe damsons. 'You are so sad,' he snarled.

'Absolutely true,' I agreed. 'Finding attitudes like yours abroad in the hills makes me thoroughly miserable. I suggest you take up football refereeing. It might satisfy your dictatorial cravings.'

This unpleasant little encounter behind me, I jogged on down the ravaged slope to Llyn y Cŵn, spent a pleasant ten minutes talking to a Jewish couple from London, very bright and precise and interesting, the woman's auburn hair shot through with red-gold where it caught the declining sun, then ground up to Y Garn, beyond which, suddenly, not a soul. The whole of that lovely ridge along to the last summit of Garnedd Elidir[1], with its little unworn paths, I had entirely to myself in the brilliance of the evening light.

On Elidir itself, the sun transformed Caernarfon Bay and the beaches along the west coast of Anglesey to burnished copper. I felt utterly at peace among line upon line of hills, golden and glowing all around me, that I have come to know intimately and to love through the best part of my life, and stayed until the shadows of the hills craved out eastwards for the return of the sun, then clattered contentedly down through the Dinorwig Quarry, by sequences of worn slate quarrymen's steps to the fleshpots of Llanberis, and food and drink and rest.

3: The Conspicuous Place

My good friend Cameron McNeish, the Scottish mountain guru, has been kind enough to concede in print that perhaps the

---

[1] Note the correct name! That given on the Ordnance Survey map, 'Elidir Fawr', is, like so many re-namings in the Celtic realms, an arrogant re-invention. For more on this theme, see the Irish playwright Brian Friel's fine drama *Translations*. As for 'Elidir Fach', words fail me!

Snowdon Horseshoe is the finest ridge walk in Britain, if you exclude Skye from consideration. That's some concession, coming from a proud Scotsman. The exclusion of the Black Cuillin is significant, though. There is a comparison to be drawn here. Both Snowdon and the Cuillin have about them a kind of similarity of architecture and mood. They are shapely and complex, bare-rocked and glacier-hewn, architectonic in the swirl and scatter of their ridges, that are so aesthetically satisfying to view even on the two dimensions of the map, and are physically unlike those of any other British hills. The sea's proximity – the gable of the Cuillin rises from the Hebridean Sea, and it is little more than seven miles from the summit of Snowdon to the shores of Menai – adds to the sense of height, the light-play, the capricious atmospherics of both. Scafell and Ben Nevis, as high points of their respective nations, have their devotees, but they're lumpen and uncouth masses in comparison. Snowdon is by far the finer peak.

It also has an astonishing richness of cultural texture, that in itself argues long allure. From neolithic cairn-builders through Dark Ages legendary to modern eco-management, by way of poets and novelists and travellers and the accounts of sporting participants in Welsh and in English, humanity has inscribed the sense of its own passage down through the ages on these stones. No other British hill has had its story told so often or so well. Snowdon possesses its own anthology of literature[2]. Its physical beauty and its wealth of tradition have ensured its popularity, and that in its turn for some has meant its ruin. There are times nowadays when it can seem managed to death – though those who criticize this seem unable to come up with

---

[2] To which I've added in the present book's companion volume, so please excuse the cursory treatment of Snowdon given here.

their own broadly acceptable and democratic proposals for how else its sheer pressure of visitor-traffic might best be mediated. And that visitor-traffic has been around for a very long time. Here's Wordsworth, forsaking his Lakeland fells for more sublime country in the thirteenth and concluding book of *The Prelude* of 1805-1806:

> ... a Light upon the turf
> Fell like a flash: I look'd about, and lo!
> The Moon stood naked in the Heavens, at height
> Immense above my head, and on the shore
> I found myself of a huge sea of mist,
> Which, meek and silent, rested at my feet:
> A hundred hills their dusky backs upheaved
> All over this still Ocean, and beyond,
> Far, far beyond, the vapours shot themselves,
> In headlands, tongues, and promontory shapes
> Into the Sea, the real Sea, that seem'd
> To dwindle and give up its majesty,
> Usurp'd upon as far as sight could reach.

A quarter-century before Wordsworth's time, Thomas Pennant had climbed with the same purpose in view:

> I... sat up at a farm on the west till about twelve, and walked up the whole way. The night was remarkably fine and starry: towards morn, the stars faded away, and left a short interval of darkness, which was soon dispersed by the dawn of day. The body of the sun appeared most distinct, with the rotundity of the moon, before it rose high enough to render its beams too brilliant for our sight. The sea which bounded the western part was gilt by its beams, first in slender streaks, at length glowed with redness. The prospect was disclosed to us like the gradual drawing up of a curtain in a theatre.

Both Wordsworth and Pennant climbed Snowdon's western flank to watch the dawn from its summit. The first time I climbed the mountain, as a thirteen-year-old schoolboy in the Easter snow of 1960, I came up from that side too, and still harbour an affection for the Snowdon Ranger route, though it's a long and rather uniform ascent. Two hundred years ago, when the head of the Llanberis lakes had to be reached by boat and there was no road up the Llanberis Pass, the approaches from Nant Colwyn or Cwellyn to the west, or by way of the long ridge thrown seawards to the north, were the only accessible ones. I doubt if a tenth of the walkers who reach the summit these days go that way. Certainly, as I set out on the last leg of this slow traverse of the highest peaks, I didn't aim to cross the Llanberis watershed and come up from that side.

Instead, I had a memory running through my mind of what is perhaps the most precious of all my hill-experiences. It is of walking up through the drizzle of a pre-dawn into cloud-filled Cwm Glas, plodding heavily on, enveloped in mist, no hint of anything other than this suffocating stuff to come, until suddenly, at Bwlch Coch, I burst through into a clearer world:

> How to describe a beauty so ephemeral that you were witness both to the moment of its existence and its passing? Its component parts were a pale-blue sky, a white cloud-sea shading to rose in the east, shadowed blue slopes of island peaks, still air, and two points of movement across the whole scene: from Bwlch y Saethau opposite, pink cloud frothed in a slow fall; on the ridge of Crib y Ddysgl above a fox flicked his brush, glanced down towards where I stood, and in a glisten of rich chestnut was unconcernedly gone.

I've had an affection for the ascent by way of Cwm Glas ever since, and if you're in Llanberis, it's the obvious way to go.

No-one in their right mind would opt for the Llanberis Path as anything other than a way of reaching Britain's finest cliff, Clogwyn Du'r Arddu, and the train is fun but it's cheating. So Cwm Glas it had to be. And besides, I hadn't been along the North Ridge of Crib Goch for some decades, remembered it as fine and virtually untrodden, and wanted to see how it had fared over the intervening years.

In Llanberis I met Ray Wood. Ray's a photographer, one of the best in the country on outdoor themes. He illustrated the book I wrote for the BBC on Snowdonia, lives in Dinorwig, and is one of my close friends. He's the best-natured man I know, vague and dilatory, always late for meetings, disarmingly silly at times, but bright and enthusiastic and the most engaging of companions – murdering the Welsh language with his London vowels, poking his curiosity down every intellectual rabbit-hole that comes his way, chattering away happily with whoever he encounters. I was glad of his company as we toiled up into Cwm Glas, and then toiled even more wearily on into upper Cwm Glas, with its little lake, Llyn Glas, on the island in which grow stunted pines, shiny and fertilized from the summit seagulls which nest and roost here.

As we sat by the lake I recounted to Ray the story of Colette Fleetwood, who was brought up here by the leader of a group of students from the University of the West of England one winter's day last century. From the lake beneath Clogwyn y Ddysgl – Llyn Bach – the leader took a bearing to the summit of Carnedd Ugain and walked his group of novices along it. It led into the steep, broken ground to the left of Parsley Fern Gully – terrain only fit and proper to the equipped and experienced winter-climber. Two of the students slipped and fell, one of them disappearing away down into the mist. Offers of help from nearby climbers were rejected by the leader. The party pressed on, their terror and the drop increasing. On the slope approaching the summit, Colette Fleetwood – an intelligent, beautiful, adventurous young woman with her life ahead of her – was plucked from her kicked steps in the snow by the gale-force, gusting wind. She went hurtling back down into the cwm below, was found later that night, dead of multiple injuries. I appeared for the family as an expert witness at her inquest. The coroner, faced with continual objection from a phalanx of solicitors representing the university, allowed little discussion and only the barest testimony. The family, bereft and uncomprehending, were left with the stark verdict of 'death by misadventure'.

It was something other than that, its circumstances thrusting a vexed salient into the whole notion of group and individual responsibility in the hills. I have seldom felt with greater force either the moral complexities that can weigh even in our simple contexts of the outdoors, or the moral bankruptcy of legal process and many of its practitioners. Mountains do not bear signs that tell: 'Whatever your leaders say, you travel here at your own risk.' Perhaps, in a world grown litigious, they should. Though litigation would never compensate a parent for the loss of a child in circumstances like these.

Beyond the glacier-smoothed ribs and hummocks of Cwm Glas is a stretch of scree slope, neither too loose nor too long, that leads to the start of Crib Goch's North Ridge. These days there is even a path traversing across it, and another one leading down from it to the start of what was once a sheep-trod crossing the mountain's east face to Bwlch Moch. But the latter is now a thoroughfare beloved of Mountain Leader training and assessment groups. We sighted two or three parties making for it in our time in Cwm Glas – engrossed in map and compass, programmed seemingly to the line being taken. I hope these enterprises warn always of how provisional confidence must be in the hills. We – gusted about in a fitful, cold wind, myself in a new pair of mountain boots slightly too big for me and Ray complaining of rickety knees – could certainly not have been accused of over-confidence as we tottered, arms waving about for balance, along the knife-edge rising to the summit. Remembrance hadn't overstated its quality. Though it's more worn these days – nowhere near as much as the ridge from Crib Goch summit to Bwlch Coch, however – it's still of a delightful, airy, mountainy character. We scrambled over the prominent quartz seams and rested again on the flat rock shelves of the top, Moel Famau forty miles away to the east clearly in view.

One of those Victorian worthies who were yearly visitors to the Pen-y-Gwryd Hotel brought an eminent Swiss guide here one snowy Easter in the century before last. Looking at the ridge ahead and the peak of Yr Wyddfa across the cwm, the guide told his *Herr*: 'We must go down. The summit is four or five hours away. We cannot make it before dark.' His *Herr* reassured him that they would be standing there in an hour. 'That,' he was told, 'is not possible!' It was. And for Ray and myself, dawdling, an hour-and-a-quarter sufficed to see us across the Crazy Pinnacle, over the gendarmes and the flaming crest, along the endless false summits of Crib y Ddysgl with its litter of recent plane wreckage, past the OS pillar with a prayer for Colette Fleetwood as we went, and up the last staircase to the cairn on top. Carnedd Arthur it was in the last-century-but-one, burial place of a giant called Rhita. An incident explaining all this from the oldest Welsh prose tale, *Culhwch ac Olwen*, locates here. But by a pleasing reversal of normal process, the former cairn has all but disappeared. Maybe that's why the mountain has shrunk by twelve feet in the last century, according to the Ordnance Survey. Or maybe they just have more accurate measuring now.

On the last stretch to the summit we came across a young

man in a garish anorak shambling down in the mist and rain that had enveloped us. I asked him about the bright yellow device dangling from his neck. 'It's a global positioning instrument,' he told me. 'So is this Helvellyn?' I queried. He looked at me askance, uncertain as to what kind of idiocy he faced. 'No, it's *Snowdon*,' he informed me with emphasis. 'You're at 3,470 feet and 218 metres from the summit.' I didn't question the mix, just thanked him. He looked concerned as he turned to descend, and told me to take care.

'No,' I rounded on him, 'don't take care – have adventures, because you learn most from them. But make sure they're charged to your own account.'

With a swift muttering glance back as though at two deranged creatures, he disappeared off into the mist, leaving us with the summit and all its litter of rusting stays and hooks from former shelters, its resonance and – on this close evening at least – its mysterious grandeur, and sense of what endures: 'Other the boys, other their transient fame,/Snowdon remains the same.' It does too, in its own hours, its own time, and despite all the irrelevance that we bring to it.

4: What we bring with us, and what we take away
So I finished my slow progress over the fourteen or fifteen three-thousand-foot summits of Eryri. It had taken me three days spread over a period of two months or more, and it had been a curiously disorientating experience. I began from the seashore at Abergwyngregyn on a sunlit August morning, and ended on top of Yr Wyddfa in the cold damp of an October gloaming. I'd been intending to make this journey in this way, reflectively, for several years.

Since I was that thirteen-year-old schoolboy in the Easter holiday of 1960, I've been enchanted by it. Wales, and that untranslatable Scottish word *stravaiging* through it, became the focus of my interest then, and a passion that has lasted since adolescence. That first Easter I climbed Snowdon by the Snowdon Ranger Path. I remember the chance middle-aged companion I'd met on the way up pointing out to me Crib Goch, and explaining its difficulties and dangers and thrills. I remember feeling then that I wanted to be able to say that I was the sort of person who could master experiences like that – remember that anticipation of self-affirming pride as clearly as I remember the malty warmth of the Horlicks that I tasted for the first time in the summit café that bitter day, and the consideration of the man I'd kept company with on the ascent (who bought me the Horlicks and later took me to where the Watkin Path slants down the steep slope south of the summit and showed me the line of descent before he bade me farewell, set off on his own route home, and I rattled off by the slanting long path into Nant Gwynant).

In the distant, retrospective view, that first day on a mountain seems to me to have been fortuitously educative: '… in this moment there is life and food/For future years.' I brought nothing to the experience then but my youth and eagerness. The weather was wintry and cold, I was clad in a tattered cotton anorak and Timpson's cheapest boots, ill-equipped and ignorant. Probably the view of all our present-day hill authorities and mountain rescue organization spokesmen and local coroners would be that I should not have been there at all. Those who do not have the qualifications deemed necessary must be excluded?

I watch my friend Sam Roberts, the National Park Warden for Snowdon, talking occasionally to youngsters like I was then. Too few of them now escape from Merseyside, or Birmingham, or inner-city Manchester where I grew up, to the hills. When Sam talks to them, there are no hectorings or forbiddings. He gets them talking, does not oppress or seek to discourage but finds out about them, informs them: of how much time what they intend might take, of what the weather is likely to do, of the things they will see, of the grounds on which they should base their individual judgements. Like the man I was so fortunate to meet on my first day...

But Sam is a very rare character, his actions informed by his own background and history of involvement with these hills. There is a more rigid structure behind him, a National Park Authority, which has some jurisdiction here. And there are also even more rigid attitudes on the part of those who come to Snowdonia. 'The keyword is acquisition,' is how the modish parlance of management-speak might have it. But what exactly do we acquire when we come to the hills? Self-belief? Self-sufficiency? Is that what the 'educational medium' of the hills has, at best, to offer?

If you arrive at the summit of Snowdon, whether by train or on foot, you can go into the café there and buy a T-shirt to tell the world that 'I climbed Snowdon'. I find that very innocent and oddly heart-warming, that you can so simply puff out your chest and expand this proclamation that you have taken probably your first step into a different world. Take a few more steps and you can become a Munroist or a Corbettista. I used to revel in all that stuff. It made me feel better about myself. I recall so clearly the weary exultation I felt a few months after this first ascent of Snowdon when I raced over all the Fourteen Peaks – there were an unquestionable, unaugmented fourteen of them then – in the course of a single day. It is like the first phase of falling in love, this attraction to the mountains – the rapture, the heedlessness of all else, the wanting more and more. And like falling in love, if it is to last, knowledge and consideration must take their place alongside attraction and appetite, or the whole business becomes a solipsistic exercise in scalp-hunting, us as the Don Juans and Donna Juanitas of the hills.

There is more to being in the mountains than being able to say that we have 'conquered' them, which is anyway always a lie, however widely peddled it may still be even by the more respectable newspapers (I have had a running feud with the *Guardian* for many years over generations of its sub-editors' insistence on changing 'climbed' to 'conquered' in pieces I've written for that paper on mountaineering. If that perception still exists even in so liberal and supposedly sophisticated a milieu, how much more widely abroad has it travelled?). It's a dangerous notion, too. In the mountains, safety and humility go hand in hand. When self-affirmation tips over into arrogance, risk enters the equation unseen. Consider the way in which institutional arrogance – the belief that if all proper procedures as laid out by the appropriate bodies in the correct training syllabuses were followed, risk could be entirely occluded and individuals made invulnerable – led to the Cairngorms Tragedy of November 1971, in which six young people under qualified leadership and supervision died. That incident should be ingrained forever into our outdoor psyche – all that confident optimism and belief in the capability and responsibility of the project and their guides frozen out of the young faces huddled together under the snow...

The more attention, knowledge and respect we bring to our hill-going, the more we derive from it. These hills are not just ciphers to augment our personal stock. They exist in their own, complete worlds, independently. That realization came to me, I think, initially through the good fortune of having come to a particular hill-region at a particular time both in history and in my own life. Fifty or sixty years ago the northern hills of Wales were a very different place – different to what they have become, vastly different to my own home environment. I was a deracinated Manchester slum-kid, electively Welsh, from a fractured home background, who made his way to a region where an essential connection still existed between landscape and population, between place, history and culture, that was thrilling, absorbing and necessary to me. I was fortunate in a way that few of my then-age could be fortunate these days. The fact that I had little but interest and need, and that this was no doubt obvious, led to my being given much in the way of hospitality, information, instruction. If I saw a shepherd half-a-mile away I would chase across a hillside and pester him with callow questions in book-learnt, half-remembered, pidgin Welsh about name and legend and hill, and often as not be allowed to stay thereafter in hay-barns from Bugeilyn to Soar-y-Mynydd to Pennant Lliw in the course of endless wanderings at every available opportunity through this land. When the focus of the hill-goer fixes on summits alone, he or she loses this dimension of instructive intimacy, the gift of which expands exponentially.

Walking the Fourteen Peaks again, slowly, deliberately, and as a planned and coherent journey after the greater part of a lifetime spent living among them brought home with clarity the attitudes we do bring to landscape in the twenty-first century. It is viewed – with some, I would say qualified, legitimacy – as a commodity to be stewarded and maintained. Other factions view it as a recreational facility, to be regarded only in the light of their own values, exclusively. At times these interests rub against each other, frictionally, and heat of argument ensues. This is the only Snowdonia – the only *Eryri* – we have. We must care for it (by which I mean preserve its essential, timeless character as near unchanged as is possible for future generations) as best we can; and care presupposes that knowledge and consideration born of love that I mentioned earlier. No, it is not enough simply to say that we have climbed Snowdon, or whatever other peak our desire may fix upon, if we want Snowdon to remain the same for those who come after us. Our presence, the wear we impart, is a form of damage to that. 'Management schemes' – to which I, along no doubt with a forceful and opinionated company of fellow hill-goers, have an instinctive resistance – are a crucial way to mediate the changes we wreak, even though I look askance at the changes the schemes themselves bring. Popularity and use bring along management as their inevitable concomitant. The number of people in these hills has increased a hundredfold since I first knew them. But the management itself must be informed and enlightened, must be born of a synthesis of all interests; and in Snowdonia it frequently falls far short of this ideal.

The idea for traversing these hills slowly took root in my mind many years ago. It came from reading a series written by that exemplary old mountain man Showell Styles in *Climber* – the first of our monthly outdoor magazines – back in the early 1960s. Showell memorably described walking over the Welsh Peaks with a tent in his rucksack; sleeping as close to each summit as he could; finding the nearest spring for water; sitting by his tent and watching as the kettle hummed and evening dammed the valleys and submerged them in shadow; waking to the unpeopled hilltop dawns. I loved that series, and it opened my eyes. To be among the hills, to reflect upon them, to come to know them – this is the way by which most value comes in upon you from the outdoor experience. This or that number of minutes or hours it took, the entry in the dusty journal, the dimming memory of excited achievement on the hardest rock-climbs – they all fade, whilst the hills' moods and atmospheres, their light and their long histories, the legends that locate so atmospherically and fittingly and the language and lives and gossip and song and folk-tales of those who dwelt here are what endure and gather force in the quiet of mind's rememberings. We receive but what we give, and that should be our best attention, lovingly bestowed. Only then will we be worthy of these hills. Only then will we preserve them.

(2001)

DESCENT INTO THE LOST WORLD

If on a winter's day a hill-traveller were to linger on the receiving end of a Welsh December downpour and skulk undecided around the car park of Gorffwysfa at the start of the Miners' Track and the Pig Track up Snowdon, whilst wind and rain lash stippled patterns across the puddles and gust through Gore-Tex layers and flurry under hood and soak up cuff and trickle down neck as even the first bend in the track retreats into the cloud, I wonder if what Theodore Watts-Dunton, in his deliciously daft Victorian romance *Aylwin*, which is set on the mountain, termed 'the mysterious magic of y Wyddfa, that magic which no other mountain in Europe exercises' would still work its spell? Or whether, given an alternative, that same traveller might opt for a less predictable itinerary than that of the summit, and one that led away from mist and rain and ascent and down into an entirely different dimension that gathers around the hem of the hill – a faded, rich embroidery of old story, association and belief the threads of which can still be discerned and disentangled from the landscape here and there?

Unnoticed in the corner of the car park near the attendant's hut, a path slips away to traverse the western side of Moel Berfedd, with the little rocky stream of Afon Trawsnant below. Circumvent the occasional stile and minor torrent and soon Bwlch y Gwyddel ('Pass of the Irish') leads up to the Pen-y-Gwryd Hotel on the left. Note the name, but we're not going that way. On the fertile ground in the valley-levels beneath, and amid the bracken of the lower slopes, suddenly from behind the shimmer of falling rain an entire pattern of habitation and use becomes apparent: hut-circles, field-systems, enclosures – a village from two thousand years ago, and the Welsh names of the hill-features close at hand or visible from here – Lakes of the Rejoicing, Pass of the Flight, Ridge of Slumber – are its only written history, for our imaginations to reconstruct as best we can. The Victorian poet and deacon Owen Wynne Jones – Glasynys to give him his Bardic name – invented his own story for the ruin of this 'town of Nanhwynen' (the latter an older and almost certainly more correct version of the nonsensical one of Nant Gwynant, which is one of too many colonial inventions or misapprehensions pasted on to the topography of these mountains). Glasynys's story involved behaviour reminiscent of Sodom and Gomorrah, murders of monks, the wrath of god, angels and uncorrupted maidens and the destroying fire falling from heaven in hues of green and blue and red, all of which reduced the 'town' to ashes and reinforced the message of Victorian morality and piety. But behind it, and more interestingly, were those threads of older tradition which had been woven and re-woven to incorporate new material and design over hundreds of years around the hearths of the old homesteads of the valley: Gwastadannas, Hafod Lwyfog, Hafod y Rhisgl. When I first came to this region over fifty years ago, the old people whom I engaged in dawdling conversations by field-gate or farmhouse porch had been a part of this process, carried its remembered richness with them still from the century-before-last. I'm reminded of a passage in Kathleen Raine's writing (it's from her impassioned introduction to *The Fairy Faith in Celtic Countries* by the American scholar and anthropologist W.Y. Evans Wentz):

...the death of any old person, whether in Cornwall, Brittany, Wales or Scotland would have been like the loss of a precious volume from a library. The 'book of the people' is oral tradition, astonishing in its retentiveness and its accuracy: and it is in the minds of the old that the unwritten learning of tradition is stored.

She goes on to note that 'many who have visited the places in fact have never done so in spirit, being impervious by their conditioning to modes of being so unlike those of our western cities.'

The note of warning she sounds there seems to me a crucial one. Do we, as *users* of the hills, represent yet another aspect of the consumerist and acquisitive society, bringing its values to an environment traditionally uncorrupted by them? Has our own failure of imagination ensured that those places in which we sought distance are now assimilated by the systems from which we attempt, in our hill-going, to escape – the recreational materialists, the hill-collectors ubiquitous there now?

Down here in Nant Gwynen – to give it the old name which I prefer and which marks out the dimension where it still exists at a remove from our trampled ways – you may put your imaginations to the test, puzzle away at old stories and their meanings, ponder the attempts they made to celebrate and understand the landscapes of human life. Nant Gwynen is as rich in these as any place I know on this planet. The people here – their imaginations working on a valley which is by turns beautiful and mysterious, intimate and grand – have told stories through millennia. There are ghosts here, fairies, water-sprites, monsters, evil kings, enchanters, magicians. Take a tour round the foot of Snowdon, past Dinas Emrys, through Beddgelert, along Nant Colwyn, by Llyn y Dywarchen and Cwellyn to Llanberis and up to Gorffwysfa again – a journey every bit as worthwhile as the *Tour de Mont Blanc* – and you can pick up everywhere on echo and allusion from an old folk-knowledge and experience that has, in three or four short decades, almost entirely disappeared from our everyday consciousness; and which was the manifestation of the human spirit engaging in complex and knowing ways with the environments to which we are now drawn.

Let me take you to the cave of the hairy man...

From that old settlement below the Irishmen's Pass, hurry past the Cwm Dyli power-station of 1906 and pick up an old path that holds to the Snowdon bank of the clear green river, skirting through woods of fantastically gnarled oak and around huge, knobbly boulders. It traverses beneath the impressively steep grass of Gallt y Wenallt (a man died here forty years ago, having slid out of control on a wet day from near the summit and crushed his skull against a boulder beneath the path); it climbs behind the cliff which juts into Llyn Gwynen and eases down along a wall on to the in-bye land of Hafod y Llan. By the confluence of the Afon Llan (or Llam, possibly, which would translate as 'The Leaping River') with the Afon Merch, keep to the near bank of the latter and follow a faint path alongside it into the woods. Here's D.E. Jenkins, from his rare and wonderful book of 1899, *Beddgelert: Its Facts, Fairies and Folklore*:

> ...its waters tumble down over a very steep and rugged bed, over which it is necessary to climb in order to get to a pool about a hundred yards higher up. That pool is fixed in a contracted place, pressed in by two perpendicular rocks. At the upper end of this pool are huddled together a number of large stones, which seem to have fallen from the rock on the left-hand side. Just below these we find an inaccessible cave, which is called... Ogof y Gwr Blewog ('The Cave of the Hairy Man')

There is a story, which Jenkins relates. It's strangely garbled, folk-tale motifs familiar from other Welsh, Scottish and Irish sources pulling it – and our imagination – in many different directions: pregnant women, stolen food, severed hands. What's apparent is that we're re-encountering the presence of the *Uruisg* here, the water-spirit, stories of whom recur throughout the Celtic countries; who – according to MacCulloch in *The Religion of the Ancient Celts* – 'haunts lonely places and waterfalls and, according to his mood, helps or harms the wayfarer. His appearance is that of a man with shaggy hair and beard...'

When you arrive at this tiny, intimate, particular place – as few, acquainted with the knowledge you now possess, have done in years, for it is little-known and less-visited – with its clear stream, its woodland of ash and holly, its moss and spleenwort, the glistening fall of ivy over its bordering rock and the fall sounding from the dark, far recess evocatively, mysteriously, what you are encountering directly is the affective power of landscape. The present magic of this old Celtic water-shrine is speaking to you as clearly as it spoke to our distant ancestors, restoring your innocence and wonder. Here's Kathleen Raine again:

> The number of those in the West who are seeking in ancient traditions for a lost inheritance is constantly growing. Nor can the knowledge ever be altogether lost since, like the laws of number or of chemistry, it is permanent in the nature of things and must be discovered anew by whoever observes the operations of the psychic world.

It is here and now and to be found in the place and moment that only require you attentively to be present.

(2006)

THE MOUNTAIN INSTINCT

In filtered sunlight and a buffeting, flint-edged wind I set off by the Llanberis Path up Snowdon one fine late-February afternoon to do a little botanizing around the cliffs of Clogwyn Du'r Arddu, which is both one of my favourite and one of the grandest places among the Welsh hills. I looked at my fellow hill-enthusiasts who were streaming up and down the route – mountain-bikers hustling and tottering their techno-steeds uphill or juddering and jouncing them down again; young men in baggy beach-shorts and singlets and their young women companions in strappy tops and denim pussy-pelmets; old stagers like myself hobbling up on stiff joints and sturdy poles – all this within winter's purlieu on the highest hill south of the Scottish border; but for sure, we were heading up or careering down its easiest line of ascent, so clearly all's permissible. I sat and drank tea on the terrace of the newly-reconstructed Halfway House, run by young Welsh people from Llanberis as it has been for the fifty years I've known it and shame on the Snowdonia National Park Authority for its misguided attempts in the recent past to do away with a unique and characterful amenity. In its former homely green corrugated iron embodiment it was so welcome a sight and stopping-place to imbibe Mrs. Williams's tart and refreshing home-made lemonade in the days of my youth when I too raced up and down this path, in the heat of long-gone summer days on my way to attempt the iconic climbs – *Great Wall, West Buttress Eliminate, The Boldest, Shrike, Woubits, Scorpio, Bloody Slab*, the *Pinnacle Arête* – on the great dark cliff encircling the cwm above.

Beyond Halfway House, beneath the scree of Allt Moses where the climb starts in earnest for Carnedd Ugain and Bwlch Coch, I took the green track to the right, surprisingly unworn even in these populous days for the high cliffs are no longer in fashion among climbers, and by the former mine barracks climbed diagonally across snow towards a prominent boulder near the entrance of an old adit. My dear friend the late Bill Condry, one of the finest of twentieth-century field-naturalists and one of the most elegant and knowledgeable of our writers on natural history first showed it to me in 1992 in the course of our filming a series of television programmes about the history of the Welsh mountains. Since then I've made an annual pilgrimage here at this time of year.

The boulder's a perfect seasonal index to the exquisite arctic-alpine flora on the great northern cliffs of Wales. On its miniature faces and facets grow roseroot, thyme, mountain everlasting, moss campion and purple saxifrage. But as I'd expected after this harsh winter, nothing was yet in flower. Feathery buds were tinged here and there with delicate purple, tiny leaves were spotted with exuded lime, the signs were there, and it seemed that a period of warm weather would surely bring forth the mountain glories. But patience was summoned, and I drifted a few yards along the slope to look across at Clogwyn Du'r Arddu. This is, from the point of view both of the climber on it and the chance beholder, the finest and most architectonic of British cliffs. Its two central and contrasting buttresses achieve a perfectly-balanced symmetry. The dark corrie lake beneath them was unrippled, mist was gauzing the buttresses, sun permeating it from behind the ridge and the 'rose-flush coming and going'. A pair of ravens seared across in rapid, hook-winged descent, opened their wings and soared up to Snowdon summit above, with its benison of tourist scraps to convey back to red throats already agape in their mine-tunnel nest on Clogwyn Coch.

These broken crags to the left of the main cliff lie directly under the railway line, which banks out with hard snow in winter, the slope beneath it suddenly steepening to their top. The Llanberis Path is the easiest way up Snowdon. The railway line, surely – proximous, a little lower down the slope – is an easier version still? Yet from where I sit, I can see the grooves ploughed through the snow above the crags in the hapless, helpless descents of three young men who had died here in recent weeks. This convex northern slope that so often in winter becomes a steepening, unbroken sheet of iron-hard *névé* where a kick with stiff mountain boots barely effects toe-purchase – to those without ice-axe and crampons it then becomes a deathtrap, as many accidents down the years (one of them in the 1960s with a shocking toll of fatalities to a London school party played its part in the setting-up of the present-day mountain leader training schemes) as well as the three recent ones demonstrate. Logic suggests the railway as a safe way down, but mountain instinct would shy away. Signs at the top of the dangerous section used to direct the descending unwary across right to the safer ridge leading from Carnedd Ugain to the descent by Allt Moses, but in recent years they have gone – perhaps weathered away, perhaps removed during the work on the summit hotel, perhaps damaged by those who believe that prescriptive notices have no place on mountains and mountain instinct should be our best guarantor of safety.

The latter's a stance with which I have a good deal of sympathy. Yes, our society is one beset by the often-moronic strictures of the Health & Safety Tyranny. Yes, our children are denied at every turn the beneficent dimension of exploratory outdoor play. I recall that the summary work of that distinguished mountaineer and educationalist Robin Hodgkin – a rigorous and delightful old Quaker friend of mine who died in 2003 at the age of 87 – was called *Playing and Exploring*, and concluded from a lifetime's experience of outstanding personal adventure and the supervision of young people in outdoor environments that only from a permitted liberty of experience does the instinct for safety derive. By extension, then, only in mountain experience will the mountain instinct grow, which raises the apparent conundrum that mountains are dangerous places in which to gather experience for survival there.

From my stance under Clogwyn Coch I look up at that slope again – how much more alarming would its profile appear if I were looking down it! – and shudder involuntarily. It is to me, from long years of mountain knowledge, so transparently dangerous a place. I would not go there in winter conditions unless I were wearing crampons. And yet, this is the line of the railway up Snowdon that I am talking about – not Zero Gully or the cliffs of Lochnagar. Note, too, that I say I'd not go there in winter conditions without crampons (and good winter boots to which to fit them). No mention of an ice-axe! I'd be perfectly happy crossing it thus shod, trekking poles for balance. Among those people I saw along the path there were plenty of ice-axes in evidence. Just this week I read a news bulletin about a walker who was rescued from beneath Crib Goch, where he'd become crag-fast. He had an ice-axe with him – no crampons, though. In all the older mountaineering instruction manuals you'll find detailed sections on ice-axe braking, with the invariable injunction to practise it first on a shallow slope with a safe run-out. Quite a good game in that context, but let me tell you this: if you're descending by a banked-out Snowdon Railway track and lose your footing, that ice-axe is no more use to you than a good luck charm, and may do you more harm than good. It stands little chance of stopping your acceleration to the lip of those imminent cliffs. I'm not by any means saying don't carry one or don't bother learning how to use one, but bear in mind that it is a tool of limited utility and there are many situations in which it will not save you.

The fine old Scottish mountain writer Tommy Weir wrote

this about an ascent of Observatory Ridge on Ben Nevis many years ago:

> We have made no plan of attack. We know each other too well for that, and as we rope, by tacit consent we shorten our line; each man takes a few coils in his hand and we move off together. This is the Alpine method of climbing, unlike the British method where only one man moves at a time; and it is only justifiable when both members of the party are equally competent on the kind of terrain they are climbing. It is exhilarating because it cuts out waiting, and it calls for constant vigilance in handling the rope, to take up slack, or avoid jerking your companion…

I smile at the memory, at the account, and not because I'm thinking: 'Well, that's a case of "If one's down, all are down"' but because I know that the technique described is incidental, and what's key here is the mutual trust in developed mountain instinct: '…*only justifiable when both members of the party are equally competent on the kind of terrain.*' You would have trusted Tommy Weir with your life in a mountain situation and his every studied easy movement told you so. He'd survived his long apprenticeship and come through to the hard-won sphere of competence and instinctual knowledge. Intuition tells me that it's harder to do that these days. Levels of performance rather than the acquisition of mountain sense are at premium. Popular survivalist epics – in the recounting of certain of which there is a strong element of the fictive or even the outright fictional – inculcate a curious belief in personal invincibility. We are not thus. We need to take guard. We need to develop an accurate capacity to judge things as they are, and not as our heroic proxies may or may not have found them to be.

In winters long ago I used to thrust out on the foulest days into the storm and snow of Welsh hills, eager to read the most difficult texts mountains can offer. I survived, and learned. All I'd want to impart here is that learning to read even the most elementary of those texts is a necessary level of consciousness to be achieved in our mountain-going. With that thought I moved away with a shudder from beneath Clogwyn Coch where those broken and wasted bodies came to rest, crossed to a bluff where the starry saxifrage was budding on ice-scoured rocks. Gargoyle boulders above the walls of the East Gully lent a sinister aspect to the scene. A straw glow infused the flanks of Snowdon's seaward ridge. A grey front moved in over the flats of Anglesey. Choughs squealed at the returning ravens' taunting play. The world went on in its fierce, natural way, indifferent as ever to all our human business....

(2012)

ON THE BLACK RIDGE

Ray Wood and myself were sitting in *Caban*, discussing a volume of autobiographical reminiscence, *Hen Atgofion: Blynyddoedd y Locust,* by the Welsh poet and scholar W.J. Gruffydd – a quarryman's son who was born and lived his early life in a neighbouring village to Brynrefail, in the northerly foothills between Snowdon and the sea. Gruffydd's a writer to whom I feel considerable temperamental affinity, his work imbued with a sense of place and regional culture, as here in this extract from the chapter 'Nant yr Wyddfa':

> I set out by car from Cardiff at nightfall, and, after driving through lashing rain and wind all the way, I reached Nant yr Wyddfa [the old local name for the Pass of Llanberis between Gorffwysfa and Penllyn by Brynrefail] about two o'clock in the morning. For a moment the black clouds had dispersed, and the vast majesty of the Snowdon crags shimmered

beneath the unnumbered stars. I stopped the car and got out. Suddenly in a flash of perception, I realized that the criticism of malignant and ignorant people is less than dust on the scales – something too insignificant even to be amusing. I was given five minutes – perhaps it was only five seconds – of assurance, of personal freedom from petty things; in the stillness of those minutes between Snowdon and the Glyders I saw how my whole life, through having been too often a prey to fools, had lost all serenity and tranquillity. I do not think I shall ever again be tormented by anything as petty as prejudice. ...my mind turns more and more to the old things and the old folk. The truth is that I have never lived in a community since I left Llanddeiniolen for Cardiff a quarter of a century ago. Here I simply reside – sleeping, working and eating. I do not live here.

This scintillating and touching memoir of a time past was written for an express purpose that Gruffydd makes clear in another redolent passage, that chimes closely with my purpose:

Sometimes, in my bed when I cannot sleep, I bring to mind the homes of my native place, and I repeat the name of everyone who lived in each of them in my time or the time of my parents; and after dropping off to sleep, I dream of the old people who have gone: my father and mother, my grandfather and my grandmother, my aunt Elin Huws of Cae Meta, Dafydd and Lewis Huws...

I look for the latter name on the map as Ray and I sit over our coffee, and find it there on a gentle southerly slope above the Afon Seiont, old woodland and an old settlement behind, the people of the place from W.J. Gruffydd's time long gone. He continues:

...for a moment on waking, I feel overwhelming happiness because I can still have their company. I don't know what Freud or Jung would say about this, and I don't care. I shall now prolong by a little the allotted period of the old community by writing the story of those times.

Well, where did all this matter go? Other plays in the repertory have been performed here since, though the backdrop – Snowdon, the Glyders, rivers and woods – has remained constant, changes in it no more than ones of detail and use. This scene has been important in my life. For years I lived and worked in a house – when I sold it, it was to Ray Wood – the windows of which looked out across Llyn Padarn to Cefn Du. My son Will grew up here. The woods and rocks and hills were his playground. On my kitchen wall in Dyffryn Tanat there hangs a large oil painting of that dark ridge opposite: Cefn Du, the black ridge...

So here in *Y Caban*, Ray and I are squandering the day, shrinking away from the glower of it and the grey clouds. It is All Souls' Night, and this vision of a hill has come to possess me. Cefn Du – few come here, and those who do mostly arrive by the tarmac road that approaches within a quarter-mile of its Ordnance Survey pillar. Few come here and yet it is the start of and the first height on the fine, rolling northerly ridge that leads over Moel Eilio, Moel y Cynghorion and Clogwyn Du'r Arddu ('the Black Cliff of the Black Height') to the summit of Snowdon itself. In every other quarter of Eryri these hills teem with folk, the more with every passing year – but not this one, not this sombre, atmospheric height between Gwyrfai and Seiont. I muse on that, remember its moods – the imperial blush of August heather, winter's snowy ermine, its solidity against the fleet scud of cloud – and envision it as an ambiguous place:

...where the damned have howled away their hearts,
And where the blessed dance.

Ray and I drive round to the path that broaches the ridge from the north-west, intending to traverse the hill back to Llanberis. We climb past pylons and under power lines that hiss and crackle at the mist, navigate through a web of stone-walled fields by gated, rocky ways, past mounds of burnt stones and the outlines of hut-circles that pre-date any written history, and are debouched finally on to the moor, which is dense and heathery and dark. This is the secret of this place – this is its notation, the key in which it resonates. This is what sets it apart, makes it special, ensures that it be left unvisited. You can acquire your summits, tread your peaks, scramble along your ridges, rattle down your screes. But a moor takes away all your definitives, leaves you errant and unsure. Its vagueness teases at Ray's map as he tries to orient himself, and the moor's perpetual ally the wind colludes to flap it away. Its heather smothers and obliterates all semblance of paths, however optimistically they are marked down on paper. Here's Nan Shepherd, from her novel, *A Pass in the Grampians*:

> For the sheep farmer, seventy years of intercourse had made the moor sit to him more closely than the most supple of garments... He had made his covenant with the moor: it had bogged him and drenched him, deceived, scorched, numbed him with cold, tested his endurance, memory and skill; until a large part of his nature was so interpenetrated with its nature that apart from it he would have lost reality.

Ray and I, we do not *live* here, have only looked on at it for years in all its changing moods and seasons, from behind glass and a near distance. We flounder; we follow faint leads through squelching, heavy ground; we chaff good-naturedly at each other's ignorance and incompetence; we crest the ridge and are battered in the wind's wuther and blast; we look out over Caernarfon Bay, all dappled mercury and pewter, and watch the white horses chasing over Caernarfon Bar; we see the squalls drift towards us as shimmering columns across the flats of Anglesey northerly; we prepare for our drenching. Before rain and hail reach us, we have slipped inside the draughty roofless ruin of Marconi's 1914 wireless station, from which the first direct radio message was sent across the Atlantic that year, and four years later to Australia. Ghosts of electricity are howling on the storm as we cower in the shell of the building and huddle into our waterproofs. That pathless mile, steep and stumbling, through the heather has eaten up the remnants of the day. Dark falls. We venture out into gale and hiss of hail to make our Hallowe'en descent through the deserted workings of the Glynrhonwy quarries. I remember Thomas Pennant's description of descending Snowdon in a storm:

> The prospect down was horrible. It gave an idea of numbers of abysses, concealed by thick smoke, furiously circulating around us. Very often a gust of wind formed an opening in the clouds, which gave a fine distinct vista of lake and valley.

The streetlights of Llanberis made our treacherous foreground of slate-tip and quarry-hole all the more opaque. From the lunar primitive of the moor, out of the skeletal remnants of technology's genesis, down through post-industrial desolation where whistle of the wind and the slip of settling spoil clacks out our sole accompaniment, we descend to connect into glimmering narrow ways whose scraped stones struck sparks from the hobnails of the quarrymen – W.J. Gruffydd's father among them, no doubt – so few decades ago in these hills' scheme of things. I find myself invoking that word *caban* as I clatter down in the unlight. It was the term used for the bleak slate huts where the quarrymen took their breaks, sheltered when necessary from the extremes of mountain weather. But it stood also as symbol for the autodidactic intensity of those former working communities, unconnected with the new world, concerned to explore and evaluate and learn, to perpetuate and amplify their own culture, to reject the merely meretricious and resist depredation and corruption.

In the dark, threading down by tenuous links, we come into the new, neon, weekend-and-holiday sensation-seeking world of Llanberis, and I walk down Goodman Street with a stanza of the old Welsh scholar-poet Gruffydd echoing distantly:

> Mor fyr llawenydd. Nid oes go'
> Ond cochni'r maes lle troedient gynt,
> A gwywder lle bu'r llwyfan dro,
> A darnau papur yn y gwynt.
> Mae'r pasiant trosodd; fe aeth Will
> I lawr y glyn...

> (How short is joy. Nothing remains in memory
> But the red of the field where once they walked,
> And the faded light of the former stage,
> And scraps of paper on the wind.
> The pageant is over; Will went
> Down the valley...)

(For Will Perrin, 1980-2004, who felt deeply and despaired of the world.)

(2010)

TWO VISIONS OF MOELSIABOD

1: *Bone Structure, Fine Skin*

From Capel Curig, early on a rare fine day in June with the flycatchers dipping along the lane under the oak trees, I crossed Pont Cyfyng and took the track up towards Rhos Farm, branching off before I reached it to follow the old green quarry-way that contours the flank of Moel Siabod's north-eastern ridge. From the clattering slate spoil-heaps and the silent pool at the old workings, a rough and squelchy quarter-mile brought me to the flats of russet grasses around the outflow from Llyn y Foel. That fine old hill-walker and lover of all things to do with the mountains of North Wales, E.G. Rowlands, in his classic little period-piece of 1951, *Hill Walking in Snowdonia* (I have an ancient and tattered copy open in front of me and note the author's good-natured dedication: 'to the youth of Britain' – hard to imagine A. Wainwright being so amiable!) writes that 'most of the pundits say that the ascent of Moel Siabod from Capel Curig is dull, but the pundits are not always right.' Indeed they're not. I have two watercolours on the wall above my desk here, studies in different light from the point at which we've just arrived, of Llyn-y-foel and the ridge behind by the Cornish artist Clifford Fishwick. Another artist and sculptor, my dear old friend Jonah Jones who died in 2003, had the following to say about this scene:

> Once the entire corrie comes into view this lake reveals itself as one of the finest [in Wales]. First the synclinal rock barrier at its foot is beautifully delineated, as though the slabs and layers had cooled and crystallized only recently. Then the ridge behind the lake, superb granite slabs ascending to the summit, is surely one of the most conspicuous in the area.

Of this ridge, which drops down south-easterly from the summit before curving round to the east and embracing the lake with that remarkable synclinal rock-barrier of which Jonah Jones speaks, Patrick Monkhouse wrote that it 'gives half a mile of very entertaining scrambling on dark, rough rock. There is neither danger nor difficulty; if there was, it could be avoided by keeping to the left...' That seems to me if anything rather lukewarm about what I would hold to be one of the most pleasant and satisfying lines of ascent on any of the central Snowdonian peaks.

The ridge is called Daear Ddu, which means 'Black Ground'. I look at these two paintings above my desk, both of which capture the lovely circling form of it. In both of them it gleams, and in neither is it black. I recall being high on one of its slabs and looking down to see in one of those startling visionary moments that the hills fine into your consciousness the edge beneath me as a gleaming silver transect across the ink-dark lake beyond. I think of how satisfying is the directness of the ridge's arrival at the exact summit itself, with Yr Wyddfa and its satellite peaks shapely from this angle across the Nant-y-gwryd, and against the sunset too if you have timed your ascent tardy and right. And I ponder too on where it might have been that the great field-botanist of these hills, Evan Roberts – Ifan Gelli, to give him his bardic name – found the purple saxifrage which set him on his life's journey into the study of mountain plants on that long-gone spring day when his wife threw him out of their house for getting under her feet, as a proper Welsh woman of her generation would. All this attaches to the mountain feature and forms a part of the texture of its attraction, and an element of explanation for my affection for it. But the basic reason is far simpler. It is nothing other than the texture of the rock itself.

Old Harry Griffin – for over half-a-century before his death in 2004 a *Guardian* and Lakeland institution – in one of his books about the Cumbrian fells which I would still count among my favourite outdoor reading, had this to say on the subject:

> It is hardly correct to think of scrambling as an end in itself – like rock-climbing. Rather is it a pleasant incident in a mountain day, a more invigorating way of reaching a summit. Rarely have I set off to do a particular scramble; usually, on a mountain walk, I have spotted a possible route away from the tracks and gone off and climbed it – or, sometimes, have failed to do so and had to find another way. Scramblers are, I think, people who itch to get their fingers on rock.

Harry goes on to elaborate charmingly and idiosyncratically around the spirit of exploration and adventure, the more complete nature of the physical exercise as compared to fell-walking; but he has surely captured the essence in that final sentence: 'Scramblers are... people who itch to get their fingers on rock.' Which brings me back to Moel Siabod and Daear Ddu. Maybe it's the long years I spent in thrall to rock-climbing – probably in part as reaction to an early and hard induction into fell-walking on the northern moors – but I still 'itch to get [my] fingers on rock', still find it difficult to pass by the smallest craggy outcrop or even the coursed masonry of some grand building without wanting to experience the feel, the tactile essence of it. Those who have never engaged in the activity tend to view rock-climbing in terms of achievement, conquest, all those spurious, testosterone-derived, ad-man and he-man concepts. For the most part, I don't believe it was thus to those of us who gave ourselves to its frights and ecstasies and consuming rigours. Yeats, I think, comes closer to the sense of it in his poem, 'An Irish Airman Foresees His Death':

> A lonely impulse of delight
> Drove to this tumult in the clouds;
> I balanced all, brought all to mind,
> The years to come seemed waste of breath,
> A waste of breath the years behind –
> In balance with this life, this death.

Thus the metaphysics plainly defined, and underpinning it, rooting it in the mountain place is the pure pleasure gained from the touch and feel of the rock. As on this ridge of Daear Ddu, where it is firm and cinder-rough, clean, frictional, its shining planes an ascending harmonic scale, its finale the top itself. Just as we might look on a beautiful human being, appreciate the fine bone-structure and the perfect skin, hope to douse out the soundness of character without which beauty is a dangerous and deceitful other, so it is for me with this perfect, alluring, embracing little ridge of the Welsh hills. The analogy is there to be pursued. I think of the Cyfrwy Arête on Cader Idris, a marvellous mountain feature which perhaps just shades over from the province of scrambling into that of rock-climbing. But it is flakey, suspect, untrustworthy, the rock splintered and likely to break. Whenever I'm on it, above those mauve drops with sea to the west, I think of the mountaineer, skier and Catholic theologian Sir Arnold Lunn, lying at its foot with his leg 'broken, crushed and comminuted' after having pulled off a huge block, a deployment of falsity in the rock, and fallen with it to the screes. Don't come to Cyfrwy if you seek something dependable in the fabric of mountain experience – exhilaration, yes, exposure and risk, but there is no solidity in this shattered matrix across which your nerves dance warily. I know of other such places: the Great Ridge of Creigiau Gleision, of the rock on which Dorothy Pilley wrote that it 'made one uneasy by its appearance of fragility';

that line on Lliwedd in the Snowdonia scrambling guide which has caused deaths and which the novice scrambler is well advised not to investigate too immediately. When I climbed regularly, rock of bad character had its appeal from time to time – the brown sugar of rotten granite in some zawns of West Penwith, the treacherous striated folding in South Stack's great quartzite cliffs, Llech Ddu's creaking Damocleans – all of these would tease at nerves eager for pathological excitement. But the solid and recurrent points of attraction – the wind-hewn roughs of Pennine millstone grit, the sea-washed limestone of Castlemartin, the sound massivity of Snowdonia dolerites and rhyolites – were those to which the pendulum, stilling itself, would return.

If there were one point to which I could return which would encapsulate all this, where would it be? I scan across these paintings by Clifford Fishwick – himself a climber, and long-time companion to one of my great rock-mentors, Peter Biven – on the wall above my desk. There is a miniature of the Black Cuillin that always has me thinking of padding up those delectable slabs on Bidein Druim nan Ramh; there are the two of Daear Ddu across Llyn-y-foel, and one also of the cliffs on Hoy, the high, dark island, its features merged into bulking abstraction. But my eye rests continually on my favourite among them – a small, intense watercolour of Corrag Buidhe, Lord Berkeley's Seat and Sgurr Fiona, all snow-dust and azure and the rose-plunge of rock down to shadowed little Loch Toll an Lochain. At my fingertips now, the scrape of that firm, rough stone of An Teallach. In a charged, synaesthetic moment, memory, imagination and desire coalesce on the summit of Sgurr Fiona, with the sun westering, and a kind of permanence, a rough endurance, under the palms of your hand as you lean back, and all the little glinting lochans of the Fisherfield Forest and a shimmer of light spreading across the Minch, the Summer Isles drawn in, everything static and permanent subsumed in its brief and recurrent glory.

(2009)

2: *Black Light*

Sunset and dawn are the great times to be on a mountain top. The physical world then settles itself down with all the sighing, rustling rhythms of darkness, or heaves and stretches itself into light. If there is one Welsh mountain I would choose above all others to watch these processes at their continual turn, it is Moel Siabod. There are one or two better viewpoints in Eryri perhaps, and even a few hills for which I have a more intimate fondness, born of memory and association, but Siabod has a particularity of feature on the face of Wales that recommends itself to me. And it has one of the best ways to reach a summit among all the Welsh hills – the south-eastern ridge called Daear Ddu that cradles Llyn y Foel and reaches to the very top.

All devotees of the legends of Wales will know about Llyn-y-foel, Daear Ddu, and their role in the epic tale of Hu Gadarn and the *afanc* (the latter ludicrously translated in most books on Wales as a beaver), which was tricked and bound in Llyn yr Afanc near the confluence of Conwy and Lledr, then dragged by Hu Gadarn's oxen over Siabod to be drowned in Glaslyn. So profound were the oxen's exertions that one of them lost an eye in pulling the monster and it rolled down to form a lake – Llyn Llygad yr Ych ('the lake of the ox's eye'). The fiery, roaring breath of the *afanc* burned the ground as it passed, and thus the ridge's name of Daear Ddu.

For all this scorched-earth pseudo-history, the ridge is a magnificent line of ascent. You can reach Llyn-y-foel either from Pont Cyfyng past the snarling dogs of Rhos farm and on through old quarries where the deep green water always gives me a little *frisson* of terror as I pass, then over the shoulder of the moor to the quartz-speckled rocks along its shore. Or through the resinous sweet forest from Dolwyddelan with low hills rolling away behind you into the Migneint. Both ways are apt preludes to the ridge's orderly theme. You scramble up its armadillo-plated spine and the texture of the rock is dreamlike. How can something so bubbly-rough be possessed of such gravity and precisely-defined form? It is over far too soon, and leaves you a few level paces from the OS pillar. Because I like to sit on my hills at nightfall and dawn, I have often slept and dreamed up here, and it was from here that I saw the black light.

I was sitting with my back to the summit cairn, facing east on an evening of absolute clarity and stillness. The sun was going down behind a shoulder of Snowdon and the cwm at my feet was inky with shadow. I was in that perfectly peaceful and harmonious state where you are so still that the gentle throb of blood around your body is as palpable, as audible, as the ticking of a clock. The whole outlook seemed of transcendent beauty – green hills and woods, a glowing softness of light. That marvelling phrase of Simone Weil's about being 'annihilated by the plenitude of being' had never seemed more appropriate. There was an emerald patch of lichen on a rock that was catching the light, capturing my attention. When I looked up from it the pool of shadow at my feet had spilled over with shocking suddenness and streamed out to the horizon. A second glance and it seemed to be pulsing back from that point to the south-east, flooding the mountain with its sharp-edged black light, suggesting such visions of despair. I had witnessed the rising of the anti-sun, knew in that moment why our land is subject to such desecration. These high places to most are a cleansing of the soul, but when their surrounding communities are lost and the values which stem from social hope with them, then the remnants who inhabit there are left desolate, desperate, unremitting in their antagonism to all who would fondly dictate. I grabbed my rucksack, fled shuddering down the hillside to the west, and rested finally among boulders suffused with the last of the western light.

(1983)

PART THREE

West of Snowdon

The hills to the west of Snowdon to my mind are the most
beautiful and shapely in Wales. The 'Ridge of the Red Cairns'
between Cwm Pennant and Dyffryn Nantlle in particular is
exquisite, its skyline like a melody. All along the Llŷn Peninsula
too there are lesser heights, sunnier than those of central
Snowdonia, a sea on either side giving them a holiday feel.
And on the whole they are far less crowded than the popular
heights of Eryri. By way of introduction, let's start with a
circular walk from Beddgelert into one of the three loveliest of
Welsh valleys.

THE HILLS OF HEAVEN

Descending Bwlch Main from Yr Wyddfa on a glum, moist
day, I go west at the fork in the path to follow the ridge above
Llechog, and suddenly the cloud all around begins to glow and
thin, is suffused with a warm orange tint, and as I walk on
through it streams past me, as though suddenly galvanized and
intent on its own ascent of the mountain. The sky above is still a
heavy and pillowy grey, but far ahead the sun has ducked under
that pall to shine a searchlight across what – a few parts of the
Western Highlands aside – is the most physically beautiful of
all British landscapes, and is transfiguring it into a dreamlike

and enchanted place where definition is lost and topography transforms into suggestion and allure. Ridge upon ridge pile up and the spaces between lose substance and become washes of colour, chasms of tint, aches of shadow. I sit down on a rock, allow my attention to be consumed by visual splendour, know that I'm entering other-worldly atmosphere, witnessing yet again the inchoate definition of this magical place.

This group of hills west of Snowdon, on that mountain's clear days, draws the eye of all those who climb there. The summit hotel itself is so aligned that its windows look on to this region, and I do not think that mere convenience or chance. Ponder the aesthetics of mountain design, think of it in terms of line, balance, proportion, and of all our British hills these are the ones to which my mind returns continually as the exemplars. They've long been known collectively as the Eifionydd hills, after the name of the commote of medieval Wales within the ancient boundaries of which they're contained. If the Tien Shan translate as the mountains of heaven, for me these little heights of north-western Wales are the hills of heaven. They are by no means lofty – only one of them, Moel Hebog, even attains the 2,500 feet necessary for Corbett status – but statistics can be spurious and misleading. We can view height as an absolute, or as a factor relative to the height from which we start (how many Munroists, after an ascent of Beinn Sgritheall from the shores of Loch Hourn, would refute this point?) To climb Glyder Fach from Pen-y-Gwryd, or Snowdon from Gorffwysfa, are ascents in both cases of little more than 700 metres. That of Moel Hebog from Beddgelert is a longer climb than either of them – consider that when you feel inclined to dismiss these as 'little' hills. Their bounding valleys are low compared to those of the Nant y Gwryd or Nant y Benglog, and that fact contributes to their sense of apartness.

I wouldn't recommend that you approach this lovely hill area from Beddgelert, though. That place – its popularity endearingly built on a fraudulently-located, commercially-motivated story about dogs and princes, wolves and babies – throngs with parking wardens and wheel-clampers, ice-cream shops and pizza parlours, trinket-infestation and National Trust way-marking. You'll find the same version of outdoor-going in Hathersage or Ambleside, Aviemore or Ingleton. Leave it to the tourists who are content to be led, and find your own way instead along the Porthmadog and then the Caernarfon roads to the Lodge Bridge across the Afon Dwyfor, at the entrance to Cwm Pennant. Come here in May when the days are lengthening and the 'glad green leaves, delicate-filmed as new-spun silk' of the beech trees around the strange tower on the little hill above are at their most incandescent, an essence of green. If you liked, and were fit and didn't mind adding a dozen miles on to a long and arduous day (it would have the benefit of bringing you back to a rare and wonderful local pub, Y Plu, in Llanystumdwy), you could follow the course of the Dwyfor up from its little-frequented, heron-and-plover-haunted estuary below Llanystumdwy, past Lloyd George's cobbled and boulder-weighted grave by riparian paths through writhing groves of oak, salmon racing through long, clear pools and leaping the cataracts alongside. But perhaps that's a walk in its own right for days when prudence keeps you off the hills? You've come to Lodge Bridge because this is the best start for the finest hill circuit in Snowdonia – the traverse of the ridges which surround the quiet, hidden heart of Eifionydd, Cwm Pennant.

I like to begin from here, for the interest and contrast in the landscape. From lush meadows and rich woodland the lane climbs up to sheep pastures, among which stands the medieval house of Isallt Fawr. Forty years ago it was quite decrepit, flag-floored, the staircase to the upper floor within the thickness of the walls, but has now been made convenient and smart. As a key to the underlying wildness or even savagery of this place, I remember from its time of dereliction how the woman who lived here in the 1970s, hearing her baby scream ran out to where she'd left it in its pram outside, to find a pack of polecats tearing at its face. The image still haunts me, plays in my mind whenever I hurry away from Isallt by pathways up the great south-west spur of Hebog. Braich y Gornel it's called, on which is one of the densest concentrations of Bronze Age settlements in Wales. From this levelled city of ancient time, you continue steeply to the cairned summit. Snowdon sprawls across the Nant Colwyn; the hooked profile of Moel Siabod blocks off the end of Nant Gwynen; your way on leads northwards into a landscape the physical, botanical and legendary textures of which are things of marvel. It's numinous with the presence of Wales's greatest historical figure, Owain Glyndŵr, whose eponymous cave is a perilously-accessed and nettle-infested, sloping and overhang-sheltered crag-ledge on the east face of the next peak, Moel yr Ogof. As for the physical fabric, let my dear late friend Bill Condry give you the picture with a botanist's eye:

> ...everything changes dramatically as you come down into the narrow pass under the north slope of Hebog. You notice that green lichens have mostly ended and that a thickly encrusting white lichen has replaced them; and that now instead of hard grey bare rocks there are brown, softer-looking rocks with many holes and ledges and fissures with green plants bristling out of them, not bilberry now or cowberry, but rose-root, golden-rod, beech fern and devilsbit scabious... Here is a little mountain everlasting, leaves pale-green above, silvery-hairy below. Next to it is the only rose of these mountain ledges, the burnet rose, with its multitude of fine sharp thorns.

What you enter into, beyond Hebog, is one of the finest rock gardens in Britain. If you're of a botanizing bent, quit your circuit here and now and head off back to the starting point down the Afon Llefrith, along which there's interest enough to detain you for the whole day. But if you're set on exercise and completion of objectives, there's another kind of fairyland in store. The ridge from Moel yr Ogof to Moel Lefn is jewelled with reedy pools set among tiny, pale outcrops. The atmosphere changes again as you pick up the old way from Pont Cae'r Gors into Bwlch Cwm Trwsgl. There are old slate quarries here, spoil heaps, deep holes, roofless workmen's barracks and echoey, stonecrop-carpeted terraces. Cwm Trwsgl itself is an impressive and rather desolate place under its brooding dolerite crags, and one I always feel glad to leave behind on the brisk climb up to Bwlch y Ddwy Elor ('The Pass of the Two Biers'). Beyond the *bwlch* a mirey descent into the forest, resinous and cool on summer days, takes you into Cwm Farchnad, and a slow, traversing ascent is followed by the steepest climb of the day up the east ridge of Y Garn. Once on that fine bold promontory, looking across Drws-y-coed to Mynydd Mawr, the elephant mountain, ahead of you is the ridge which is one of Snowdonia's supreme delights – the Nantlle Ridge, or 'Ridge of the Red Cairns', elegant and swooping, narrow-crested and switchback, deeply sculpted and gouged to the north by glacial ice, the ground underfoot grassy and accommodating, sea to the north and south with all the tricks of light and mood its proximity can play.

It will be afternoon by now. You'll make your way along it, over Mynydd Drws-y-coed and Trum y Ddysgl, up to Mynydd Tal y Mignedd with its quarrymen's high slate jubilee obelisk for Queen Victoria, then by scrambling steps to Craig Cwm Silyn with one of the finest rock-climbing cliffs of Snowdonia beneath, and on to Garnedd Goch. Since the day is hot and has been long, I'd recommend that you turn aside at Bwlch Cwmdulyn, descend through Cwm Ciprwth with its fine waterwheel made by Dingey & Sons of Truro, brought up here in pieces on horseback to serve an unproductive mine, neglected for a century and now restored by the National Park's archaeologist. The path by the side of Ceunant Ciprwth leads down to Cwm Pennant again, at a perfect bathing pool, after the refreshment of which the couple of miles along by the side of the alder-shaded and trout-darted stream will seem all too short to reflect on as perfect a hill itinerary as Britain can provide.

CIRCUMAMBULATORY

Sometimes I get a notion to set out in the opposite direction to the one in which I'm heading, circle round, and study the object of whatever quest I'm on from the angles. From the campsite – a noisy place – on the Nant Gwynant side of Beddgelert I turned my back on the morning glories of Moel Hebog and strolled along riverside paths through high bracken wet with dew. The rocks and oak-woods of Dinas Emrys were sun-gilded, and I whiled away the mile to Llyn Dinas by rehearsing the story from Nennius of the first appearance of Ambrosius (who was later to become famous as that mysterious presence in the Matter of Britain, Merlin the Magician) – a story of which modern archaeologists have vindicated much of the context at this site. I stopped at the footbridge below the craggy old fortress. Tint and texture of weed in the outfall from the lake, wavy russet and vivid, mottled green, held me gazing for minutes in delight. I cast a casual glance across the lake at the great pyramidal form of Moel Siabod, and trudged up by a popular and carefully-reconstructed path to the heathery col that leads over into Cwm

Bychan, the narrowest and least pretty of those three parallel valleys – Bychan, Nantmor, Croesor – that score south-westerly through the foothills of Eryri towards the great *Traeth* and the sea.

This brief circumambulation had brought me to a point I could have reached in a quarter of the time from the Beddgelert campsite, but the saving in minutes would have been at the cost of encountering scores more people. Also, though both routes would have brought me to Pont Aberglaslyn, the one I'd chosen had certain advantages in the matter of outlook, and this was the theme that was taking root in my mind as I ambled along. Thomas Pennant, over 200 years ago, extolled Aberglaslyn, and it must then, roadless, have been a terrific defile leading down to the sea: 'The mountains approach so close, as to leave only room for the furious river to roll over its stony bed; above which is a narrow road, formed with incredible labour, impending over the water … The scenery is the most magnificent that can be imagined.' The anxious register of that chimes well with the National Trust's posting of contemporary warnings about the dangers of this selfsame Fisherman's Path as it's now termed.

I prefer little, mine-scarred Cwm Bychan to Aberglaslyn for a – circuitous, it's true – route out of Beddgelert. It's more open, airy, surprising in its outlooks; it gives you a sense of how lovely, shapely and sylvan are these hills to the south and west of Snowdon. Both ways bring you to Pont Aberglaslyn, old and of single-span, thrown across the torrent by the Devil for human use on condition that he took possession of the first soul to cross it. But the Devil made a mistake! He went into the bar of the nearest public house, Tafarn Telyn, and there met with the magician (they were thick on the ground in these parts formerly) Robin Ddu, whom he attempted to lure into the crossing.

Black Robin, with a loaf under his arm and the pub's little terrier at his heel, looked askance at the Devil's work. 'Will it bear the weight of this loaf?' he asked disparagingly. 'Sure, go ahead, roll it over,' sneered the preening demon. Robin did just that, the little dog gave chase, and hence the reason why terriers are such bad characters...

I don't think the story quite ended like that in the original, but never mind. I had nothing to worry about. A thousand people had already crossed that morning as I idled over, turned left, and then sought out the old way, moss-walled on either side, that leads through woods of birch, beech and pine up to Oerddwr. This, and its associated guardian hill fort of Pen-y-gaer, is one of the prime and quiet places in the Welsh hills. After splashing through a quaking morass, a regular *fign*, in quest of the lost path, I stretched out my limbs to rest in the sun on sweet turf, and was descended upon: 'Sorry to intrude on your patch,' fluted the cultured accent, 'but could you tell us where the path to Pont Aberglaslyn goes?'

My short-term memory not being what it was, I gestured vaguely one side or the other of a green hummock, and told of a moss-grown, beautiful, narrow and abandoned lane down through the woods. At which point a fourth, and detached, member of the group began braying in a high, cross, insistent whine from the knoll above, scolding the woman who had spoken to me, reminding her of the walk she was soon apparently assigned to lead. So she, apologetically, shuffled away in the direction she was bidden, and I, bridling at all the presumptuous lexis of authority, was left muttering wryly a phrase of Gwenallt's about *Bratiaeth Saeson y De* before I lapsed into reciting stanzas from a favourite poem of mine by the great poet of the Welsh hills, T.H. Parry-Williams. Here's a stanza from it. It's called 'Oerddwr':

Nid daear mo'r ddaear yno, nid haen o bridd;
Mae ansylweddoldeb dan donnen pob cae a ffridd...
O feudy'r Cwm hyd at feudy'r Hendre draw
Y mae llwybrau'n arwain i leoedd a fu neu ddaw.

(Earth is not earth there, no mere crust of soil;
There is insubstantiality under each calloused field and
sheepwalk...
From the cowshed at Cwm to Hendre beyond
Paths lead to places past or unborn.)

There were cows grazing across the slopes above the old farmstead, and the few fields below the *ffridd*, wrested and smoothed from stony acres, were summer-green, the blackthorn leafy around old grey barn and house. As if emanating from the ground itself, there is the feeling Parry-Williams tuned in to; of the not-quite-real, of a small region apart from the physical world, of a *cantref* of the otherworld where the fairies and the former inhabitants still throng. Is that slipping shape glimpsed at the corner of my eye Ann Jones, perhaps, who lived in Ty Cerrig here, now a small and crumbling outhouse, from 1720 to 1826 before her light corpse was carried away to the Beddgelert burying ground? The sense of a way of life departed is as livid upon this quiet place as the scar up Bwlch Main to Yr Wyddfa, the best and most dramatic and unusual viewpoint on which mountain is from here at Oerddwr.

Nor on Snowdon alone. With every foot of height gained towards Bwlch Cwm Ystradllyn above, the view south and east towards hill after beloved hill – Cnicht, Moelwyn, Arenig, Rhinogydd, Cader – blossomed into glorious display. How could anyone not think these hills of Eryri's seaward margins to be one of the supreme delights of our British landscape? I turned my back on them at the *bwlch*, clattered down through the inclines and spoil-heaps of the Gorseddau quarry, and fetched up at another Welsh hill delight – the old green tramway that contours round from Ystradllyn to continue as a high, grassy belvedere that ends at the very head of Cwm Pennant. With the larks singing and pipits flurrying among the rocks and the lovely little flycatchers flitting ahead I paced along under the wave-like stone wall that protects the tramway from spoil falling from above. This little abandoned industrial area at the head of Cwm Ystradllyn, with its utopian village, Treforys, of which the two-street ground-plan and foundations are still visible on the flank of Hebog, is one of the oddities of the Welsh mountains, and was ruination to those who invested in it. The slate was not workable, did not cleave. You can read the history of an economic disaster just by looking at geology exposed in these old workings. Yet what's left has such dignity and aesthetic appeal – particularly the slate mill at Ynysypandy, like an abandoned cathedral of the hills.

At the old school close by two rowdy dogs lolloped out to remonstrate at my presence, and as I spoke Welsh to calm them the woman who'd followed them out engaged me in conversation and offered tea but I hurried on, eager to re-enter the valley which is still, somehow, my *cynefin*. In 1973 I went to live in an isolated cottage a mile or so from the head of Cwm Pennant. The four years I spent here were the most formative of my life. If this valley is known to our recreational outdoor community at all, it is for its surrounding circuit of hills. Throughout the years I lived here, I walked some part of this circuit, in the course of the shepherding by which in part I was earning my keep, almost every day. To have that closeness with a natural landscape is a life-changing experience, taking you into dimensions previously unsuspected, initiating you into the earth's mysteries. It was a time of gifts, and – in its way, though perhaps more in retrospect than when in process – of spiritual discipline. In all weathers, in all lights or no light, at all seasons, these hills became my intimates, disclosing, confiding. I slipped among them in the company of chough, raven and peregrine; of fox, polecat and hare. I came to know: where, in the moonlight, the hares would race and box; by what paths badger and stoat would cross the twilight fields below the mountain wall; or on what rocks the roseroot and the burnet rose, within what streamside spray the hay-scented buckler fern, might grow.

On this bright summer's afternoon with a dark sky closing in from the north, instead of heading for Cwm Trwsgl and the end of the tramway at Blaen Pennant – a place where I've had eerie and troubling experiences in the past – I turned up into Cwm Llefrith from just above Cwrt Isaf. The little farm down there, where my friends the Owen brothers lived with their mother, who had no words of English, and which once would have been busy and thriving with animals and activity and children, was deserted, silent, tidy. But high among the rock bluffs of Cwm Llefrith and alongside the splashing stream bright heather and gorse were in bloom and the rarer plants too, and I re-made their acquaintance as if seeking out old friends, and was surprised in doing so by walkers tripping down off Hebog, smiling, in the state of happiness that beauty of day and place and fond company can bring.

At Bwlch Meillionen I left my sack behind a rock and raced up to the summit of Hebog to see the peninsula curving out west into the lowering sun, and little Mynydd Enlli offshore at its end, Ireland's coast faintly beyond and Pembrokeshire's hills far away to the south. How lovely it is, this land of Wales, and how delightful to wander towards your objective, discovering and re-discovering along the way, instead of making straight for it, appropriatively. Back at the *bwlch* the path led down into a waste of clear-felled forestry ground, messy and stumbling and difficult, and the descent through remaining trees in the encroaching twilight was miry and fatiguing. But down in Beddgelert I sat in comfort outside a pub, drank my beer and listened to locals talking in their own language of the coming quiet seasons. A bright moon glided out from behind Hebog. I slipped back by riverside paths in the dew of evening to the place from whence I'd set out, with that Daoist sense upon me of the oneness of the way, however wandering.

(2005)

THE LOVELIEST VALLEY

On a bright Sunday afternoon in October, out of Garn Dolbenmaen I headed upwards by zigzag footpaths between high, jumbled walls of boulders. After the recent rains, a sound of rushing water rose from hidden ditches and culverts. My route threaded through old steadings that grew ever more derelict and neglected the farther up the hill I climbed. Gables lean, a roof-tree sags, broken doors creak on their hinges at the touch of a breeze. An occasional pony crops the sweet grass of the small fields. Down here no other livestock is to be seen. These paths have the feel of those *boreens* on Inisheer, worn rock outcropping across them, green turf softening your footfall to a whisper. They are all-but-abandoned ways that even as recently as fifty or sixty years ago – even within my memory – would have seen the traffic of people on foot between the valley beyond the *bwlch* and the village from which I've come. A Welsh family was ascending in front of me – a young woman cajoling and jostling along her two small sons, their sprightly grandparents heading off the boys' erratic breaks from onward progress, for all the world like a pair of sagacious collies anticipating the wilfulness of the flock. All the while an animated chatter in Welsh was kept up between the five of them that put my own breathlessness to shame. My memories centre fondly on talking with that fine old Welshman Ioan Bowen Rees about the local-community use and enjoyment of native hills – its deep, long knowledge of them – that is so often ignored in the visitor-recreational mentality. We wended disparately, circuitously, through small, impressive outcrops and arrive at the spiky crown.

An east wind blustered round these summit rocks of Craig y Garn. I slipped into the shelter-cairn and took a flask from my rucksack, a spyglass and notebook from my pockets, then sat down, back to a boulder, to survey and record the immediacies of bliss that come simply from being here. This little seaward hill of Eryri is a perfect viewpoint into Cwm Pennant – *y cwm tecaf* ('the loveliest Welsh valley' in the view of many). There are other contenders, of course, throughout Wales – Cwm Croesor, Cwm Doethie, Cwm Gwaun, or maybe the Olchon valley and the Vale of Ewyas – but for me, Cwm Pennant has always been pre-eminent. All around me heather was still in fragrant bloom, loud with bees. Peacock butterflies, strangely late in their presence, danced by fast and close. The lower valley-slopes were russet with bracken. Dark heather above the thousand-foot contour, towards the hill summits, was patched silver with scree. On beech trees around an old tower above Bryncir Hall, the leaves were yellowing. I remember sitting there often on summer evenings, on the plinth by the then-ruinous tower (it has since been restored as a holiday cottage) and watching badgers play across the slopes beneath, their dense coats silvered and bouncing in the moonlight. Beyond the tower on this golden afternoon a westering sun burnished the sea, and 'blue, remembered hills' processed along every horizon – Rhinog, Arenig, Moelwyn, Cader. This land of Wales, that is so beautiful, and so abused...

From my vantage point I looked down and searched out farms

along the dearly-remembered valley where I dwelt and worked in my youth, in a time when the long traditions of Welsh hill-communities were coming to an abrupt end: Rhwngddwyafon, Cwrt Isaf, Gilfach, Brithdir Mawr. 'I name their several names/ Until a world comes to life.' Through my mind are running the verses of Patrick Kavanagh's poem, 'Kerr's Ass' – one of the subtle and haunting evocations of dispossession, of the interplay between rural memory and urban reality which defines our modern life. '…the God of imagination waking/In a Mucker fog', is how it ends. For me, this was how a deep connection with landscape began, here in Cwm Pennant. In a time of solitude. Through daily contact with the hills at all hours and all seasons; and through companionship with the native long inhabitants of place, and their knowledge and beliefs.

I am reminded, by this direction of thought, of a passage from one of the finest living writers on natural themes, the American author Barry Lopez. It's from an essay entitled 'The Stone Horse' on a 300-year-old *intaglio* made by the Quechan people at the head of a remote *arroyo* in the Mojave desert – an acutely-descriptive and celebratory design in stone that has miraculously remained undisturbed and unvandalized, and which, for Lopez, comes to stand for the crucial significance of all our lost knowledge:

> Today, the distinction between draft and harness horses is arcane knowledge, and no image may come to mind for a blue roan or a claybank horse. The loss of such refinement in everyday conversation leaves me unsettled. People praise the Eskimo's ability to distinguish among forty types of snow but forget the skill of others who routinely differentiate between *overo* and *tobiano* pintos. Such distinctions are made for the same reason. You have to do it to be able to talk clearly about the world.

Patrick Kavanagh is making the same point in 'Kerr's Ass':

> The straw-stuffed straddle, the broken breeching
> With bits of bull-wire tied;
> The winkers that had no choke-band,
> The collar and the reins...

From my shelter-cairn the stones of which commemorated who now knows what character or event from before the written histories of man in this region, I face out to the long western slopes of Moel Hebog, and they too in their turn set me thinking of something that was lost. In six days' time I was to give a memorial lecture on the work of the most distinguished writer on the natural history and landscape of Wales. One of my favourite passages from all the late Bill Condry's writings is set on this sunset flank of Moel Hebog, from the chapter entitled 'Hebog, Moelwyn, Siabod' in his *New Naturalist* volume on *The Snowdonia National Park*. Here's an extract:

> I sat so long in the warm dusk at the top of Hebog that it was already dark and starlit as I made my way down the west side; yet it is surprising how much light the pale grass holds and all the way down I could see the difference between dark rushes, light grass and palely gleaming rocks. I unrolled my sleeping bag by a murmuring stream and went to sleep looking at Jupiter bright over Hebog and thinking of the botanist J. Lloyd Williams who, when a young schoolmaster here years ago, found the Killarney fern, Snowdonia's rarest species, along one of the streams on this side of Hebog. It has not been seen since because the precise locality was never recorded; but it probably grows there still in the spray and shade behind some little waterfall.

It does indeed, and before the end of his long and honourable life – sworn to utmost secrecy as to its location to protect the plant from the like of those who Lopez describes as 'aimless wanderers with a flair for violence and a depth of ignorance' – Bill was taken to see it, in just such a place as he intuited and described, by that exceptional local field-naturalist Dewi Jones of Penygroes.

So was I, and seeing this frail and exquisite little plant in its secret place became a kind of epiphany, apotheosizing for me every small thing cumulatively lost from the once-rich natural texture of our lives. I am glad it was here in Pennant that I saw it, glad that Bill came by that experience too. He for me epitomized the modest rigour, the applied knowledge, the close attention which is the hallmark of the great observers of the natural scene. Elsewhere in his writings, Bill commented about Gilbert White that he gave us:

> the facts cleanly and frankly without trying to sell them to us in a wrapper of fine writing. And for chatting with us so amiably and teaching us so much without for a moment giving the impression that he is trying to teach us anything. And for communicating the delight of finding things out for ourselves. 'And for so subtly appealing to our sense of wonder about the world of fields, woods, hills, swamps, stars, planets and all the winds that blow.

On the way down from Craig y Garn I paused on the high moorland apron where the Bwlch y Bedol leads over from Garn, climbing through those smallholders' cramped fields into great walled sheepwalks of the Enclosure Acts. The isolated cottage of Llwynybetws, up here on the col, is cracked and ruinous now. Fifty years ago this was home to a hale old woman. She in her time lived in solitude, facing the sunrise, without electricity, far from roads, supplies carried on foot from the village shop. If hers was a harder life than ours in many ways, I doubt it was a poorer one.

OLD CALVINIST UNEASE

There is a famous, and rather sentimental, poem by Eifion Wyn, which poses this question:

> Pam, Arglwydd, y gwnaethost Gwm Pennant mor dlws
> A bywyd hen fugail mor fyr?'
>
> ('Why, Lord, did you make Cwm Pennant so lovely
> And an old shepherd's life so short?)

The thought's commonplace enough, though no less affecting for that. But the location is sublime. Through the years I lived here the sense grew on me of a landscape thick with ghosts, where generations had arranged and re-arranged stones into the temporary shapes of two or three hundred years, borrowed from here to build there, let frost and wind collapse and the grass wipe clean: '*Y mae lleisiau a drychiolaethau ar hyd y lle,*' wrote Parry-Williams ('voices and phantoms throughout the place'). It is one of the loveliest valleys in this most lovely of all countries: streams and woods, close turf with orchids and scabious, church and chapel, ridge and dome of hill, a drift of bluebells like woodsmoke across a green shade.

For me the people were as much a part of it as river or hills: old faces, lingering conversations, companionable crises of the farmer's year: the frenetic sweat and itch of stacking hay, pandemonious sadism at dipping, the shepherding – a time in the late snow, the ewe tired with long labour, no option but to bare my arm to the elbow, push the breech lamb up and round before pulling it out, lamb and my arm both marbled bloody and yellow against the white ground; and a few days later, in a field now patched with green, a hare reared up to box with this same lamb. I remember talking with old Mr Morus, Gilfach, asking why sheeps' heads hung in the trees above the stream by his house:

Duw, it's cure for the *pendro*. When the sheeps die, I cut off
its head and hang it there. Blowfly lays eggs, maggots eat the
brain, fall into the stream, and the sickness is washed from
the land.

You'll not find beliefs like that current in Cwm Pennant these
days. Acre-millionaires, seekers of subsidies, have bought into
the valley. The land wire-fenced, huge grey wintering sheds
dominate. It is made to work, to repay investment in it. Rather
than this exploitation, I am not sure that I do not prefer a certain
old Calvinist unease at its beauty, which spoke at least of the
power and mystery of place, and a certain reverence.

(2012/1996)

GARN FADRYN

Across the canted summit of Garn Fadryn wintry heather is
a dark chocolate-brown, pocked with hut-circles, the plateau-
rim chased with silver of stone fortifications and steep rock
outcrops. This ancient volcano, looking down on sea to north
and south from near the tip of the peninsula, has one of the
finest-situated hill forts in Wales. Its ramparts give views to the
west over Bardsey to the Wicklow Hills. Eastwards the peaks
of Snowdonia are ranged along the horizon, fractal shapes that
reiterate the region's complex geology. I climbed by a steep and
zigzag path to the top, with its spiked crest of crag, in the late
afternoon when a haze obscured all distances and the near-at-
hand was accentuated.

With gaining height a sheen of bays became visible. Mist
resolved in a thin, luminous film from pastures at the back
of Hell's Mouth. Cold weather was moving in from the Irish
Sea. Streaked rags of cirrus above drew up last red of the sun
and scrawled it across a pale sky. Snowdon and all her crew
retreated into mauve shadow. Immediately below was a ruched,

buckled and ice-smoothed landscape. Islands and almost-island headlands beyond floated on a grey sea indistinguishable from cloud. Boats clustered in the shelter of Porth Dinllaen northerly. Isolated, bird-sown conifers rooted among scree, and a single beacon of gorse was chance-shaft-flamed with sunset.

On this high-seeming, solitary hill the only intrusions on silence were the distant 'pop' of a rabbiting farmer's shotgun, muted roar of a tractor, and the gulls' cries. An unkindness of ravens convened among the heather, sweeping in from the west with air hissing through their pinions, and launched into harsh and measured discourse. The sun rolled down behind the tide-race island. As I descended rough cobbles of the path, a bright moon hung above the great bay, casting its glow back over the fields. Suddenly they were shot through with brilliant spectral flare of post-sunset illumination, as though the land itself emanated light.

(2007)

PEN DRAW LLŶN

This crab's-claw land's-ending pincers you in its mood, nips at old nerves. What is it about this place – *Pen Draw Llŷn* in Welsh ('Furthest Llŷn') – that I should come here so continually? As if for refuge. (As if for refuge from what?) If I were to meet you, I would want to know maybe of your particular place. Yet now that I try to tell you of mine, I sink only into quietude, and images rather than words resolve out of the stillness in my mind. All the headlands, from Cilan in the south round Mynydd Penarfynydd, by way of Pen-y-cil and Trwyn y Gwyddel, Anelog and Braich y Pwll (whose names are breathy as the mutterings of the sea, sonorous as music), past all the little porths – Oer, Iago, Colmon – and promontories of the north to the tip but not the bay of Porthdinllaen – there is something here that is more than landscape and comprises a part of my knowledge of the way the world is.

'Why,' asks Thoreau in *Walden*, 'do precisely these objects we behold make a world?' As in so much of Thoreau, the apparent simplicity of the question is deceptive, the question itself touched with genius. Our worlds – those amorphous strange atmospheres, bundles of bizarre perceptions, codified and supportive ways of seeing and interpreting that we drift among or utilize, with which we fend off the different, make sense of the contingent, and that inhabit our waking and dreaming minds – are precisely made up of 'objects we behold'. How does favoured landscape transmute into potent presence, and into what shades of meaning does it branch out there?

> In cities that
> have outgrown their promise people
> are becoming pilgrims
> again, if not to this place,
> then to the recreation of it
> in their own spirits.

Thus, from his poem 'The Moon in Lleyn', these headlands' own poet, R.S. Thomas – incumbent for many years at Aberdaron, dweller on the morning-sun slope of Mynydd Rhiw that looks down over Porth Neigwl – Hell's Mouth of the surging breakers and southwesterly gales unobstructed between Wales and Brazil. His lines chime so closely for me with a passage from the best book of another rare, grave giver-of-voice to all our inarticulate longings – *The Story of My Heart*, by Richard Jefferies:

> I walked almost daily more than two miles along the road
> to a spot where the hills began, where from the first rise the
> road could be seen winding southwards over the hills, open
> and unenclosed. I paused a minute or two by a clump of firs,

in whose branches the wind always sighed – there is always a movement of the air on a hill. Southwards the sky was illumined by the sun, southwards the clouds moved across the opening or pass in the amphitheatre, and southwards, though far distant, was the sea. There I could think a moment. These pilgrimages gave me a few sacred minutes daily; the moment seemed holy when the thought or desire came in its full force.

A time came when having to live in a town, these pilgrimages had to be suspended...

He calls them 'these pilgrimages' and you might think the word too big, too deliberate and portentous for the daily amble he describes – a walk up a road, a glance across the downs, a flooding sense of detachment, release and relief. And yet – pilgrimage! Is not the word's root in the Latin *peregrinus* – 'coming from foreign parts, wandering abroad'? Which brings me back to this place apart, these headlands of Pen Draw Llŷn, where the *teithiau pererin* ('the pilgrims' ways') of medieval Wales converge before crossing the sound to the island of the tide-race. This last fist of hills and knuckled headlands clenched against a wild sea is more abroad, more detached and remote, than the visitor-melee of Snowdonia, the holiday camps of Pwllheli, the caravan parks of Abersoch that hide and precede it might lead you to believe. I tried to explain once to a young poet about this otherness. 'Oh yes,' she'd responded, and with a shine of recognition behind the matter-of-factness she concluded, 'one of the thin places!'

Celt, Greek and Hindu alike have believed in those – the sites, the regions where the barriers seem to shimmer between worlds: Varanasi, Tapovan, The Dakotan Black Hills, Pen Draw Llŷn. But I don't. I simply don't know. I just feel a detachedness, a remoteness entering me in these places. So that when I round the stacked and razored points from Porth Oer and descend

into little Porth Iago that is maybe my favourite cove along all
the world's coasts I know; so that when I walk upon its beach
of sand the quartz crystals in which squeak beneath my heel
in praise of the perfection of their symmetries; so that when I
rest and shelter from a lancet-keening wind behind some black
fin of Precambrian rock and feel momentarily disconsolate and
alone, then the pulse of ultramarine waves, the high slow streak
of cirrus across the azure, the silent waving of moss-textured
vermilion weed in a pool lift me, permeate, make still. And I hear
the squeal of the choughs, watch their fold-winged tumble and
soaring scatter of flight, and such peace comes. As Wordsworth
wrote:

> These beauteous forms,
> Through a long absence, have not been to me
> As is a landscape to a blind man's eye:
> But oft, in lonely rooms, and 'mid the din
> Of towns and cities I have owed to them,
> In hours of weariness sensations sweet...

These places imprint on our minds, like shibboleths aimed to
catch at some deeper, some truer level of meaning. Which resides,
surely, in their elemental simplicities, their accidental harmonies
of colour and form, their actual insusceptibility to the imposition
of any form of meaning other than that of their existence. Each
of us 'half-lives a hundred different lives'. These headlands just
are. And so for me they become less headlands than Head Lands,
to which I have continual recourse in both mind and body, and
which bring joy. There is a moment, for example, when you
have followed the long cliff path from Porth Meudwy, rested in
the sun perhaps among tufts of thrift on rocky Craig Cwlwm,
continued over Porth Cloch and Porth y Pistyll and Hen Borth,
through the bracken and gorse with the sea far below, and you

are making your way across the ancient field-banks, traversing the rough slabs towards Pen-y-cil's stepped and lofty profile, when in a shocked instant you arrive at a natural belvedere, the great ridge of the headland rearing above you; and out across the water, like some vast presence of the deep, animate almost, Ynys Enlli – Bardsey, the island of the currents. The sight is so sudden its currents course through your psyche and cleanse and purge – and bring joy.

These moments of imprinting vision are almost too pure, too powerful, to inhabit long. You cannot always view your lover naked. However strongly you retain that sense of them, for the most part they must walk clothed through the world. And the clothing, the texture of this landscape of Pen Draw Llŷn is a fascination in itself. On a still, cool evening I sit on the terrace of the Ty Newydd hotel looking out over Aberdaron Bay. Wood smoke from a garden fire drifts across a thin crescent moon, the pale sky's seared with pink, the bounding headlands green and golden, a blanched rim of rock at the base of umber cliffs separating them out from a sea cold as blued steel. Time shifts into another mode. All those who have come here, over centuries, their marks and fragmented testimonies...

There is Ffynnon Fair, which many do not find and at which I have puzzled and visited for years. There are no traditions here, only affective evidence of its power: a few verdigrised copper coins in its depths, scraps of folkloric tradition concerning strange ladies, wishes, circumambulations of the chapel above carrying water from the well, and the steps down to it, chipped, carved or worn into rock that looks as though it was stilled in time's yesterday but that's as old as any in the world. These are merely responsive, and not the thing itself. The well is that, in its shelf and dark alcove above the tide-flow. It is planed in all directions as though to express the Trinity or some older mystery, fronded with bright weed, and its water has a clarity, a sparkle, a depth that in that sombre place seem to transmute light into liquid emanation. I have brought people here over years, and none have gone away unaffected.

But this is a place of obvious power, and there are others where the sense of distinction steals more discreetly upon you. You could be walking along one of the innumerable going-nowhere lanes of Pen Llŷn when suddenly it bursts upon you. Is it the heavy fragrance rising from the meadowsweet's flowers of honeyed lace, or the red campion's tangle-starred profusion, or the speckled bells of the foxglove and the yellow broom flecked as though by blood that catch your heart and lead your eye down past the road's bend to the blue bay and the jut of land, beyond which the world presses? You don't know or care. You are simply suspended in the beauty of a moment that, even when it has faded, will continue to bloom.

Later, it is a midsummer evening. On a wire that crosses and connects the distances of the moor raven exchanges harsh talk with a long-tailed tit, the pair of them comically disparate. I carry on down, the sun descending slantwise with me to the edge of the trees, gilding them. At the forest edge I rest a knee on the old stone of a stile and look in. A young fox, ginger as the spruce needles across which he pads, has emerged from his earth in the roots of a fallen tree. Our eyes meet. Ears erect, he approaches. He attends to me, knowing my foreignness here. He is very near now, curious. A lambskin, chicken feathers, gleam behind him in the tree-shadow. Suddenly he's away, glancing back, sidling, gone. I enter the dark wood. The paths are vague but there is something I want and must find. The feeling of the place is spikey, oppressive. After a half-mile I double back along a lower path by an old wall lost in the trees.

And come across the well.

A shaft of sunlight in a forest clearing illuminates it. Steps down in two corners, fern, the slight, bright issue of a spring on to gravel. Ffynnon Saint it's called. One sentence of knowledge I have: 'Women visited it on Dydd Iau Dyrchafael[3] to wash their eyes and offer pins.' I let the drops fall on to my eyelids and see them now, laughing, momentarily grave, here in this wood with life's secrets falling from them.

To connect, if only for an imagined moment, with well, spring and source…

(2000)

MYNYDD ENLLI

The places to which I return most frequently are not the objects of past trips of grand or exotic or ambitious design. They are those intimate places that were once – at one stage or another of my life – no more than a few steps or at most a few miles beyond my own front door.

I can bring these places back to mind with an aching clarity of detail that I would be hard-pressed to match from other scenes. There's a little rough buttress of gritstone at the northern end of Windgather Rocks on the eastern border of Cheshire where maidenhair fern grows in a shady crevice and I can see it now, feel it brush across the back of my hand. There's a ribbed and submarine sandbar that curves across the mouth of the Dwyryd estuary, by which you can cross from Portmeirion to Llanfihangel-y-Traethau if you know tide and the sands' design well enough and dare take the risk. I can feel the waves against my thigh and the sense of distance and space and hear the flocks of pintail at their parliament right now, because once I was there almost every day. There's an incline, its steps sculpted by the

---

[3] Ascension Day

facemen's hobnails, leading down through the Dinorwig quarry into oakwoods loud with the woodpeckers' laughter. I feel the contour of each one of those steps, and will continue to do so though I may never pass that way again.

And I see also another scene, from another form of intimate landscape. It is on an island – Ynys Enlli, off the westernmost tip of Gwynedd and separated from it by two miles of perilous tide-race. On a cold April morning I'm walking the ridge of Mynydd Enlli, the island's sheltering hill, behind which it hides its western seaward garden from prying mainland eyes. The air's like crystal, Ireland to the west near enough almost to touch, but it's the immediate context, the small compass within whose dial I'm contained, that enchants. There is a small bird preceding me along the hill-crest. His flight is dance-like. He soars, glides down with a lovely, liquid, trilling call, displaying in his every action his dapper pied plumage. He is unafraid, shows no wariness at my presence.

He's a snow bunting. I've never seen one before. What storm brought him here, what wayward impulse? For a few days, wherever I go on this mile-and-a-half long by three-quarters wide scrap of land, I'm aware of him, almost always by daylight can see him somewhere. The seals moan and bask on their rocks and he trills; at twilight the little owls come out from their rabbit burrows to quarter the fields and osier beds, and in the night the ethereal disturbances of the shearwaters craze the darkness. Until I depart this place I am simply content to be in their presence.

PART FOUR

Between Glaslyn and Dyfi

The variety of hill scenery to be found between Porthmadog and Machynlleth has been a perpetual source of delight to me through the greater part of my life. Here are some of the well-known attractions, and some lesser-known ones too. We'll start with two of the latter.

DIMINUENDO

Drops of cold dew on every hazel twig and blade of grass are crystal-bright in contrast to the diffusions of mist. I climb out of Nant Gwynant, blue densening into azure overhead as the vapours thin, and take steep paths broaching the rocky defences of Dinas Emrys. This rocky kop rising from riparian pastures has a wonderful sense of the miniature mountain about it, and is one of the most redolent and story-rich places in the Welsh hills. In this blue-gold dawn, echoes from history's infancy ring clear. Vortigern, who invited the Saxons in, had his stronghold here; here Myrddin Ambrosius – the enchanter Merlin of Arthurian legend – was brought as a child to be sacrificed, proved himself wiser than wizards, foretold conflict in the land. Back in the realities of the present century, slant-wise early sun gilds the old fort on its top, islanded above the cloud-sea, its ramparts and its ruinous tower searched into definition. Heather – more glorious and fragrant this year than any I can remember – fades and bracken rusts across the encircling southern slopes of Yr Aran; leaves in the sessile oakwoods are warmly imbued with the fire-tones of autumn; a buzzard mews.

Under the footings of this square tower-keep, on the collapsed wall of which I stand, dragons fought according to the legend. Time, and not their subterranean battles, have tumbled it. Now, apart from a few querulous sheep calling from those streamside meadows below, all is silent. I wander across to rest against a wall on the outer defences, look out from the crag. An eager, mounting sun burns down, bizarrely illuminating a garish, inflatable bouncy castle in the tourist attraction on the far side of the valley. A fog-bank pink as candy-floss rolls up the hillside, in front of it a lone heron in slow, creaking flight. I watch as it rounds a protruding bluff, sights the waters of Llyn Dinas, glides across to land, stalks into the shallows, and stands motionless like some grey martial ghost, deadly and spear-intent. The hills of Eryri are clustered all around above where it keeps its vigil. Later, on impulse I drive to Pont Croesor on the Great *Traeth*. Along the river bank on this still autumn evening the ordinary and unregarded life of the place asserts itself: pied wagtails bathe from a sandbank in the pool on which are footprints of otters; a flotilla of swans with ruffed wings glides by; plump great tits chase little, delicate long-tailed tits in and out of bankside hazels, and the wide river gentles down over the weir under the bridge.

Shelley thought this view up the Glaslyn estuary – reclaimed land these past two centuries – incomparable, peerless. At Pont Croesor it wraps itself around you. In front are the high peaks of Eryri. Moel Ddu ('the Black Hill') to the north, its summit strangely cleft and scarcely visited, is fading at twilight into milky indigo shadow, all detail lost of woods like old brocade across its flanks. To the south, bare rock slabs of the northern Rhinogydd have a metallic gleam in the last light, and sage and blond tints of upland pasture glow softly. Suddenly a full moon bounces into the sky from behind Foel Penoleu ('Hill of the Head of Light') and soars, silvering the river. Across the wide pool a Daubenton's bat flickers low, wing-tips glancing the surface to send filigreed ripples spreading. From a fence post, the barn owl looks speculatively on before gliding ghostly away along the line of a ditch.

My attention is caught on the twin barbs of intimacy and privacy. This scene in front of me – a panorama of hills I've known since my early teenage years – is grand and beautiful; but I know that what appeals most strongly in the scene to me now are the quiet places and the smaller and less frequented heights. That formulation of Ruskin's about hills being finer to look at than to look from holds some truth for me, though I'd hasten to add that viewing the grander hills from their less stridently impressive neighbours is perhaps best of all.

There in the foreground is Mynydd Sygyn, and to its south Moel y Dyniewyd, between the grassed and mined gash of Cwm Bychan and the sylvan lower reaches of Nantmor. I know this latter craggy, heathery, lone little hill because of a friend of mine, Paul Orkney Work, who farmed on its western flank for years at Carneddi ('Place of Stones'). I would visit him there, sit in his kitchen by the old Aga that had revived the chilled lambs of Welsh springs year after year, listen to his stories of Colin Kirkus and Menlove Edwards, the great pioneers of Snowdonia rock-climbing in the 1930s. He kept llamas – delightfully disconsonant presences when you came across them unawares along the woodland paths of the valley. Up on the crag behind Carneddi there is a satisying little rock-climb – slabby and intricate and graded *Very Difficult* in rock-climbers' parlance, which means, perversely, that it is not at all hard. The rock up which it threads its too-brief way buttresses the summit ridge of the hill, and I've often sallied and sauntered up this way to reach the crest. Moel y Dyniewyd doesn't even breast the four-hundred-metre contour, and yet it's a fine, singular micro-mountain, set apart as though intending to take a good look at its neighbours rather than enter into competition with them. And what neighbours they are!

There's Moel Siabod pyramidal and elegant to the north-east, and to reach it from here you would traverse some of the most rugged and complex terrain in Wales – a land to itself, of rocky hollows and craglets and rowan-blessed boulders into which only a solitary single-track road intrudes itself peripherally and where you're more likely to meet some lone fisherman casting a fly at Llyn Llagi or Llyn Edno than the striding hordes of popular Snowdonia. Eastwards, shyly peeking above the heathery bluffs of Yr Arddu, is the unfamiliarly homely aspect of Cnicht's level north-easterly ridge, with the comical contrast of the two main Moelwyn peaks – the one bluff and rounded, the other hook-nosed and beetle-browed – beyond. Due north is Yr Wyddfa itself, massive and black from this aspect, and all around the compass, glimpses of other hills, the names of which have their own rhythm and music, as though terrain sought its counterpart in sound: Arenig, Rhinogydd, Hebog. I love to come up here, the paths winding through the bracken of the *ffridd*, past the old *corlannau* under the crags where peregrines nest. In this place I once watched as a pigeon was killed, decapitated in the stoop, the tiercel feeding afterwards on the rock just over there. For me, that insignificant life transmuted into the special providence of a visionary moment.

HYMNING THE DERELICTION

The meadowsweet has not yet flowered in the verges at the head of Cwm Croesor. In the valley's new community-run café, I nurse a procrastinating cup of unwanted coffee and watch as columns of warm July rain stride past the windows. Maybe today's not ideal for the elegant, fascinating and occasionally gruelling circuit of Cnicht and the tops of the Moelwynion, that was one of my favourite Welsh hill-rounds. So many times I've walked it, and in such good company: with Cameron McNeish when we took in a HVS rock-climb on the Tremadog cliffs in the afternoon; with Nick Shipton, son of the great Himalayan explorer Eric Shipton, lithe and springing in his step, vigorous from start to finish of the day, his intense blue eyes shining with an endless curiosity about place and history; with my old Labrador towards the end of her long life, plodding steadfastly alongside me; and with my little terrier The Flea often in the youth of hers.

Today the trickle and merge of drops on the outside of the pane keeps pace with the blustering wind, and promises no let-up any time soon. I zip myself into waterproofs, pull down my hood and step out through the door. First stop is back at the car, to collect trekking poles and Phoebe, the Parson Russell Terrier who replaced The Flea after a dog-less decade and who's my canine companion now. She looks nonplussed, rolls brown eyes at the drench of the rain and, tail between her legs, slinks resentfully to heel. We edit out half of the planned itinerary and forget about Cnicht for today. It's easy to do this when you view the mountain from Croesor, for at this angle it appears as a dark and brooding bulk instead of the shapely pyramid that acts as centrepiece to the view of these southern and western hills of Eryri from the Glaslyn estuary. With their refined ridges, their long and secluded sylvan valleys, rapid streams and proximity to the western sea and the going-down of the light, their position at a remove from the high, rocky peaks of Eryri and their retained sense of Welshness and otherness, these hills for me are one of the heart-places, with which few others compare. So Phoebe and I set off up the old quarry track that scores its easy diagonal across the northern slope of Moelwyn Mawr. Leaning on a gate by a cattle-grid filled in with gravel washed down the track, I scan round the houses of Croesor and find myself recounting histories and revivifying faces and characters of those who lived in them. Here's Clough Williams-Ellis, architect and playmaster of Portmeirion, aquiline and spare and angular, marching up the road to survey his valley domain in plus-fours and brogues and canary stockings with green garters, looking every inch of the six-and-more-feet of him the last of the line of eighteenth-century aristocrats from which he was descended; he's stooping now to chat with little Nellie Jones who had eight or nine children by different fathers and lived in the top terrace here, always ready to talk and offer tea as you came down parched from the hill; and here's Dei Huws, poet, former volunteer in the Free Wales Army, who claimed to have blown up with quarrying black-powder the monument in the square at Tremadog (an event for which I can find no record in any contemporary newspaper files); shaman, face twinkling with roguery, tongue quicksilvering around a torrent of new-age chicaneries and lapping the credulous in, a good man for an hour in a pub any day of the week or time of the day; years dead now, of liver cancer (too common a cause of demise in these areas downwind of the old Magnox station at Trawsfynydd); down there among the trees is the second home of Marxist historian Eric Hobsbawm, and a half-mile down-valley from it that of the late Oxford mathematician Robin Gandy, whom I remember in his college rooms, dressed in black motorcycle leathers, preparing toast at his fire and serving it with *Patum Peperium* – The Gentleman's Relish. He was associate and lover of Alan

Turing, whose input was central in the development of modern computing and whose contribution to the breaking of the Enigma codes was vital. Just over the ridge towards Rhyd was Geoffrey Hill's Welsh base. In the doll's house cottage tucked beneath the incline as I start to climb lived Patrick O'Brian of the Napoleonic naval warfare novels, and also of a neglected, masterly fictional insight into Calvinism, his early novel *Testimonies*, set in Croesor village. This was a galaxy of talent, a thrilling and cosmopolitan community in the latter half of the twentieth century – perhaps still is, though I've scarcely known it in these latter years.

In a tiny cottage high on the slope of Cnicht opposite me here – a new skylight illuminating what I knew as a dark loft bedroom – I spent the snowy winter of 1978, choking as the wind fell off the ridge of Cnicht and blew the fire smoke back down the chimney. I was looking after a black and mettlesome Lipizzaner stallion stabled in the buildings right below me here at the gate whilst his owner was away in America. If I rode him through the valley pastures the mares wintering there would gallop up and bite him – or me, if my limbs got in the way, so this track I'm now loafing up at the slowest possible speed would frequently be the way we'd come to avoid them, and we would carry on if the gates were open right to the top of Moelwyn Mawr itself, he sure-footed and high-actioned across the snow. I wonder if anyone has climbed all the Corbetts – of which Moelwyn Mawr is one – on horseback? You couldn't do it with the Munros, certainly (The Inaccessible Pinnacle by Lipizzaner? I think not!), and even some of the Corbetts – Y Lliwedd, for example, would need a very sure-footed mount. A few years ago the Cambrian Mountains Society wrapped me in Glyndŵr's flag, set me on a sturdy cob and had me ride to the top of Moel Hyddgen to address an anti-wind turbine rally. It wouldn't surprise me if a travel book on the horseback hills were to appear one of these days. And on a day like this, I was feeling decidedly nostalgic for equine assistance to the hilltops.

The advantage of this route out of Croesor – an old work road which at one time was a main line of communication by way of Cwm Orthin between the Ffestiniog villages and those clustered around Traeth Mawr – is the gradual angle of its ascent. You can amble up it, never losing your breath, generating a glow rather than a sweat, gradually gaining height, the valley floor dropping away to the left, broken power lines attached to fallen poles reaching up from it. On my right stonechats bounced and bobbed on the breeze from outcrop to lancet outcrop of slate, chittering as they flew, and before many minutes had elapsed I arrived at the old barracks for the Croesor quarry.

The wall below the terrace in front of the barracks building is startling in its bushy profusion of plant life. Swelling emerald mosses protrude between vertical groves of ferns and spleenworts, a few fronds of parsley fern break the grey slate scree gently in to this unwonted intrusion of greenery among the overall grey, and the tiny pink flowers of herb Robert work a certain magic within the overall palette. The whole dense and variegated organism ripples and thrashes to the wild movement of air around the ribs of the Moelwyn. I scramble up to the terrace, and peer in to these low dank spaces where the quarrymen slept and ate, two to a bed and four to a dark, earth-floored room under a poor and leaking roof. Low footings of the walls, rubble, broken sills and chimney breasts of massive stone standing piled and gaunt as Inuit cairns in Arctic wastes marking ways long untrodden – these are the evidences left from labouring lives led in conditions that to us now seem unimaginably harsh. Our tendency is to sentimentalize them, and dwell on the sense that Alan Llwyd captures epigrammatically in his fine line of *cynghanedd*: '*Bywyd gwâr mewn byd gerwin*' ('a civilized life in a rough world'). I think of the outdoor community's favoured wholefood and organic café in Brynrefail, *Y Caban*, named after the slate-quarrymen's extempore debating societies held in their lunchtime huts and shelters high on the exposed mountainsides. *Y Caban* serves provender of a quality and variety these workmen of a century and more ago would never have known. The ironies of our modern society are so frequent and strange. I find myself brooding on our modern sense of entitlement, look at these stark and cairn-like chimney-breasts again and think of how they point back to a lost way of optimistic and ameliorative analysis of social structures, to a passionate desire for self-instruction now scarce in society. One of the proudest moments of my life was to be made an honorary fellow of the university in Bangor, the great neo-Jacobean college building of which was paid for by quarrymen's subscriptions, fixed sums freely given each week from their wages, every man willingly contributing – men who lived week in week out under conditions like those in the barracks here. This example is worth more than all our sentimentalizing. It's worth remembering how much our education and progress owes to what was given from places like this. When I encounter – as inevitably happens time and again – the grasping materialism, the sense of entitlement, the vacuous philistinism so rampant in contemporary society, then I come to places like this to remind myself that it was not always so, and it may not remain so. In their dereliction the barracks memorialize something that was altruistic and fine.

The view from the top of Moelwyn Mawr above me, Showell Styles suggested, 'might well claim to be the finest in all Wales for beauty, variety and extent'. But one thing was for certain, which was that today it would be unavailable. The mist which had been feathering round the crags on the way to Rhosydd was louring and thickening around the 1,500-foot contour. To ascend was to commit to the blank and the damp. The rain having abated, I set off over slate scree where a lone foxglove bloomed, and also rust on abandoned machinery. A solitary raven resolved darkly from the general gloom, croaked a brief alarm and slithered away on the wind. I arrived at the desolate shore of Llyn Croesor, most sombre of Welsh mountain lakes, hard under the northern spur of Moelwyn Mawr. Tennyson is supposed to have based his description of Bedivere casting Excalibur back into the lake after Arthur has received his mortal wound on Llyn Llydaw, under Yr Wyddfa, but if he'd wanted the true stygian, Llyn Croesor might better have suited his purpose:

> I heard the ripple washing in the reeds,
> And the wild water lapping on the crag.

I circled round above it with a shudder, kept to the contour path between chasms and spoil-heaps in this ruined landscape, traversed beneath Craig Ysgafn and through Bwlch Stwlan to reach the old tramway along Ceseiliau Duon that would lead me back down to Croesor again and its little river frothing and rolling between close alders. As I went, I remembered back to meeting an old man here on a fine June day nearly fifty years ago. He had been a quarryman, bore the scars. We had talked, perhaps for several hours, and I learnt much. He told me where he lived and invited me to call. Months later I did, at the little terraced house he'd named in Tanygrisiau. He had died weeks previously. His wife invited me in, gave me tea, and cucumber sandwiches on fine china plates in her front parlour.

'I don't know how he got about in the hills with his lungs gone,' she told me, 'days when he couldn't get his breath...'

Something about him has long stayed in my mind. I know more about him now than I ever did, and honour him the more for that. *Genius loci...* Of rock; of a community; of a society.

(2011)

CNICHT

On one of those dull February days when not so much as a glimmer of sun penetrates the cloud, I force myself out and head for Croesor. The steep climb out of the village up the Roman road leads through winter-grey pastures where pregnant ewes crowd round sileage feeders. A stile takes me into an oakwood of writhing branches and mossed boulders, beyond which the path curves north-east and makes directly for Cnicht.

The name of this shapeliest and most striking of Eryri's lesser hills is an oddity. Saxon in origin, the same word as the English 'knight', it's thought to have been bestowed on the hill by sailors a millennium ago, because of its fancied resemblance to a Saxon knight's helmet. Today, as I toil up the path along the approach ridge, its hero-head remains stubbornly in the mist. A mile to the west, the little, rock-girt lakes amidst the crags of Yr Arddu have a cold, pewter sheen and not a soul moves in the whole, elemental landscape. I pause before the last climb. The slatey buttress which leads to the summit is dappled with may-green lichen – the only vivid colour in the entire mountain scene. The holds for a direct ascent are slick with moisture. I opt for discretion, turn it on the right where a few steep moves bring me round above it. A slight breeze ushers away the capping cloud, I arrive suddenly on the sharp ridge-crest and look steeply down into Cwm Croesor. Its farms and cottages are miniaturized in the plunging perspective, yet at the same time brought into focus by the mist occluding all distant views. It feels like looking down into a small and secret world, glimpsed momentarily – and so it proves, as the cloud swirls round again.

Light fading, I skitter back down the steep path, a solitary raven putting on a virtuoso display of aerobatics, wind whistling through its pinions as it rolls and dives. It comes to rest on a boulder to observe, communicates with me in rich gutturals, wings hunching into a ruff of throat feathers. All the long ridges of these hills, stretching south and west, are merging into darkness, night and shadow consuming their detail. Lights are coming on in Porthmadog, and faintly across the two estuaries in Harlech. An owl ghosts past on hushed wings as I reach the wood again, seconds later from among the trees lets out a long and quavering scream.

(2007)

OWL

A full moon glints on the waterfalls by Gelli as I make my way down by the old way along the western side of Croesor. There is a silvery light among the oakwoods, liquid whispering of the river beneath. From a darkness of trees, the long quaver of a tawny owl. It is autumn, so no harsh answering call tears at the stillness. I think back to an April morning years ago. Walking down the valley road, I came across a ball of down on the tarmac – a tawny owlet, only days old. With no obvious nest around and no parents in view I took her home, fed her on cat food that day, in the evening took her back to where she'd been found and called for her parents. No response. She came home with me again, was installed in a box in my study and fed on minced beef wrapped in fur from grooming my long-haired cats. Her rate of growth was impressive. Within weeks a large bird-of-prey was sitting on a perch atop my filing cabinet. From time to time she'd ghost across on hushed wings as I worked to sink her talons in my bald patch, chew gently at my ear-lobe, click and croon for food. Mice the cats brought in were traded for extra rations and fed to her. When she was a few months old I'd set her on the garden table, tie cotton to the legs of the dead mice, and pull them through the grass for her to pounce upon. Eventually, like an errant teenager, she'd roost in the sycamore tree above, but still fly down for her food. Soon she was flying farther afield, hunting successfully on her own account. She still came for food when I saw her in the oakwoods along the estuary, but inevitably this became less often, and then not at all. I hope and believe that, unlike the majority of her kind, she made it through, perhaps is even alive in that lovely place to this day.

(2009)

THE OLD WAYS

> Roads go on,
> While we forget, and are
> Forgotten, like a star
> That shoots, and is gone.

Edward Thomas

Out of Croesor village I climb steeply by the old way that leads through woods of sessile oak, the leaves of which are rimmed already with fire-tones of autumn. After a breathless half-mile it broaches the long spur flung down to the south-west from Cnicht, that stands sharp sentinel over the flat, reclaimed lands of the Great *Traeth*. The path to the summit of that grand and shapely miniature mountain branches off right, but I keep to what's known locally as the Roman Road, and at the stone-slab bridge over the tumbles and torrents and clear pools of the Afon Dylif slip down to drink and rest on the green bank. A serious-faced runner with a plastic water container on her back pounds by, glancing at her watch as she crosses the bridge, not noticing me lounging there. Her brief presence having wafted past, my imagination conjures in its place the long generations of farmers, miners, wanderers, maids, packmen, itinerant vendors, preachers, young and ardent lovers, of whose former line of passage through these hills the recreational community of the outdoors has become the sole inheritor.

I delight in these old pathways and all the long sense of former times bustling at you from the quiet they now assume. I love to see the worn stones in places no traffic now disturbs. I love all the signs and notations by which their former significance can be read: the cairns and standing stones, the hill forts and hut-circles that guard or cluster around, the grooves that iron-shod wheels have worn in stone. Treasure-houses of ancient memory, these old ways thread through the hills (if on a winter's night a traveller, under a bright moon, were to follow them, who knows to what dimension they would lead, and what tales could be told if the traveller were to return from thence? But how few of us now travel at the magic times).

Not just in Wales. I remember the thrill of leaving the train at Bridge of Orchy and taking that long, wild approach in to Lorn that slips away from under the loom of the Black Mount. Set your tent by the shielings alongside the Eas a'Choire Dhuibh in readiness for the great circuit of Stob Coir'an Albannaich, Glas Bheinn Mhor and rough, remote Beinn nan Aighenan above Glen Kinglass, and by the old walls in the autumn twilight as the kettle bubbles to keep the silence at bay, the same tremor along the nerves, the heart-stopping sudden intimacy with that which has gone. The memory of stone…

There is a pass called Bwlch y Ddwy Elor ('Pass of the Two Funeral Biers') that leads over from Rhyd Ddu into the high, rocky hollow of Cwm Trwsgl. Years ago I used to come here often to explore the cliffs. On the fine, diamond-shaped slab of impeccable dolerite that looks down on Bwlch Cwm Trwsgl there's a climb of which I did the first ascent thirty years ago called The Exterminating Angel (one of the pleasures of doing new routes is that you get to name them, and in its day this was a difficult and dangerous one for which that appellation was appropriate). Before I could climb it I had to abseil down to strip off the fields of turf and caterpillars of grass that masked out its every feature. I did so on a day of mist, and throughout the hours I hung on the rope peeling off the sods, from the deserted cwm below, from the hut-circles and sheep-folds, voices, whisperings.

Another time – maybe it was later in the same year – I was up higher in the cwm, which is the strangest and eeriest place I know in the Welsh hills. In the old quarry barracks on a terrace below the *bwlch*, I remember sitting on a windowsill, trying to will into existence some sense of the men who'd inhabited here, but there was not so much as the flicker of movement glimpsed by an averted eye to register on my conscious mind.

So because I was young, impatient, not yet practised in stilling down into a landscape, I climbed on to the pass above, the weather turning, a wind blowing in from the north-west and bringing rain in luminous, drifting, grey columns that swayed like phantoms as they approached. The heavy drops slashed down before the wind, and I ran back the way I'd come, seized suddenly by a strange terror. I hurled down a slope of slate scree, all but slithered over the lip of a deep quarry hole, scrambled rigid around its edge and reached the stonecrop-carpeted terrace where I'd been sitting half an hour before.

Far from that place feeling like safety, the experience shifted there into another phase. As I carried on down, walking now, struggling to keep composure, there came an overpowering sensation that I was being watched, and what succeeded it was even more sinister – the sure sense that I was being followed. The skin on my back crawled, my scalp was prickling with fear. I would stop to listen; and hear nothing beyond the suggestion of presence. I would look round; nothing beyond a kind of ripple about the air that discomfited. But after each look behind, each pause to attend, always the something that was behind, keeping pace, speeding up if I speeded up, holding back if I slowed down.

When I burst into a run, it kept up with me effortlessly, until I was right out of that high cwm, when it went as suddenly as it had come.

There was an amiable version of that same sense once when I was walking with my son Will up to Bryn Cader Faner in the Rhinogydd – 'arguably the most beautiful Bronze Age monument in Britain', according to the archaeologist Frances Lynch. As we climbed up past Y Gyrn to come at it from the west, the mist closed in. Will – who was maybe eight at the time – stole his hand into mine for reassurance, and in that old landscape with its innumerable signs, the mystery and the intangible presence...

I can assert nothing definite from any of this, except that such resonances abound among these old hills of Britain. There's a beautiful passage from the writings of T.H. Parry-Williams that, neutrally, without conjecture, conveys the enduring echo of the past as it touches our nerve-endings. He's describing any one of the innumerable little spills of rock from quarry or mine with which the hills of his home region west of Snowdon abound:

> Some time or other, every stone has been through someone's hands, lifted on to the waggon and thrown with its fellows over the edge of the tip. Sometimes a saw-mark can be seen on one, and on occasion the trace of a gimlet – the gimlet of someone who was, in his day, trying to make bread out of stone. ...it is a mute community; but in the silence of the night or on a fine summer's day, the occasional stone is moved to speak – to speak in movement, as if some vanished quarryman was still at work 'treating the stones'. There is a strange dread to be felt when one hears the sound of a slate or a stone moving thus in an old quarry tip, and rolling down a little, as if in search of a more comfortable position. It may not move again for centuries, if left in peace...

All this material I was musing over, on my sunny bank by the Afon Dylif. An adder slithered from the undergrowth on the far side of the stream and curled itself to sleep on a sun-warmed rock as a dipper worked busily upstream. I stirred myself, cut across to the path, and followed the old road to Croesor once more.

(2007)

BRYN CADER FANER

On the flank of Moel y Geifr I sit on close turf and my eye is drawn by the constant flitting and breathless trilling of a wheatear. I love these little dancing birds of the hills with their abrupt cascades of song and bowdlerized name. (The original and accurate 'whitearse' was too robust for Victorian ornithological taste.) Their return is one of the true signs of spring, along with that of the curlew to its breeding grounds across the damp and rushy hollows, where its haunting soft crescendos are a defining sound of the Welsh uplands. Keeping very still, I watch as the male wheatear returns continually to a hole in a dry stone wall. Derek Ratcliffe, the authority on mountain birds, in one of his books talks of the frequent disappointment when a small pale passerine proves to be not a snow bunting but 'only a wheatear'. For once I'd disagree with him. At close quarters the wheatear is astonishingly beautiful, its pied markings perfectly set off by overall pale hues of cinnamon and grey. The commonplace is so often marvellous: 'Could we but look with seeing eyes'. What purpose, I wonder, in this design, that is so consummate? Yet I know as I ask that the question is unnecessary. I rouse myself and wander on along the Bronze Age trackway that led from the coast at Mochras through this wild land and down along the Dee valley into the soft shires.

The day is hazy, sky a faded blue, tones of the landscape subdued – tawny grasses, ash-coloured rock. There is a subtlety to it, and a potency too in the stark evidences here of geology and geomorphology, in a design groined from forces for the currency of which the ashen sky serves as reminder. The green path leads to one of the prime places of the Welsh hills – Bryn Cader Faner, a spiked hill-top corona, the most beautiful Bronze Age monument in Britain. It is utterly silent. No planes fly. A raven nearby pulls at the broken carcase of a sheep. Distantly above Y Gyrn a buzzard hangs on the wind. Down in Nant Pasgan the oak is out before the ash. I chant the old weather rhyme to myself. Yellow cast of bronzy new leaves harmonizes with cadmium flare of gorse running along surrounding ridges. I look up from them and glimpse the Ridge of the Red Cairns slipping behind the massive bulk of the hill of the hawk, and emerging again on its western side. I transcribe it into musical notation, ponder in what key it should be and settle on humming it in B-flat.

The Seven Birds of Rhiannon pass overhead and a sentinel chat holds its pose on a Bronze Age marker stone. From up here familiar peaks show new perspectives, like artists' models shifting their pose. Instead of struggling to identify and impose name, I seek to fit them in to the greater geological scheme. When I sidle round the ring-cairn to find shelter from an unexpectedly cold wind from the west, suddenly there confronts me the majestic swelling clarity of the Harlech Dome, its pale strata scored across rising slopes that climb to the hill of the hare. The hill at the head of the light is craggy and notched behind it. I translate these names for you out of their beautiful native assonances so that you will know their meaning and not just pass over them as riddle of alien consonants – Moel Ysgyfarnogod, Foel Penoleu.

When I leave Bryn Cader Faner – and always this is with regret and many a backward glance to imprint in the mind the resonant presence of it in this blanched and silvered lonely landscape – today instead of returning by the familiar tracks that have been used, and latterly most sparingly, through millennia, I saunter up the unpathed hill to the west and drop down to Llyn Caerwych. This is one of the least-visited of Welsh mountain lakes, 'a bare-margined tarn' Bill Condry calls it, in the only written reference to it I know. Perhaps in the Bronze Age or the Medieval Warm Period, people camped here through the summer months, tended their stock, churned butter and made cheese as shepherds still do in remote high valleys of the Pyrenees. Maybe latterly a lone fisherman with deft dip of the wrist has dropped a hopeful line into this water. The peaty shores crowd in and across the surrounding *fign* black braided buds of the bog cotton are unfurling their wild little flags of white. Brilliant white too is a hank of fleece caught in purple lichen on an erratic rock marooned on the rim above. In it a seam of quartz pebbles sparkles, on the sunlit side spreads may-green lichen, and the skylarks are singing and soaring and tumbling suddenly earthwards.

Under Moel Ysgyfarnogod, where the ice laid bare those rock-ribs of the Harlech Dome – structuring principle of these North Walian hills – one bluff was undercut, and from the scoured slabs above enormous blocks have peeled away to fall in cyclopean jumble below. The gauzed sky above, unblemished by vapour trails[4], tells that Earth is still at her old games. I sit on a drumlin among the heather and look down. Like a fly cast far across the surface, the eye is drawn farthest first, to Ynys Enlli at the end of the Llŷn Peninsula, the tide-race between it and the mainland a silver thread. Then I reel in my gaze past all the ripple of fretted headlands where seals sing from flat rocks under cliffs. It rests for a while among a swirl of channels that gleam across the sand in the estuary of the Dwyryd.

---

[4] The 2010 volcanic eruptions in Iceland had grounded flights at this time.

Behind me the cleft and broken, in front this fluid dance of water and light. Twenty years ago a set of photographs was given me by the sculptor Meic Watts. They were long late evening exposures taken in the valley into which I am looking down, a stream winding through its flat marshy ground. Meic had set candles in paper boats. The faltering paths of their light, so fragile and tenuous, somehow linked perfectly the fluid and the fractal, and all the dimensions of time they have inhabited. In brilliant daylight I follow their ghost-glimmer down to Caerwych ('the Marvellous Field') with such a gladness upon me in this old and lovely land. Not a soul has crossed my path all day.

(2010)

YR HINIOG

This was many years ago – that summer when the reservoirs dried, and walls of drowned houses rose once more into our consciousness. *Cofia!* But when a thing is gone, we never remember it as it truly was. The sentimentalizing. The idealizing. Even the distortions of animus. At best, we might come close to a sense of what could have been learned. Or is that too a trick of temporal perspective?

Sometimes the accretions delaminate.
We gain a glimpse of how and from what we're made.

I was young. It was morning. The sun had blazed for weeks, wheeling daily round a cobalt dome of sky. Rucksack on my back, I took the train from Porthmadog, alighted at the little halt beyond Pont Briwet. Hook-beaked black sea-hags, wings spread to dry, roosted on the estuary pylons. My Labrador Kigfa, a young dog then, lolloped and panted to heel. We climbed by way of Caerwych and Nant Pasgan into the hills. Into the

Rhinogydd. The rough hills. The threshold place. That may stand for our life's journey if we ponder it this way, in the way of correlatives. By identifying our feelings with the texture of a landscape.

I splashed the cold water of the stream by Nant Pasgan Bach across my face to wash salt-sting away, and followed the course upwards, grass crisped by drought, past the hut-circles of the older time, past the enclosures and the piled stones, climbing by cold water in the heat of the day; climbing to the crest of the hill of the hare, to spend the night beyond, in a dark and quiet place, apart, in stillness; to journey for days through lonely hills; for this reason: *a riveder le stelle* ('to see again the stars'). It's how Dante ends the *Inferno*...

I love the naming of places – loved to hear the old keepers of land and memory, the remembrancers, the *cyfarwyddion* with all their onomastic guile and invention, recount them – stories that shimmered beyond need for explanation. Though I loved their fun and their dreaming too, their melodic richness – notations of the heart-land. Magic kicked from the dew...

On scratched, bare rock in the uplands of Ardudwy I spread across phantom filthy straw my yellow ox-hide wherein the fleas crawled, and lay down to dream, heard and laughed again as the mythical, appropriated king and his inward-gazing court, oblivious, were subject to pricks of our satire.

The other hero – our hero – wins at *gwyddbwyll*. Heraldry scatters the clues.[5] Warriors are turned to stone of the landscapes they inhabit. Caerwych indeed! Often the valley-dawn was misted, this summit floating above. The foreign writers, *Weallas*

---

[5] cf. *Breudwyt Rhonabwy* – the earliest British political satire, written to mock Edward Longshanks' appropriation of the Arthurian stories – 'The Matter of Britain' – and promote instead the alternative heroic tradition of Owain ap Urien. For an excellent close de-coding, see the article in THSC 1958.

but not of the *Cymry*, tell of northern Rhinogydd how they are without parallel rough and arduous, advise to avoid. Here is easy enough to find; to attain; to understand. By feeling. By contemplation. By reading the land and pacing yourself to meet its demands.

How I love these hills! Down there, ice-scoured Ynys Gifftan is a barge to bear the dying king to Avalon, and the sea-hags look on. Times, memories – they conflate. These hills – they are the *Rhinogydd*. They are the threshold hills. They are the liminal place. This is why cultures of achievement, concepts of conquest, Saxon certainties, will warn you away. For these it seems too alien, too difficult, too taxing here, where nothing is straightforward. To tease out the complexities of a route through rough ground; to listen with sensitivity; to study the lie of the land as it affects our passage and our lives – all these are superfluity and preciosity to colonists and conquistadors; to those who would annexe, appropriate, thrust on through.

The *Brut y Tywysogion* tells of how, in 1164, Henry the Second, king (but not of Wales) from the Scottish borders to the Pyrenees and unprepared to tolerate the impudence of independence in this little country of ours, marched with a mercenary composite army – English, Norman, Gascon, Flemish and Angevins – on the heartland. Wales was ready, forces massed along the banks of Dyfrdwy (name of which river translates as 'water of the divinity'), harrying his flanks, cutting off his lines of supply, forcing his army to camp at Foel y Gwynt above Carrog, 'where he remained a few days. Then a tremendous storm of wind and foul weather and driving rain broke on them, and they lacked food. He withdrew his camping place back to England, and in his fury he caused to be taken out the eyes of his [Welsh] hostages whom he had long held.'

The Berwyn. The White Barrier. Another threshold. *Eiry*

Mynydd, gwyn to tei[6]. Envious rage. Hostage-takers. A terrible price exacted, 'in the country of the blind', upon those who can see. What echoes our landscapes hold. Attune!

In my own family a whole historical process enacted, over and over. This Huguenot name I bear. After the Revocation of the Edict of Nantes, they fled westwards. Last month, lecturing in the university at Nantes, a sudden subliminal halting chill came on me mid-discourse. Of collective memory; and afterwards, walking the narrow dark streets, such unease. This was how we came to Wales. Repeated over and over, from diaspora to assimilation, and back again. Now, electively, I belong.

Centuries pass. My people drifted eastwards again, as the Welsh among whom they had settled had done of necessity over centuries. To where the work was, accepting subsistence for themselves to create wealth for others. They too became *Cymry colli iaith*. Exchanged Fron Deg, Bryn Goleu, Llwyneinion of their settled place for Factory Lane, Barrow Street and the East Ordsall Road. Such depletion and poverty, of the language, of the life. I wake from a heat-of-the-day slumber and wander across bare rock to Foel Penoleu. To look on which hill is happiness to me.

This is why I come here so often. It is a place, a feeling, a connection back into the essence of that which was lost. For the most part lost generations ago; though instinct still thrills to the possibility of return; to the primal place, the elemental place. Here in the Rhinogydd the deep structure of Eryri is revealed in every rock-rib: under a cobalt dome the glinting silver dome of Harlech, curving, inverted, chased with delicate beauties, earth-

---

[6] An early Welsh nature-gnome, first transcribed in a fourteenth-century MS but in origin certainly much earlier. It translates as: 'Mountain snow, white the house-roofs'.

power implicit in vast form, up-heaved – naked resonance of stilled magma.

When I was young, on my own quest to connect, I had to climb out; of the city, which was always down there. My city was hill-rimmed, height-encircled, moorland edges rearing beyond each mean street's end. In the year's spring, in my life's spring, I found my way out beyond its confines. To where the forms of land were weather-sculpted – frost-riven, wind-carved, wuthered into resistant shapes; in the high land where the cold tilts slow into the cusp of spring and the mountain hare, the little *lepus timidus* that is white in winter, kicks a diamond glitter against the light.

On the stem of the rose among the hooked thorns the red spot, tiny, that becomes leaf, bud, flower; so too our attentive awareness, hooked into growing and flowering. When you go out into the natural world, it is best not to look on that experience acquisitively. Focus down instead. Explore intimacy, delight at increase of knowledge. In the jewelled elsewhere of Wales a term of approval: *'dyn ei filltir sgwar'*. Persons 'of our own square mile' we can each become. It is to take the sign of belonging; the red spot that grows into branch and blossom.

I look back on my time of first venturing both as gift and as spiritual discipline. In all weathers, in all lights or no light, in sunlight and by moonlight, at all seasons, the hills became my intimates, disclosing, confiding. I slipped among them in the company of wild creatures, and along the customary paths they travelled.

What I saw then and there; what I see now and here, on the elemental pavements of the hill at the head of the light: rocks balance; the crags are seamed and riven; streams thread down; through and through, the same fault-lines, the same pattern, the same design. Our fractal universe, faces and creatures in the rocks, what we perceive.

There was a winter's night when a round moon silvered the stream, imparting a radiance, a soft mercury sheen to the moorland grasses. All was silence. Shadowy secrecies of the night held sway, summer glories were dimmed: subtle pastels, points of light, patched glimmers of infinite shades of green and purple and brown, the pungent fragrance of bracken and heather-bloom and bilberry. The ring ouzels that flitted restless by the *nant* below; the plaintive lovely call of the golden plovers, the chirring, frantic flight of red grouse; a hen harrier ghosting alongside the long path winding southwards into noon light – all those gifts of summer day lay winter-stilled, out there in the moonlight, which transmutes everything to longing, gives otherness to the themes of landscape. Among the surrounding landscape glimmer and drift of water and wind, spectating the dark. A theme hovered in liminal space. What comes to you on a moonlit ridge is a different thing entirely to the more customary illuminations of life.

To walk alone in a wild place in the moonlight is a kind of ghostly and distant variant to our normal customs – is to take ourselves to a place we may sense but do not often go, and to find something expressed there achingly, of which we have profoundest need to know. You remove yourself from the everyday in order more closely to connect, in order more clearly to counterpoint clarity of imagination with the mundane detail of life. In the darkness, understanding comes, suffusing it with a pale light more magical than anything mere possession can bring. Here in obscurity the riches of mystery and suggestion are objectified.

Would you count cost? I am talking typologies here. A squall of sleet, the dimming of the moon by cloud, a stumbling long descent through woods, solitary footfall of self along the silent forest road. The way we follow is of what's within; is our own energetic and loving spirit, that is better released and allowed to flow. It is Camus's 'invincible summer' of the heart. It is the ghostly fifth theme from the *chaconne* of Bach's great Partita in D, written for the memory of his wife Maria Barbara. To listen attentively to the devotional melodies of our own attuning spirits is to cross into liminal space – to find our way to the edge in the moonlight and wander there, among whatever presences we may encounter. Things come again, in all the sufficient, beautiful strangeness of their being, making the unknowable briefly known, if we dare to venture there.

Much of this is what I learnt when I was young, in the course of many journeys that led into the liminal space. My dog and I on top of Foel Penoleu in that hot summer, for example. The rough country alien writers so revile stretched for miles ahead of us. Clip, Craig Ddrwg, Bwlch Gwilym, Twr Glas – we have named them, and come to know. At Llyn Morwynion I slept, swam in the morning sun that streamed across Migneint, across Rhobell and Arenig. Kettle boiling on the stove; mingled scents of heather and coffee; a curlew calling; the mirror-lake and the great peace.

A warplane screamed past as I lay naked and drying. I heard a woman once, to whom I was close, tell of how such sudden dreadful Tornado-thrust, the noise, the energy, brought her to instant climax. The snub-nosed bomb is delivered from bloodied thighs and rent flesh. That my genes should have swum in the pool of her arousal. Hussar on the roof looks down in fearful wonderment, all-seeing; looks down on the world's contagion. That brilliant trope. Angelo squeezes through skylight, descends; a woman at the foot of the stairs holds the candle, herself illuminated by its flame.[7]

---

[7] The reference in this passage is to Jean Giono's visionary historical allegory, *L'Hussar sur le Toit* (1951) – a romantic counterpart to Camus's much more widely known *La Peste* (1947).

She feeds him goats' cheese, wine and bread. I wander for more days through the hills, following leads through the heather, through crags, sleeping by quiet and rock-bound tarns. At Bwlch Drws Ardudwy an old man, the age I am now, bare-chested in the heat, pushes a bike along the stony track. He hails me. I walk over to him, notice the scars.

'Heart by-pass surgery', he tells, following my glance. We part in our different directions. By Dulyn with the sun westering behind Enlli I make camp again. Goats approach warily. Kigfa shivers close and groans. A sleeping-bag spread on dry and springing turf.

On the ridge above, next morning, the nature of the ground I traverse has changed. Smooth sward rolls along towards sun's destiny. By green paths I slip down to Dinas Oleu, down into Bermo, with its behemoths, its pubs brimming with good-natured orotund vowels of Brummagem; and am content.

Which remains, though all of this was years ago…

(2012)

GLOYWLYN

When you are still amongst a landscape, and become an object fixed temporarily within it, the landscape itself starts to come to life around you. Those who have written about the Rhinog comment on what they see as its sterile and lifeless quality. Perhaps they were too busy passing through, too intent on destination to see what's here. I begin to be aware of how much is moving around my bed in the heather. From a rock behind me there is a fierce fluttering and chipping of small birds, as pipit and wren argue over territory, take up aggressive stances on prominent boulders before joining brief flurries of battle in the spaces between.

On the shining lake-levels there is a convergence which threatens more trouble. I see it all from this vantage point. A drake teal – a lovely small duck made shy and fearful by the depredations of the wildfowling fraternity – is gliding round the margin of a reed-bed, whilst unseen to him in the next inlet a moorhen jerks and bobs along. They meet in an explosion of wings, clattering away across the water, the teal airborne and wheeling back to alight in a clearing amongst the reeds before the more aggressive moorhen has even raised her trailing legs from ripples that follow her. A bemused fox comes down to the farther shore to drink, watches with one foreleg held aloft, points delicately to where the teal has landed, pricks its ears at the metallic call of a snipe that rises from the sedge.

The accent of light falls differently now. Carreg y Saeth has become black, the stony detail of its crags entirely gone. Its ridges serve as dark frame for the peak of Yr Wyddfa, twenty miles away and purple with coming night. The bright lake itself is a map, its countries sketched out in quicksilver, in wavering lines of rushes, reeds and sedge, in undisciplined clumps of bushy heather and the stirring, tawny grasses that catch the last rays. These light up also rock strata that dip at a steep angle into the water, bearing the scars of glaciation, erratics scattered across them from the yesterday of geological time. It catches too and glitters on the rings which surface tension has pulled up the brittle grey stems of reeds furred underwater by green algae and standing in soldierly groups. The hillsides, hitherto plain and dark, are glowing with rich greens of plaited bell-heather stems, and the dusty pink husks of last year's flowering in the common heather. Two ravens creak across the indigo sky. I imagine them as the 'twa corbies' of the old ballad, discussing in this stately progress their next meal:

The one of them said to his make,
Where shall we our breakfast take?
Down in yonder greene field,
There lies a Knight slain under his shield.

A scimitar-winged peregrine flashes by. Colour ebbs away, then suddenly surges above the horizon again. An arc of robin's-egg-blue in the west modulates down through sunset's palette to a glisten of sea beneath. Above the rim of the *cwm* the lights of Cricieth and Pwllheli register, and beyond them the beam from Ynys Enlli pierces the haze. The moon is up, climbing above Rhinog Fawr, the lake still bright with its reflection. I watch the stars come out one by one, as though switched on.

Across from my tent snipe are still drumming in the marsh. The sound is eerie and yet comforting. Noises of the stream mingle, stilled momentarily by a breeze. As it traverses the hillside, on the farthermost ridge scarlet flames where the heather is burning leap as vivid and temporary within this landscape as our lives, tugging as they do so at the most primitive emotions. Streamers of livid smoke furl round the moon, extinguishing in their short sway the brightness of the lake.

(1996)

THE CLEAR SIGHT OF JANET HAIGH

Mountains are no place for memorials to Man, but there are one or two which are affecting enough in their way. I doubt if anyone coming down off the Brecon Beacons in a winter's twilight could fail to be moved by the obelisk above Cwm Llwch to little Tommy Jones. And the great slab of slate with its simple inscription carved by Jonah Jones on a knoll among the tawny grasses of Bwlch Ehediad sets up a strange resonance between itself and the sinister pool with its single alder in the marsh below, from which for many years a DC-3's tailplane protruded, and deep within which are bodies of some of those whom the stone commemorates. The memorial which has the greatest emotional force for me is a fragile, plain tablet of local slate which stands beside the old Harlech-to-London coach road where it climbs out of the Nant Ysgethin and on to the broad, grassy height of Llawlech. Its inscription runs thus: '*Gogoniant i Dduw*. To the enduring memory of Janet Haigh, who even as late as her eighty-fourth year, despite dim sight and stiffened joints, still loved to walk this way from Talybont to Penmaenpool.'

I know nothing about Janet Haigh other than the above, and the two additional facts that she died in 1953, and that her son Mervyn was sometime Bishop of Winchester. What matters is the sense of due reverence that her stone imparts to this remarkable place. It is nothing to do with her spirit lingering here or any like sentimentality. Stone, inscription and landscape together present an extraordinary and poignant specific expression of the great poetic commonplace which is the endurance of natural beauty by contrast with human life. That 'dim sight', those 'stiffened joints', labouring up this hill in their 84th year with the burden of mortality upon them are the fate we all share. Her capacity to delight in the glory of the place which the Welsh words suggest is not so general, though.

Let me describe the context of her stone. I may have misled you by that reference to the coach road, for it's almost incomprehensible that the London Stage, with or without its Pickwickian complement of jovial, be-toppered gents and genteel crinolined ladies, could ever have passed along this ancient line of communication. The old green track eases its way through ice-scoured bluffs and over hillsides of bleached grass. It traverses a bare, wild valley stretching up into the innermost recesses of the Rhinogydd, most rugged of Snowdonia hill-ranges. It bumps across the narrow, humped bridge of Pont Scethin and strains up zigzags on to the ridge of Llawlech at 550 metres above sea-level, before edging gingerly down into the valley of the Mawddach. This is no ordinary 'road', and the landscape through which it leads is one of the most fragile and exquisite in Wales. Even the statutory bodies for the most part recognize that fragility (with one ignoble exception which we shall come to in due course). In 1979 a huge acreage with Pont Scethin at its centre was designated an Ancient Landscape, with a strong consequent presumption against any form of disturbance within it. The lake of Bodlyn, a mile above Pont Scethin, is now a Site of Special Scientific Interest under the Wildlife and Countryside Act of 1981. A Management Agreement for 135 acres lower down the Afon Ysgethin has been negotiated under conditions laid down in the same Act. The whole area, in the words of Snowdonia National Park archaeologist Peter Crew, is 'the most important archaeologically in Wales, and stands comparison with anything in Britain. The valley has an exceptional range of relict features, of which Pont Scethin is only the most obvious.' Richard Kelly of the Gwynedd Archaeological Trust, with whom I visited Pont Scethin recently, adds that 'What's important here is not just the number of scheduled monuments, but more particularly the context in which they're to be found, which shows with remarkable clarity the patterns of land usage and settlement over millennia. It's vital that nothing be allowed to affect any part of this whole landscape.'

And of course, it is also beautiful. From Janet Haigh's stone you can look out over that serpentine scar in the cerulean of Porthmadog Bay which is Sarn Badrig ('St. Patrick's Causeway'). You can look across northwards to Snowdon: 'Give me the stones of Snowdon/And the lamps of Heaven' wrote Kingsley, and from this angle you see the aptness of the collocation. The very end of the ridge you stand upon was the very first acquisition of The National Trust – Dinas Oleu – the citadel of light; and it is light which illuminates the divine and priceless manuscript laid out before you – hill-light, western light, that glowing, changing, suffusing light, flooding into these western valleys beneath, around, through the clouds and making them at times among the most ethereally lovely places in God's creation. I talked with the photographer Fay Godwin about this unique and particular quality of light and Pont Scethin came into the conversation. She has a photograph of it, the hills heavily black and clouded behind, middle distance a field of cloth-of-gold, and the elegance of the bridge, the exuberance of the foreground stream, picked out in a gleam of lichen on old stone, a crystal string of bubbles in peat-dark water. 'God forbid that anything should ever happen to that place!' was her instinctive response, the pain which is never far from her eyes focused on the thought.

Well, it has happened, and this is what it looks like now. At the point where you cross the spur which ends in the Iron Age fort on Craig y Dinas and leave the harsh new track that Welsh Water Authority, in its wisdom, has forced through to the high mountain lake of Bodlyn, there is a pile of alien aggregate dumped over the green moor grass, dwarfing the standing stone which marks the old route. A few yards further and you look down the latter towards Pont Scethin, but its line is no longer to be seen. Instead, there is a scar, a dark slash, a quagmire in places fifty yards wide. It ends a hundred yards beyond Pont Scethin. Walk along it and note the details. Those rocks breaking the surface of the moor, which the long-departed ice smoothed and ground to a fine sheen and in which the iron-hooped coach wheels later wore their grooves – the steel caterpillar-tracks of the JCB have crushed and shattered their way across them. More aggregate, from-God-knows-where, is scattered about here and there to ease the juggernauts' progress. Almost certainly, archaeological remains have been affected, and the ancient trackway, which dates at least from the Bronze Age, has in places been erased. The sparse mountain vegetation will not recover to its former state in my lifetime. By the stone abutments of little Pont Scethin stand discarded drums of lubricant for the digging machines, and in the Afon Ysgethin likewise – in that pure, rapid stream, cast-off oil drums! On the greensward of Fay's photograph and across the first stones of the bridge concrete has been mixed, rubbish strewn, bottles smashed. Beneath it they have made a ford. On the other side, a hundred yards above, a great hole has been dug quite possibly on the actual line of the old road, though it is now impossible to tell. The peat all around shimmers with the iridescence of spilt diesel fuel and stinks of the same and the monstrous machines which have made the mess stand idle nearby, claws stuck fast in the flesh of the moor. In the hole is a huge, shiny metal tank, a pipe, stop-cocks – too huge ever to be fully concealed! It is all to relieve pressure on the water mains, the pipework of which needs to be modernized and set in good order before being sold off. If it shows above ground when work is finished – as it clearly must – then planning permission will be needed, but this will be granted to Welsh Water Authority retrospectively and automatically.

Is it the workmen's fault? It would be easy to point the finger at them, and some of their behaviour – if they were responsible – has certainly been remiss. But after the first rape, how easily does gang morality plunge. I talked to these men. They are sub-contractors, decent, tolerant, doing hard physical work often in bleak weather and under difficult conditions. Each one of them found it bewildering that they should have been ordered to put the tank here, that they should have been told to gain access by the route they did, that they should at no time have been overseen by WWA planners. But to question is to send tremors back along the chain of command, is to be difficult, and to be difficult is to be dismissed – the Thatcherite bind, and a hard option in an area where there is little employment. In abjuring their responsibility to individual witness, undoubtedly they are culpable. But theirs is not the basic lack of perception towards that treasure of a landscape. They have worked in it, and their effect on it sits uneasily in their conscience as their consciousness of its worth grows. The real destructive arrogance has its root elsewhere.

The Welsh Water Authority, which is engaged in this work, has no need to gain planning approval for what it does to the landscapes through which it has rights of access and among which its interests lie. I remember its past dissonant brutalities in the Welsh hills: the Bodlyn track; the tarmac road to Ffynnon Llugwy; the destruction of archaeological remains in the bulldozing of improved access to Llyn Anafon. (After the furore caused by this latter, the WWA grudgingly acceded to the implementation of consultative procedures with the Gwynedd Archaeological Trust before future work at sensitive sites. At Pont Scethin – which of all sites is perhaps the most sensitive, these procedures were ignored.) The men who can countenance, condone and promote these actions are brutish. Invested with power, yet unaware of its effects and excused its responsibilities, their behaviour is an outrage. And these are the same people to whom the Government wishes to hand over private executive power!

Let's take this story as a metaphor. There is one image from this whole scene of physical and spiritual desolation which I cannot overstress – it is the mud, which is deep and all-pervasive. The potency of that image haunts our dying century's consciousness. It transports us in an instant to the Somme and

Passchendaele. The sepia images of nightmare flicker back at us – the slippery mire, the severed limbs, the putrescent flesh, the uniforms fouled, bloodied and torn. And the terrible antiphony of those names – what sleep here? What passion and suffering in this vale? *Pro Deo, Rege, et Patria*! Men doing their duty, acceding to force of circumstance, be it social, economic or whatever: 'We shall miss you, we shall kiss you/But we think you ought to go…' To keep the perspective, though, this is simply building-site mud, not that of a killing-field where 60,000 men – my paternal grandfather among them – will die in a single morning. And the jets which fill the shining chamber here will not hiss with Zyklon B, however much their technology repels. However close the crucial and underlying lack of life-reverence may be, there are no deaths involved here. Except, that is, for those insubstantial and unprofitable ones of beauty and hope. Those are terms which Janet Haigh, whose dim sight surveyed the scene where this dereliction was to take place so many times from the hill above, would have recognized and understood. But we no longer live in her age, nor in that of her son.

We live in an age when public utilities such as water (the land for which was taken from people, for the most part by compulsion, for the greater good) must now be modernized and made efficient in order dogmatically to be sold off for private profit. And when that has happened the land must be made to pay, so the public will be excluded. We live in an age when so-called freedom fighters can explode bombs at Remembrance Day parades; can place explosives in the holds of aircraft so that the mutilated bodies of innocent victims are strewn by the hundred across just such bare hillsides as this; can commit rape, murder, infanticide, with American financial support and training and tacit British approval, against the free citizens of Nicaragua. We live in an age when politicians, after a *respectable* gap of time, are rewarded with knighthoods for their serviceable lies; when politicians who have overthrown all parliamentary and environmental precedent in driving a new multiple-carriageway road through a National Park are rewarded for the same with the post of Secretary of State for the Environment; when political leaders in the West glorify, defend with sophistry, and allow to proliferate, weapons of genocide the use of which is totally against the words and spirit or the Geneva Convention; when our own political leader can *lie* about the details of an engagement which led to the deaths of 368 seamen of another nationality, and treat those deaths as a credit to her self-proclaimed martial spirit and beyond that an irrelevance – neither of which they can ever be.

You, if you have a trace of human fineness and sensitivity instead of the crudely corrupt self-interest, jingoistic blood-lust and philistinism which presently hold sway in our society, will know how long this bitter catalogue could stretch. So try to imagine something with me. This leader of whom I've been talking – I could almost envision taking her, for all that graceless and unnatural means of locomotion she has, up to Janet Haigh's stone, and pointing out this devastated scene to her: 'If *you* seek a monument, look around!' I could *almost* imagine it, but not quite, for of course she has no place there, and that is the crucial point. We are talking leaders, role-models, paradigms, examples. So how could this affected creature of the image-makers, with her deformed gait and undiscardable social armour, hope to reach even the modest heights which Janet Haigh, with her 'dim sight and stiffened joints' regularly attained into extreme old age? Who, then – self-publicizing stances aside – is the heroine? It would be impossible for Mrs Thatcher, in reflective solitude, to climb that hill. Which is, I think, cause for pity. Because there is thus for her no hope of release from the artificiality, meanness, moral turpitude and narrowness of vision which her mode of life entails.

I never knew Janet Haigh. When she died I was a six-year-old slum-kid in Hulme – the seedier end of Manchester's Moss Side. When I was of an age to do so, I escaped its narrow, shabby streets to the hill-country of Derbyshire, then Wales, and the joy and the fulfilment their wildness brought me was liberating. I believe that you cannot go about *by yourself* among the hills without them having a beneficial, a salutary, an improving effect on your character. It is demonstrably so – take your arrogance, your self-conceit to the hills. and circumstances will soon conspire to make you lose them. How easy is it to stumble the wet miles down through the mist to shelter, lost and alone, with your self-congratulation intact? How ridiculous to retain the large sense of your own importance when you sit, dwarfed by your surroundings and silent and utterly stilled, in some mountain cwm? I have no doubt whatsoever that Janet Haigh knew these things. (Yes, yes! Writers should not put thoughts into the minds of the dead, but will you, as readers, deny this?) But what of Mrs. Thatcher? Where I cannot see her is climbing the hill of vision in penitence for the effect she has had upon it, learning her own inadequacies, seeing her mistakes, having imparted to her the humility and hence, perhaps, the magnanimity which can come from a simple-hearted response to natural beauty. The Nant Ysgethin provides one tiny example of what is happening throughout our hill-country. Elsewhere, the examples proliferate: forestry, farm roads, second-home developments have all boomed in the last ten years, devastating the quiet places. And just as child murder and child abuse appear to have increased in our brutalized society under the Thatcher regimen, so too have activities like badger-digging in the countryside. Ten years ago I scarcely knew of one dug sett;

nowadays the undug sett is an exception and the export trade to city dog-pits flourishes.

Keith Thomas, in his monumental and masterful book *Man and the Natural World* (Allen Lane, 1983) writes that 'nature parks and conservation areas serve a function not unlike that which toy animals have for children; they are fantasies which enshrine the values by which society as a whole cannot afford to live'. It is probably the most fatuous statement this excellent historian has ever made. Far from not being able to live by the values we enshrine within these places, it is vital to our continuing physical and spiritual health and even our continued existence that they are liberated and brought to play in society – the balance, the wisdom, the detachment, the quietude, the humility, the quiet courage as of a frail octogenarian labouring up a steep hill-slope, are as humanly indispensable as they seem – to our Government and its executives – unavailable. Which is why, when I have sloughed through the mud which at present fouls Pont Scethin, I can arrive at Janet Haigh's stone and feel a profound sense of gratitude for her son's action in recording how, 'even as late as her eighty-fourth year, despite dim sight and stiffened joints, [she] still loved to walk this way'. For if ever an age needed that love of landscape expressing, and the human gifts such benediction brings, it is ours.

Footnote, 2016: The above piece, written in 1989 in some despair after witnessing the savage environmental depredations of the Thatcher decade, I include here not only as historical record and warning, but also for a more heartening reason. After its publication I sent it, with a portfolio of photographs, to the then chairman of Welsh Water, John Elfed Jones. His response was honourable, outraged and immediate. Those responsible were disciplined, and sustained and serious attempts were made at landscape restoration. I wish I could think the same willing acceptance of responsibility and desire to make amends conceivable in Britain's current management culture; but much has changed there in twenty years, and I think it unlikely.

CADER IDRIS

> What is so beautiful in Dolgellau, seen from the hill on the
> station side of the river is the sense of appropriateness, of
> rightness in the arrangement of slate roofs and grey and white
> walls. When the eye passes from the town to Cader Idris ...
> one feels that there is a sort of family likeness, a relationship
> between the works of man and his maker.

Thus, appreciatively, wrote the architect Henry Wilson in 1895.
To idle here before setting out on a luminous winter's day maybe
for the summits is one of the pleasures of life. The Reverend
Francis Kilvert – most amiable of our great diarists – did so, and
left a delightful account of it, in 1871 before taking the Pony
Track up Cader by the Rhiw Gwredydd. But I prefer Fron Serth,
that leads up from the outskirts of town into an exquisite region
of oakwoods, sheep pasture and little ridges at the north-eastern
end of the Cader range. An old, flagged pony track runs over
to the top of the Tal y Llyn pass, and is a good way to gain the
eastern gable of the longest and finest mountain ridge south of
the Scottish border.

From the state of the paths, by far the greater number who
do climb Cader don't come this way, nor even venture so far as
Mynydd Moel, easternmost of Cader's three main summits and
a great hill in its own right, massive in presence as you approach
it from this direction. Its top is particularly fine, with a shelter-
cairn and a little cockscomb of rocks above plunging crags. You
can see from it straight down on to Dolgellau, a bare two miles
away, and that gives you the clue as to why, in Elizabethan times,
this was considered the highest mountain in the British Isles.
Penygadair – highest point of the Cader range – may only be 892
metres above sea level, but sea level is just down there. Dolgellau
is at it. Ben Nevis may be nearly half as high again but it is twice

as far from the sea. Those sandflats and long, low saltings of the Mawddach estuary give Cader its uplift, its subjective impression of height. It *feels* a tremendous mountain.

From Mynydd Moel, you look right along the northern escarpment, lakes flashing silver from glaciated hollows around which elegant ridges glint skywards. Walk a few yards down the southern slope and you're confronted by a view a version of which is one of the masterpieces of eighteenth-century art. Richard Wilson's *Cader Idris, Llyn-y-cau* of 1765 is in the Tate in London – a surprisingly small canvas, not much more than eighteen inches high by two feet or so wide, all russets and Payne's grey with the palest blues and greens and a touch of gold on foreground boulders which root its conceptual diagonals firmly in the landscape. It always shocks me with its capacity simultaneously to be like and yet unlike. It's less the depiction of a mountain scene than its re-ordering, the interpretation of its essence by a man with a kindly, respectful and loving view of nature and its power for harmony. I love it, and the place it so wonderfully expresses.

I was last here on a day suffused with the golden light of a Claude landscape. I've seldom seen so far from the hills: Snowdon seemed almost within touching distance to the north, and Snaefell nebulous behind it, whilst to the south-east and the south-west the Malvern hills and the Preselis closed off the horizon, so clear their every summit was identifiable. A blustery wind scoured the plateau between Mynydd Moel and Penygadair. As I arrived at the summit, the ravens grated their welcome.

These birds and their parents I have known for forty years. This was the first mountain I climbed in Wales, in that burnished summer at the end of the 1950s. They were there then, tumbling joyful acrobats around the summit whose flight spelt freedom, but whose presence was a stranger longing, the exact words for which remain fixed only in feeling, refusing ever to succumb to our quest after definition. If I could never return, each bird would dance a memory there for me: of running up on a wet autumn day to find, as we reached the top, the world peeled clean of cloud and gleaming as though renewed; or picking our way down the Fox's Path after the first ascent of one of the hard ice gullies on Cyfrwy over 30 years ago, with the sun slanting up the estuary, strewing the slope with fiery rosettes where ice ringed rocks which had melted through the snow. These most beautiful places imprint themselves in perpetuity on our consciousness. On this last visit the wind froze fingers and cheekbones, and I shuffled rapidly down to Cyfrwy, the arête on which is my favourite way up any mountain (be wary, though – it is most definitely a rock-climb). I raced down the broad ridge over Rhiw Gwredydd, where the ponies once climbed up from the Dysynni valley, and on past Tyrau Mawr to Braich Ddu, the ridge's unvisited seaward gable, descended in the gathering dark with the light of Ynys Enlli flashing 30 miles across the bay.

By Cyfannedd a gibbous moon cast latticed shadows of branches across the road, an owl's wavering scream tore at the woods' silence, curlews descanted in the estuary as I took the footpath across the Barmouth railway bridge with slick, black water running fast beneath, between the baulks which the shipworm gnaws. Maybe to ask for more than glimpses and memories of the perfect state is to ask too much. Maybe only in moments – as accessible in the mountains' simplicity as anywhere – does the landscape of our life approach the harmony of Richard Wilson's vision. Maybe Cader Idris is as close as we get to the perfected place…

(1996)

WAUN Y GRIAFOLEN

My habit in recent years, at Epiphany, has been to go to Ffynnon Fair at Penllyn – the elemental and exquisite spring-pool just above high water mark in the cliffs at the westernmost point of the Llŷn Peninsula, that was the holiest well in medieval Wales. This year – whether because I had moved house to a different part of Wales just before Christmas, or from some chthonic sense that the landscape had a different lesson to reveal – I thought to set out for a different objective, and one that I'd had in mind for some time to revisit. I thought to go back to the source of the Dee.

The morning deterred me. It was cold and heavy, sightlines to the ridge across the valley all obscured by drizzle and cloud, the temperature risen barely enough to glisten with moisture the ice of the preceding week's freeze. All writers are experts at diversionary tactics, can spin the thread interminably before winding it on to the spool of decisive action. I cooked my cat a particularly delicious breakfast and watched her pick it piece by piece from the plate, shake it fiercely, deposit it on the carpet and chew it contemplatively. I told her about where I'd be going in the course of the day, and she purred a distant and entirely notional approval. I made phone calls, wrote letters, packed my rucksack with particular care. It was 1.30 before I left the house, and 2.15 before I'd driven up the valley of Pennant Lliw, negotiated sheets of ice across the track below Castell Carndochan, and parked the car by the old way that leads up through deep shade of a spruce plantation towards Waun y Griafolen.

John Berger, in one of his seductively intelligent and stimulating essays on art, comments that 'as soon as I begin looking at a field, an escarpment or an orchard as though in it there were some code to be deciphered, it becomes unfamiliar. Even the result – that is to say the "message" transmitted – remains mysterious… this is not just because of the problems of finding words to describe formal revelations; it is because the longer you spend with them, the more mysterious all visual images become.' He goes on to describe the way in which, he believes, because of 'a development in our understanding of reality... objects no longer confront us. Rather, relationships surround us.'

That sense of a deeper unfamiliarity beyond familiar surface appearance, of an inhering mystery in which the concept of interrelatedness is central, floods in on me continually, increasingly, from the landscape. Much of what I write is an attempt to reflect – and only to reflect, not define, for each of us will encounter it differently – some part of this. I look back on recurrent motifs present even in my earliest essays on mountains, and realize that this instinct for 'something far more deeply interfused' has always been a part of their appeal, a crucial element in what draws me to them. There is, of course, a paradox in trying to write about this dimension of the mountain experience. Because the dimension itself is almost best expressed by the characteristic phrase of Krishnamurti's 'freedom from the known', and is worlds apart from what F.R. Leavis, in spittingly parodic language, termed 'the Benthamite, technologico-positivist Enlightenment' with which, in the earnestness of its desire to grasp at meaning and significance, the writing project might be thought to have aims in common.

So, on a bleak January afternoon, light already fading, I set out on the gruelling two-hour walk to one of the mountain places that most haunts my imagination. A flock of gregarious bramblings, the stripes across the females' crowns a rich cinnamon colour, flitted noisily and erratically around the edge of the trees. Within the wood owl-pellets littered the pine needles, and a few solitary oak seedlings straggled up from beds of moss. I climbed briskly by the rough, steep path, old fallen boundaries radiating into shadow of the trees, reached the watershed and hurried on down to the gate from which you look out across Waun y Griafolen and see Dduallt for the first time.

Maybe there are lonelier places in the Welsh hills, but there are not many of them. Human intrusion here is minimal. No habitation's visible, no power lines, no roads. A fence here and there, a drainage ditch, a salient of spruce provide scant contemporary counterpoint to a map-notation that's of melodic richness: the moor of the rowan trees, the whistling crag, roebuck stones, the black height. It was three o'clock, scarcely an hour of daylight left and the best part of three miles of deep heather and bog lay between me and my objective – the old chapel that, following the river, I'd found my way to eighteen months before, built over the first pool of the Dee. The face of Dduallt was shrouded in cloud. A wind thumped and scudded across the moor. From the sedge in front of me a jack snipe rose briefly, lethargically, without a sound and, feathers plumped, dropped back into the heather maybe ten yards further away. No other living thing was in view.

Of course I should have turned back. I had none of that stuff you're supposed to carry – torch, compass, rations, space blanket, first aid. But I had food and a flask and my own consciousness, and they seemed safeguards enough. I carried on.

Waun y Griafolen is a great bowl in the hills, an extraordinary place of pathless bog where the heather and ling grow knee-high or higher, the acid, sodden peat beneath swelling each year as the vegetable life dies back into it. It took me over an hour to flounder across it to the chapel. Once under the face of Dduallt, tracks of a fox clearly imprinted in the snow led me through boulders to shrine and source.

Inevitably we come at places eager with expectation, and perhaps I had hoped for some gift, some sign, some sight in which I could invest symbolic significance, like the raven that had revealed the chapel to me when I first came here. But there was none. Most of us 'follow wandering fires,/Lost in the quagmire.' What we find at the end of our quest, properly, is a darkness, a mystery, for it is these, and not the dazzling conclusions of the explained, that lighten our understanding. I stepped inside the walls of the old chapel, drank from the pool below the boulder that forms its eastern wall. The mountain face above me was an intense black, its gloom alleviated only by flashes of ice on the rocks. Tendrils of mist stretched down to root themselves in the marsh and flower wanly in the last light.

What did I do, as a single human consciousness in this place so entirely apart? Simply, I prayed: for the wellbeing and safety of those whom I love; for an end to animosity and an access of understanding in our world; for deliverance from our obsessions with power and materialism that lead us inescapably into disharmony, blindness and abuse. I took from my rucksack bread and broke it to share with the raven, who was not here. I unwrapped Christmas cake, rich and reeking of brandy, that my dear friend Polly Biven (whose husband was so good a mentor to me in earlier years and who fell at his son's feet and was killed whilst climbing in the Avon Gorge a quarter of a century ago) bakes and sends to me each year, divided it and left on the topmost stone the raven's share. I drank warm, spiced tea from my flask. And I listened. Beneath the wind's insistency, what I could hear was this – the infant river, the name of which in Welsh means 'water of the divinity', flowing away under stones:

> Once
> I heard him
> He was washing the world
> Unseen, nightlong,
> Real.
>
> Paul Celan

What am I trying to tell you? That realization comes in the darkness of our understanding, not in its light... Here's John Berger again, from a seminal essay of 1985 entitled 'The White Bird':

> Art does not imitate nature, it imitates a creation, sometimes to propose an alternative world, sometimes simply to amplify, to confirm, to make social the brief hope offered by nature. Art is an organised response to what nature allows us to glimpse occasionally. Art sets out to transform the potential recognition into an unceasing one. It proclaims man in the hope of receiving a surer reply... the transcendental face of art is always a form of prayer.

In the gathering darkness of a winter night, without light, I turned to the rough miles for home. Flurries of snow whirled on the wind, ridges elided, hill-shapes merged, until I no longer knew this place. I was not lost. Some sense guided me, each step I took fell safe. Like an *ignis fatuus*, from a gap that looked down a long valley lights glimmered once from the farther shore of the great lake below. As I came down through unrelieved blackness of the wood, I knew the child to be stirring in the earth's womb, and I willed term of its succour there and safe delivery, hoped for the health of its mother and her long happiness.

(2001)

ABERGEIRW

Pont y Llyn Du on the Afon Gain, in the lonely moors east of Trawsfynydd, above the old gold mines at Gwynfynydd, is one of those places at which you'd never arrive except by design. It's one of my favourite haunts in the Welsh hills. The peaty hill stream rushes down through a miniature rocky gorge under the old humped bridge to debouch into a round pool of amber depth, green-pasture-encircled. You can traverse through on rock ledges beneath the arch, plunge into it if you're hardy and of the 'wild swimming' persuasion. What most appeals to me are the spirits of the place.

At this time of year, reliably, you'll find a pair of grey wagtails nesting hereabouts – ravishingly pretty little birds, by no means common even on the mountain streams of Wales that are one of their chief habitats. To call these wagtails 'grey' somehow sells them short. Of their plumage – gleaming dove-grey wings, white eye-stripe, black gorget and canary waistcoat – W.H. Hudson, soundest of ornithological judges, wrote that 'the effect is most beautiful, and pleases, perhaps, more than the colouring of any other British bird.'

He's right, though appearance isn't their sole attraction. I love them for the quickness of life they display, constantly in motion. The fine Northumbrian poet Katrina Porteous perfectly evokes their dynamic quality of apparent weightlessness in her couplet: 'The wagtail somersaults,/Light as a gnat.' Slender and graceful, they dance out of the gorge in undulating flight to hover among clouds of insects over the water, feeding and singing in light hirundine cadences as they do so. I lean over the parapet and watch their ceaseless activity, marvel at its anti-gravitational grace. They seem spirit-presences, free of substance, pure manifestations of energy, their long tail-feathers ever beating out a music of effortless movement. I have known them here for fifty years, come back each green June to witness them anew. Were they ever to desert this exquisite, wild, miniature landscape, an aspect of the land's essential life would have passed away.

(2016)

'WHO SHALL DWELL IN THY HOLY HILL?'

This is the time of year at which my dear old friend Bill Condry, the best of our natural history writers over the last half-century, died in 1998. I like to do things to commemorate the people who have been precious to me; thus took a walk that Bill himself at this season had often made. Here's his general description from his masterly volume on Snowdonia in the *New Naturalist* series:

> To go to Arenig Fawr in May... is to go at a delicious time of year. The approach from the south... is particularly delightful just when the slopes are loud with cuckoos, and countless pipits are coming down the sky in song; by the last habitation... the beeches are a fresh new green, and here and there if the sun is out the little green hairstreak butterflies rise from the turf in front of you, their underwings flashing brilliantly emerald.

Bill liked to make his ascent from above the hamlet of Parc to the east, but I have a perverse preference for the longer and boggier one from Blaen Lliw to the south-west. The preference is chiefly because of the valley of the Afon Lliw, with its continual flitting of pied flycatchers and its ancient oak woodland, its rocky spurs and waterfalls and the narrow, twisting road rising on to the high shelf of moor between Rhinog and Arenig. This is remotest Snowdonia, little-visited, a place apart.

Writers have commented on 'the wet and uncompromising nature of the terrain which encompasses [the Arenig]', and are right to do so. The broad and quaking circlet of quagmire from which the Arenig Fawr rears up is decorative in effect as any golden torc round the neck of a Celtic chieftain. It accentuates the fine head of the mountain, keeps all rival distraction at distance and at bay. From every angle, Arenig impresses. Here's George Borrow, who was not always a great connoisseur of wild landscapes, from his *Wild Wales* of 1862:

Arenig is certainly barren enough, for there is neither tree nor shrub upon it, but there is something majestic in its huge bulk. Of all the hills which I saw in Wales, none made a greater impression upon me.

A hundred years later, Showell Styles commented on how dominant a landscape feature Arenig Fawr is:

> ... because of its isolation in the midst of a huge tract of marsh and moorland, Arenig's twin humps are a familiar but distant part of every landscape between Snowdon and the Dovey, seen usually over the crests of lower ridges and suggesting a Bactrian camel of enormous size cruising along just behind the horizon.

If anything, Showell underestimates the Arenig's dominance. From the end of the Llŷn to the west, right across to Rhiwabon Mountain or even, on clearest days, the Roaches of Staffordshire to the east, it is the one instantly and unmistakably recognizable feature in the Welsh landscape. To glimpse it there, hovering among its wild uplands, as I drive back into Wales over the border hills is always to have the sense of coming home.

So, on a bright morning after days of rain, I drove alongside Llyn Tegid with the Aran mountains wave-like across its end and bluebells incandescing in all the woods, turned up Pennant Lliw and parked as close to Hendre Blaen Lliw as the discouraging signs that have proliferated in these parts over recent years would allow. For reasons on which views will vary widely, there has been a hardening of the Welsh rural arteries of late. The farmer at Twr y Maen (a couple of miles to the south and ruinous beneath the alien conifers now), who had called out his friendly greeting to Patrick Monkhouse when he passed this way in 1930 – "'Good day! Fine day! Ever been here before?" as if there were so many people passing that he really couldn't remember whether he had set eyes on us before or not' – would not, I think, be so welcoming now. There is a sad frisson of hostility about this place, some share of the responsibility for which cannot entirely be avoided by our own at-times-insensitive, and often careless, community of the outdoors. Nonetheless, I parked my car as far away as possible from all the veiled invitations to leave, locked it in the hope that it would be driveable and undamaged on my return, laced up my boots and set out for the hill.

The old track over to Rhyd y Fen by way of Amnodd Wen, that would have been a regular line of communication in former years, branches steeply off the little road to Trawsfynydd. I dawdled up it, conjuring spirits from the hazy air. And one materialized. As I glanced up, sailing serenely, wings half-folded, a red glisten slipping along the wind, there above me was a kite. Crowding into my mind in its wake came memories of being taken to the kite-roost at Tregaron by Bill Condry, forty or fifty of the fork-tailed birds drifting around in easy flight at twilight. And since I am by nature fanciful, and convinced that my little dog The Flea has come back as a cat, I fell to wondering whether this was the form Bill had chosen for his return, and mused too on my own future transformation into a raven, so that I could swoop and harass and play around his stately progress, and him unperturbed, as we would in the province of words on outings in his life.

These thoughts and fond memories quickly brought me to the old farm of Hendre Blaen Lliw, more or less abandoned now, the everyday life drained from it apart from at the crucial events of the shepherd's calendar, which are themselves passing. In the slate above the door was carved *Arglwydd yw fy Mugail'* ('the Lord is my Shepherd') a beautiful sentiment that strikes home ever more poignantly as the years pass. The loving spirit within us is our only worthwhile guide and keeper. But do we these days, for all our material comfort, truly 'not want'? I'm reminded of a passage from D.J. Williams's classic Welsh text, *Hen Dŷ Ffarm*:

> I do not think there is any occupation in as favourable a position... as that of those who dwell on the land and obtain their living out of it. In this work one has to do daily with one's fellow-creatures, man and animal, and with nature herself in every aspect. From cradle to grave, the inheritors of the earth are in closest touch with all the secret powers of life.

It was a thought that sat comfortless and askance alongside the great corrugated-iron wintering shed and the trodden dung of the grassless in-bye land, where even the mired lambs seem too dispirited to play. The shepherds are consigned to their own factories now. So I wound my way past and came with relief to the gate where the old way broached the moor. I wrote above of my 'perverse preference' for this approach. Its perversity lay in front and it's called Cors y Foel ('the Bog of the Hill'). Right up to the broad watershed from which you look down on Amnodd Wen, this is quaking ground, best forged through fast, for 'it may be that the gulfs will suck us down'. The twinned summits of the great Arenig seem a long way off, and buzzards wheel and mew mockingly, rising on thermals off the slopes of Moel Llyfnant as you toil towards them. I crossed Ceunant Coch – an exquisite little stream flowing clear over pebbles, dipping valleywards, wheatears and pipits darting and chasing around its banks – and traversed the hillside diagonally towards the *bwlch* on the summit ridge. Soon Amnodd Wen was in sight, a tiny cottage, growing derelict when I last visited, at the corner of a vast quadrant of forestry plantation. In the spring of 1911, the artists J.D. Innes and Augustus John stayed there, Innes in particular taking Arenig Fawr as his subject and producing a series of luminous, inspired paintings of it. Here's John, from his autobiography, *Chiaroscuro:*

> Innes's activity was prodigious; he rarely returned of an evening without a couple of panels completed. These... usually meant long rambles over the moors in search of the magical moment. perhaps he felt he must hasten while there was time to make these votive offerings to the mountains he loved with religious fervour...
>
> When he was moved to a nursing home in Kent [Innes died of tuberculosis in 1914 at the age of 27], we went with his Euphemia to see him. The meeting of these two was painful: we left them alone together: it was the last time I saw him. Under the cairn on the summit of Arenig, Dick Innes had buried a silver casket containing certain correspondence. I think he always associated Euphemia with this mountain and would have liked at the last to lie beside the cairn.

And so to the summits. There is very little difference in height between them, the southern perhaps twenty metres lower than the northern. The former has an attractive little rocky crest, the dip between the two is scattered with grotesque volcanic boulders, and the higher top has a cairn that is probably Bronze Age in origin. This latter summit is a place of great atmosphere and power. It has a separate name – Moel yr Eglwys ('Hill of the Church'). From it, Wales is visible. North-west in a long line, unfamiliar in aspect from this angle, are the hills of Eryri from Yr Wyddfa to Tal y Fan above Conwy. Far out west stretch the little hills of Llŷn down to offshore Mynydd Enlli, and all around near at hand the lesser, but infinitely characterful and beautiful hills of Snowdonia: Cnicht, Moelwynion, Rhinogydd, Rhobell. To the south-west through my glass is the dark face of Dduallt, a pale strip beneath it where the holy water of the Dee rises. The great ridge of Cader Idris lazes out seawards beyond, Pumlumon shadowy between it and Aran Fawddwy, and Abdon Burf above Ludlow is a pale smudge south-easterly. All around the base of the mountain is the Migneint, lakes rich in story flashing around its perimeter: Serw, Tryweryn, Morwynion, Conglog, Conwy, Cors y Barcud. Its quaggy moorland leads the eye north and east into Mynydd Hiraethog ('the Mountain of Longing') and the mood suddenly changes. A wind turbine, like the pale shoot of some invasive weed colonising the soul's garden, is savagely sprouting there. Roads and pylons circumscribe space. Out of the faded blue, three small warplanes scream in, their pilots hurling them in mercurial and gravity-defying manoeuvres that would allow no such attentive knowledge as lights the reflection in a raven's eye. I go and sit in the robbed and reconstructed summit cairn, where the secreted letters of love would once have lain.

There is a memorial tablet, poppies and balsa wood crosses beneath it in gesture to one form of reverence. Those that the wind has scattered I carefully rearrange. The carved slate tablet, cracked and thin, reads: *'In memory of the crew of the Flying Fortress which crashed on the Arenig 4th August 1943.'* Beneath are the names – boys from Michigan and Pennsylvania, from Illinois and Idaho, from Kentucky and California and Queens. I think of the lumbering warplane, in mist or dark, all vision lost, sheering into the mountain at two hundred miles an hour, and the instant cessation of all consciousness and future and hope. *'Sergeant Walter B. Robinson, Sacramento…'* I think of riding on a Harley Davidson up through Sacramento and the foothills of the Sierras into the redrock of Nevada, the saltflats glimmery in the last light. *'First Lieutenant James N. Pratt, Boise, Idaho…'* I remember crossing the high desert on my way to Boise next day, pulling into the Rome Café on the banks of the Owyhee River under Big Grassy Mountain and the three young guys, same age I suppose as these, coming in with their father after their trip through the Owyhee Canyon, talking of river otter and warm springs and bears and thousand foot rock walls, shining with the touch of the wild upon them. I sit in the shelter cairn of the hill of the church, where Euphemia's letters of love to the dying artist were buried, look at the immediate beauty of this volcanic rock – its pale tints, its textures, its sienas and purples and ochres, its pinks, yellows, umbers – and am ravished by the splendour of it. Descending from the summit, I wonder what kind of world my daughter will inhabit, and the things for which she will want, when our 'civilization' has destroyed the wildness it ignores or abhors, that succours us. And a quiet kite glides along the ridge, keeping company as the curlews call.

(2002)

CAIRN OF THE GREYHOUND BITCH

As I made my way to the hill this dreary afternoon, the startling geometries of sunlight, suddenly cloud-freed, lit up a heavy-berried rowan like a lamp against the slate-grey sky; and wheatears drove like blown petals across the shadowy green of the slopes. These were auguries enough. I sat by the crossroads that looks down into Cwm Penanner, gave thanks for freedom to roam, and considered by what route I might gain the heights? Call me misanthropic if you will, but I was looking for a place where, in the course of a day, the probability would be that no other human being would cross my path. I was seeking solitude. And wondering, too, how much the presence of people militates against the experience of wilderness? I could have gone westwards to rockier hills, grander in form, and joined the queues ascending to their summits, and nodded to the wardens, paid the parking fees, read the signs. I didn't want any of that. These October days, louring skies, a sort of melancholy on me – I wanted to find something of what we have lost.

Cwm Penanner is a little bit of medieval Wales hidden from the sight of hill-enthusiasts who hurry past on Telford's old A5. When the boundary for Parc Cenedlaethol Eryri – the Snowdonia National Park – was being negotiated in the late 1940s, some nefarious agency or lobby managed to have Cwm Penanner excluded, a great dent in the yellow marking-line on the map commemorating the iniquity. So one of the few, old, precious places is now, ironically, all the more at threat from those who think the paltry amount of energy generated by wind turbines is compensation enough for the imposition of their alien presence on prime landscapes – planning regulations outside national parks being more malleable than they are within. Cwm Pennaner, so we are told, will soon be surrounded by the monster variety of the species. The owners of land on which they are to be sited will welcome the rent paid on them, and hill-goers, whose counter-arguments are in substance merely aesthetic, will bear witness to further and grievous loss of the wild's presence in our lives. What weight does philosophy have, against capital and expedience?

That yellow boundary line around the salient of unregulated land into the national park – I'm surprised no walking guide to Wales has yet promoted it as 'The Cwm Penanner Horseshoe'. Did you pick up already on the hint that Cwm Penanner is one of the sweet and secret places, *'Darn o Gymru Biwritanaidd y ganrif diwethaf'* (Gwenallt – 'a sliver of the old, last-century puritan Wales')? Well, the circuit of its surrounding ridges is one of Welsh hillwalking's little-known riches. I left my car in a lay-by above the infant Afon Ceirw and set off to savour it again. There are few occasions when lines drawn on a map to indicate territory also denote itineraries worth following on foot, but this is one of them; and recent right-to-roam legislation eases your mind of a few anxieties – boundaries not necessarily being rights-of-way – in so doing.

These days, respectfully, you can climb the long spur of Trum Nant Fach without the least qualm about trespass or possessive-aggressive farmers. All you need worry about, in fact, is how the sedgy leads through the heather interlock as you make your way up on to the broad moorland crest. This land is the eastern sector of the Migneint. 'Black and barren' is how George Borrow characterized the great swathe of wild country when he passed through in 1854, before noting that 'one must not be over-delicate on the moors'. For us, black barren's all that's left. It is a region that is no respecter of those who like dry feet. That name derives from *mignen*, which means a morass. Parts of it are just that, but I won't direct you into those. If the appeal of the place begins to exert a hold over you, then surely you will discover them for yourselves. Try finding your way, for example, by any other means than the track above the Afon Serw to the loneliest house in Wales, Cefn Garw, deep in the sodden heart of the Migneint, and you will begin to see what I mean.

This little round of Cwm Pennaner is at worst splashy so long as you keep a weather eye open for the occasional bright-green and waist-deep-pool-concealing patch of sphagnum moss. I pieced my heather-avoiding way on to the whale's back, the red grouse chirring away, a couple of ravens passing overhead with a call that sounded for all the world like a deep and sonorous 'Hello!' To the south, slopes of deep heather descended to remote and unvisited Llyn Hesgyn. All around the southern and western horizons, suggestions of peaks among the clouds, glimmers and flashes of lakes the locations of which I sought to identify, the names of which I strove to remember and the associated stories to recount to myself as I ambled along, the moorland vegetation rain-beaded and glittering as the sun seemed itself to dart in and out of wreathing mist. Behind me Foel Goch, at the summit of which Augustus John attended in 1931 the scattering of John Sampson's ashes, danced with the clouds as lightly as those present had danced to the gypsy fiddlers' and harpists' tunes.

From Bwlch y Pentre, to climb up on to the higher gable of Waun Garnedd y Filiast looks on the map to be a small matter – barely four hundred feet of ascent. But there is a rule always to be observed in these moorland heights of the national park's margins. Never insist on the direct line! To do so will often punish you with deep and uphill heather. Instead, an elliptical approach may well reward you by saving time and hard labour. It is arduous enough once you are up on that gable, as it undulates along at about the two-thousand-foot contour. There are peat-groughs here to rival those of Kinder Scout or Bleaklow – slithery black gulfs into which you must leap, and weirdly-shaped, isolated, heather-capped hags looming at you out of the mist; and old cairns of white quartz rather phantasmal in the greyness, against the dark cast of the land. And I saw neither sign nor footprint of another soul as I toiled along in enveloping cloud to the summit cairns and scatter of splintery stones and shelter-encircled, moss-grown Ordnance Survey pillar, all of which tell of your arrival at Carnedd y Filiast. (So too, unfortunately, does a Land Rover track that has been driven up from the shores of village-drowning Llyn Celyn – *Cofia Dryweryn!* – to ease the passage here of shooters, blood-sports enthusiasts who desire to kill the grouse but would prefer not make too much physical effort in pursuit of that end.

A gap cleared in the mist. A distant flash of water to the south was Llyn Tegid. Scanning round, not twenty yards away a hare loped, came to a halt, reared up on its hind legs, fixed its soft gaze in my direction and suddenly, through this shamanistic creature, the old redolence was upon me, place and association giving up their riches through solitude and chance encounter. I had climbed out of the everyday into the sphere of the magical, by which our ancestors, who were surely in certain ways wiser than we are, sought to comprehend.

I'll tell you more, but in brief. You must fill out narrative here with your own understanding and experience. Llyn Tegid ('Bala Lake' the watersports enthusiasts call it) takes its name from Tegid Foel, Bald Tegid, husband of Ceridwen, enchantress, who distilled in her cauldron knowledge and insight and deadly poison. She set Gwion to stir the brew for a year until the time it could be given to her hideous son Afagddu ('Utter Darkness') but as the year drew to its end three boiling drops splashed on to Gwion's finger, and to cool it he sucked them, thus receiving the inspiration she had prepared. The cauldron split as he did so, spilling the poison that remained and alerting Ceridwen to what had happened. His chance gift detected, to escape Gwion changed into a hare and Ceridwen into – a *filiast*, a bitch-greyhound; and the chase and the shape-shifting and the stranger births and poetry itself all began...

These old stories – they are still happening, they are all around us. They give us such keys and clues to understanding our planet, our place upon it. They give us such warnings. I believe in them, as I do not believe or have faith in politicians, profit and growth, and other such perfidies...

So – I continued on my way. The boundary stones lead from Garnedd y Filiast north-west to the rim of Cwm y Gylchedd and a steep, knee-jarring descent to the *corlannau*, the sheep-pens, at the head of that strange place, the atmosphere of which has always unsettled and disturbed me, as though bad things had been done there years ago, and not just sheep had been penned in. Each stone is of slate, set into a cairn of white quartz, and bearing the letters 'C.D.' on one side (County of Denbigh) – and 'T.I.' on the other (Tir Ifan), about which experts on land-tenure in medieval Wales have written much. This was land belonging to the Order of the Knights of St. John of Jerusalem, who established a hospice here in 1189 to help travellers across these barren wastelands. They left. The place became a haven for robbers and bandits. Nowadays much of it hereabouts is owned by the National Trust. I left the map-drawn line, headed out compass-less into the mist to drink from Ffynnon y Waen ('the Well of the Moor'); and then by the feel of contour alone eased round on to the spur of Foel Goch, dropping down out of the cloud in the course of its gentle descent to see diffused sunlight catching at the moor grasses on Foel Frech beyond Bwlch Blaen y Cwm, and transforming all to a russet glow, that faded slowly around me as I toiled over Copa Ceiliog and strikingly-cairned Garn Prys. I stumbled down in the last glimmerings, the afterglow, to the ancient cairn-circle by Bryn Ffynnon. On the descent into Cwm Penanner again, slew of a twittering bat against my face and the owls' screams from the trees. These creatures, again...

Such magic, within this old world's cloak of darkness and mists. Please understand what, from every unadulterated source, we are being in every living instant told – of the world, its value, its beauty, its truth.

(2005)

CRAIG YR ALLOR

Flycatchers danced ahead as I took the old road out of Rhos y Gwaliau, that ascends by a clear stream through woods of birch, alder and sessile oak. Little groups of long-tailed tits, delicate and vulnerable, were trilling and wheezing from the topmost branches, my heart gladdening at their vulnerability having survived the snows and the north wind. The tarmac gave out into sheep pasture, the mountain ewes heavy with lambs that would in another fortnight be playing among the clumps of sedge and the knolls, the brown hares I could see cowering there now rearing up to box with them. Two old wagon wheels, steel-rimmed, that had worn down the ruts I followed, rested broken-spoked in the back of a barn at Beudy Bryn Bedwog, and at the house beyond I spoke of stock and weather and land to the young farmer there, who told me of the hill to which I was bound, and the church built in to the rock there. I would see it, he vouchsafed, up on top, as he guided me by a dry way through farmyard mire to a mountain gate, and as I walked on the oldness of this landscape and its mystery became ever more apparent, its turf-concealed testimony everywhere around in mound and tall stone and line of grassed and tumbled boundary. At the hilltop, in front of me suddenly, Arenig Fawr, which you see from every point, which I had seen clear a hundred miles away against the sunset from the ridge of the Roaches in Staffordshire not a month before, twin-breasted and in recline, the great mother mountain.

From the summit I had sought, the Arenig's presence was startling, overpowering, this viewpoint unexpectedly the best for one of my country's finest hills. Snow-streaked, and with swirls of snow drifting across in front, she seemed elusive, like a phantom beyond the beech-copses by Parc. Though I would not reach them today across the cold waters of Llyn Tegid, I thought of those two high points, the lower crested and rocky, the higher with a cairn that is probably Bronze Age in origin, and a name of its own – Moel yr Eglwys ('the Hill of the Church'). From it Wales is visible; north-west in a long line the hills of Eryri from Yr Wyddfa to Tal y Fan above Conwy; and from where I stood too in the gathering dusk with the storm approaching, they were grey presences.

Arenig is little visited, the hill I was on even less so – the shepherd maybe, from time to time, who had told me the old tradition of the church here that the hill-name seemed to bear out. Turning around, the russet ridges of western Berwyn that curve down into Cwm Hirnant in front of me now, I went looking for it, found the rock and the enclosure and the suggestion of walls of which the shepherd had told me, and I sat there utterly alone with darkness falling, and the shadow of the hill from which I had descended – Craig yr Allor ('the Altar Crag') – ever deepening into that solitude from which, alone, comes intimacy with the natural world from which we are so divorced.

(2005)

THE COUNTRY BEYOND

There is a word in Welsh, *bro*, which translates literally as region, but the resonance of which transcends that literal meaning. The earliest of Welsh poets, Taliesin from the sixth century, gives us the clue when he writes of his home country as being '*bro sêr hefin*' ('the land of summer stars'). Wherever I travel among the hills of this small, inexhaustibly rich and jewelled country of Wales, I am conscious of nuance, demarcation, shading difference that fascinates. Maybe the textures are those of history, or settlement, or the defining tones of geology. But always there is the sense of boundaries, of a continual moving through into the country that is beyond. Even the names of the hill-groups themselves reflect this: Berwyn, the white barrier; Rhinogydd, the thresholds. Nowhere, to my mind, is this sense more pronounced than on the great hill-scarp that dominates the westerly view along Llyn Tegid from its Bala shore.

Aran, it's called in Welsh. Its two main summits along a ten-mile ridge that stretches from Llanuwchllyn to Dinas Mawddwy are separated by a bare twenty metres in height. View them from the east, as you drive up the wild pilgrims' pass of the Bwlch y Groes by way of which medieval penitents made their slow way towards Ynys Enlli, and these tops give the appearance of comprising virtually a level gable. The higher of the two, Aran Fawddwy, at 905 metres, may be the highest summit in Wales outside the heartland of Eryri, yet there is no sense in which it queens it over its marginally lower sister, Aran Benllyn. The curious thing about these two main summits of Aran is – despite the obvious unanimity, their rising from a common base on which Thomas Pennant commented in 1781 – how contrasted they are in character. The two high points of their solitary ridge – most easily reached by rather a gruelling ascent over endless false summits from Llanuwchllyn – may only be separated by a short mile and a descent of only a few metres, yet they seem to inhabit quite different countries. Bro Aran has always been a place of contradictions, a land fought over and apart. To reinforce distinction, each peak is named for a different *cantref* of medieval Wales. To emphasize mutual belonging, well – walk over them. They are like an old couple, utterly different, utterly dependent, their grey crowns speckled with white quartz, their mutuality and their marriage as strikingly obvious as their independence of character.

Aran Benllyn is the presiding peak of Penllyn – a region echoey with myth and legend, sheaved with poets, preachers, educators who made their mark on Welsh cultural life – that stretches around Llyn Tegid. Its broad back carries in its train the other two enchanting, remote and little-visited hills of Rhobell Fawr and Dduallt above the headwaters of Afon Dyfrdwy, most magical of Welsh rivers, that rises below the Black Height and flows through Llyn Tegid without, according to legend, ever mingling its waters. The outlook from Benllyn is all northerly and easterly, stretching round from Moelwynion, Arenig and Glyderau to the ramparts of Clwyd and even the little, lovely, redolent heights of Shropshire. Aran Fawddwy, by contrast, seems to belong, as its name suggests, much more closely to the high, riven moorland heights above Llyn Efyrnwy – wastes as inhospitable, rough and trackless, apart from the odd forestry or shooters' incursion, as any in Wales; or with the region at the head of Afon Dyfi, and with the sinuous switchback hill-ridge that stretches from Bwlch Llyn Bach above Tal y Llyn to Foel Dinas above Dinas Mawddwy and is generally known as the Waun Oer ridge, after not-its-highest point; or alternatively and collectively as the Dyfi Hills. The outlook from the highest Welsh peak south of Yr Wyddfa is of the whole of our western land of Wales: of moorland, of distant Cader Idris against the westering sun, of Pumlumon to the south and all the rolling little hills of Radnor and Montgomery along the Welsh Marches.

The traverse of these two hills, from Llanuwchllyn to Dinas Mawddwy by way of the rocky, beautiful cwm of Cywarch, is one of the great Welsh hillwalks. It has a loftiness and spaciousness about it, a sense of crossing watersheds both physical and cultural – for this ridge is the east-west watershed of Wales, and the north-south divide of language and history: '*Mangre dawel fynyddig ydyw, lle ardderchog i enaid ddal cymundeb a Duw*' ('This is a silent, mountainous retreat, an excellent place for communion with God'), O.M. Edwards wrote about Bro Aran. This greatest of Welsh educators (tutor at Oxford, incidentally, to surely our best-loved landscape poet, Edward Thomas), had his home in Cwm Cynllwyd above Llanuchllyn. He might have felt that his motto, *Codi'r hen Wlad ar ei hôl* ('Raise the Old Country to its Former Glory') had something of an ironic ring to it if he could have viewed what has happened to his home region in the last fifty or sixty years – the marring, fencing, afforesting, turbining of wild hill-country, which is so precious, of which we have so little.

Enough complaining! The rocky character of the Aran summits is still something to rejoice in, and if you set off on a summer's day after a pint of good beer in The Eagles at Llanuwchllyn, and enjoy another one in the twilight sitting outside the Red Lion in Dinas Mawddwy, you'll be stretched of leg and contented of mind. And unlikely these days to find here, as George Borrow did in 1854, 'a collection of filthy huts', from which 'fierce-looking red-haired men, who seemed as if they might be descendants of the red-haired banditti of old, were staggering about, and the sounds of drunken revelry echoed from the huts'. This was an outlaw region in the sixteenth century, stronghold of the *Gwylliaid Cochion Mawddwy* ('the Red Robbers of Mawddwy'), eighty of whom were captured and hanged in 1554, and buried in a common grave just down the Dyfi valley at Mallwyd. The pub is the only red thing around these days.

I look back fondly to a summer's day in the early 1960s when I first completed this traverse of Aran, setting out in the morning from Rhos y Gwaliau, and sleeping by a small fire in a hazel wood in Cwm Cywarch as the dew fell. Sweet though the memory is, and good though this straightforward traverse of Aran may be, sometimes I think that our hillwalking itineraries can be a little too linear, a little too unimaginative, inclined at times to miss out on some of the less obvious delights of a region.

For example, if you want to enjoy the best that Aran has to offer, you might consider approaching its main summit by a considerably more circuitous and interesting route. It takes the footpath that winds through the *ffriddoedd* of the farms of lower Cwm Cynllwyd to Plas Morgan and on into Cwm Croes. You'll meet men and women of the farms of these hills along the way, and I would vouch for their friendliness, helpfulness, interest. When you enter Cwm Croes, there is a little diversion to be taken that should not be missed – to a place celebrated as of interest to visitors to these hills since the seventeenth century. Here's the great naturalist Edward Lhuyd, writing to his cousin David Lloyd in 1686:

> Aran Benllyn is I hear too far from you, else I am sure you might find there twice as many plants as on [the Berwyn]. Divers gentlemen have gone from London, Oxford and Cambridge to Snowdon, Cader Idris and Flinlimmon [sic] in search of plants... to my knowledge [Aran Benllyn] produces as many rareties as Cader Idris [in] ye rivulets that run through ye rocks above Llyn Llymbran.

Llyn Llymbran, courtesy of the Ordnance Survey down there in Southampton, now appears on the map as Llyn Lliwbran ('Crow-coloured Lake'), pleasantly descriptive enough, but which may have served to conceal an older, mythological allusion. What is not in doubt is the visual quality of the lake and its surrounding cwm, the magnificent columnar cliff of Gist Ddu, with its soaring, angular arêtes on which delectable and rarely-visited rock-climbing is to be had, leading your eye up to the summit ridge of Aran. This is one of the great mountain places in Wales, and the chances of your sharing it with anyone other than a very occasional angler, botanist or climber are remote indeed.

Don't climb to the summit ridge yet, however enticing a scramble it looks to be up the back wall of the cwm alongside the cliff. Descend instead back into Cwm Croes, follow the ancient way from the farm of Nant y Barcud over to Dinas Mawddwy by the Bwlch Sirddyn, but branch off at Gors-lwyd and contour round the spur of Foel Hafod Fynydd to Creiglyn Dyfi. Here, you are in another of the untrodden places of the Welsh mountains, by another of these jewels of lakes. Savour it, and the rich natural life of the place, and its undespoiled beauty. And then, if your urge is for the summits after all, climb up the monstrously steep flank called Erw y Ddafad Ddu ('Black Sheep Acre'). You'll soon find yourself equidistant between the two Aran summits, the choice of which way to turn all yours. And in your mind, fixed there, will be the memory of the country beyond what's normally seen, as we pass through on our way to our hills.

(2004)

COLD MOOR, WIDE HEAVEN

This narrative, which concerns a day spent walking over certain Welsh hills, begins in a place that directs my thought into an awareness of the complex framings of memory, and reminds me how crucial a part that plays in our humanity. It is an August morning, with a slow stream of air down from the north that renders every mark on the canvas of landscape as a thing of exquisite clarity – the kind of day that, in the Welsh writer's phrase, gives *'telyn i glogwyn ac organ i geunant'* ('a harp to the cliff and an organ to the gorge'). I drive across from my home in sight of the Berwyn to Dinas Mawddwy under the Aran. The latter village is spruce these days, unlike the place of broken windows and small, shabby dwellings and hearteningly friendly, though timid, people that the early traveller wrote of two hundred years ago:

> Although in England I appeared like other men, yet at Dinas Mawddwy I stood single. The people eyed me as a phenomenon, with countenances mixed with fear and inquiry. Perhaps they took me for an inspector of taxes; they could not take me for a window-peeper, for there were scarcely any to peep at...

The cottages now are pebbledashed and UPVC-windowed and white-Kentucky-doored, and if you park on the road in front of them, as I soon learned, out from within bristles some former inhabitant of Birmingham, loudly to denounce this intrusion of an incomer and to ask me to be more respectful. So I retire to a sunlit table in front of the Red Lion pub, which I've known for fifty years (is the Welsh singing here on Saturday nights and into the small hours of Sunday mornings still one of the local glories?), and order a pot of tea to share with a companion who's driven over here from her home in the other direction to join me for the walk...

Her presence opens another of those vital dimensions of memory. She reminds me of change – not only of change in our lives, its dynamic and impersonal force there, and the means by which continually, fearfully, we seek to resist and define rather than wisely ponder and accept it – but also, and especially, of change unkindly written across the landscapes we love. She and I are no longer as we were when first we knew each other. I was young then, shepherding in Cwm Pennant. She was the daughter of a farmer down that loveliest of valleys, encircled by the ridge of the red cairns. Just as we have changed, the place where we met has changed. In another context, I wrote this about it recently: 'A stiff knot of baling twine secures the rusting chapel-gate. Acre-millionaires and seekers of subsidies bought into the valley. My old friends no longer farm their land, now fenced around with wire. Grey wintering sheds of corrugated iron dominate. It is made to work to repay investment in it. Rather than this exploitation, I am not sure that I do not prefer the old [Calvinistic] unease at its beauty, which spoke at least of the mystery of the place, and of a certain reverence.'

In remembering all this, in dwelling on it, I'm reminded of a passage in Nan Shepherd's lapidary, soulful celebration of the Cairngorms, *The Living Mountain* (Aberdeen University Press, 1977):

... at first I was seeking only sensuous gratification – the sensation of height, the sensation of movement, the sensation of speed, the sensation of distance, the sensation of ease: the lust of the flesh, the lust of the eyes, the pride of life. I was not interested in the mountain for itself, but for its effect on me, as puss caresses not the man but herself against the man's trouser leg. But as I grew older and less self-sufficient, I began to discover the mountain in itself. Everything became good to me, its contours, its colours, its water and rock, flowers and birds. This process has taken many years, and is not yet complete. Knowing another is endless. And I have discovered that man's experience of them enlarges rock, flower and bird. The thing to be known grows with the knowing.

Well, there was some getting-to-know of a particular hill-massif to be done for us on this day – the sinuous switchback that stretches from Bwlch Llyn Bach above Tal y Llyn to Foel Dinas above Dinas Mawddwy, and that's generally known as the Waun Oer ridge, or alternatively and collectively as the Dyfi Hills. We'd both been there in the past, she in the moonlight on some night exercise whilst instructing at Rhowniar Girls' Outward Bound School, me in some long-past youthful Welsh *stravaiging*; but neither of us for years, so re-acquaintance – re-minding – was the order of the day.

There's no real mystery and several plausible explanations for the general neglect of these hills by mountain walkers. It's not that they're unattractive to view – far from it! When you see them from the road between Dinas and the Bwlch Oerddrws, they have a kind of smooth and convoluted massivity that's unique, appealing, and I have to confess rather misleading. Bill Condry summed it up pretty exactly: 'If your ankles and your breathing are good enough there is a splendidly rough and undulating ridge walk from Dinas Mawddwy to Talyllyn Pass by way of the top of Maesglasau rocks, Craig Portas and Mynydd Caeswyn.' So although these 2,000-foot summits between Cader and Aran are not extensive, nor are they without a certain ankle-taxing arduousness. Also, this is one of those groups of hills that creep across the margins of more than one map, so getting a sense of them in their entirety from the map is difficult, and further compounded by great blocks of forestry plantation to the south that blank off any sense to be derived from the map contours of the fine sculpting of spur and cwm. For such reasons, people don't come here in any great numbers. These are lonely hills, awkward to negotiate if you plan to start and finish from the same place, not lending themselves to our habitual circularities. You pass over them necessarily as on a journey, starting at the one end, finishing at the other.

Fortunately, we'd arrived in our respective cars, so mine is left in front of the house of some other re-planted scion of the Black Country, and in hers we drive round to the pass-top car park where Llyn y Tri Graienyn ('the Little Lake of the Three Pebbles') once glinted, before road 'improvements' necessitated its being filled in. The pebbles were vast rocks that the giant Idris – whose chair, Cader Idris, is just to the west – shook out from his shoe on top of the pass. The road constructors blew them up (designated trunk roads, after all, have to be a statutory and non-negotiable minimum width between appropriately broad verges), as well as draining the lake. In all probability the rocks had fallen from the impressive tower of Craig y Llam ('the Cliff of the Leap') that rears conspicuously above the pass, and was used in former times, Thomas Pennant tells us, for capital punishment, felons being brought up here and forced to leap from its top, their broken bodies left as the ravens' food. In my dark moments I could wish such fate on those who steal from us the beauties of the land – that in their last and terminal flight they should view its splendours as their arms flail at empty air…

But let me not be mad, sweet heaven! A short way down from the pass the old pack-horse trail, that threads through ancient oak woodland over Bwlch Coch from Dolgellau, crosses the road and continues up a slatey, steep gully on its way to Cwm Ratgoed and Aberllefenni. Nowadays there's a motorable tarmac road past the ruins of Fotty'r Waen and down to the Llefenni valley – part, apparently, of the Sustrans 'green' network of 'eco-friendly', 'sustainable' transport routes throughout Wales. We meet two people who are walking it, and smooth going it makes for them. They seem a little dismayed for our sakes as we jump a fence, slosh through a bog, and head up the steep flank – ripped and scarred by mountain-bike tyres – of Mynydd Ceiswyn. But each to his or her own. We're soon on the long ridge that zigzags away in front of us, not a soul in sight along the whole length of it, and scarcely a path either, so we lope happily along and a few minutes bring us to the Ordnance Survey pillar on top of Waun Oer.

Cold moor, wide heaven! Behind us, ant-like and industrious along the ridge of Gau Graig and the dome of Mynydd Moel, the insect-crowds encroach on Cader. To the north is Yr Wyddfa and all the peaks of Snowdonia, etched across the skyline with startling clarity. Out west, Ynys Enlli floats cloud-like away from the grasp of the peninsula, and to the south-west Carn Ingli hovers above the misted glass of Cardigan Bay. Pumlumon seems close enough to touch. Behind it Pen y Fan and Corn Du – high points of the Brecon Beacons – peep over the moorland ridges of militarily-despoiled Epynt, and the cairns on lonely Drygarn Fawr are perfectly visible. Eastwardly the Shropshire Hills and the Berwyn block out sight of England's industry. Heaven, yes, and every hill with its own store of memory, association, culture;

but man must needs colonize and reduce it all to what's useable. Wind farms – that vexed issue on which reef the coherence of the green movement founders – mar the view south and east, and – 'sustainable' energy source that they are – in that direction are likely to increase exponentially in coming years. Nearer at hand and all around us, forestry plantation is approaching its maturity, will soon be clear-felled and the land will be denuded of its soil, the rains will silt up the clear streams and lakes, the slopes made barren for generation upon generation to come – all to enrich a few wealthy and tax-concessioned investors, 'demented by the mania for owning things'.

I remember places before the alien trees came to enrich the few and rob the many; I remember the undespoiled places without four-hundred-foot-high sustainable-energy-producing turbines and all their grand ancillary works in celebration of man's ingenuity and spurious needs; I remember the story and texture and people of a landscape that I love and have long celebrated after my own fashion, and have wanted others to come to know for the bliss it brings. Bright gold of a mown field gleams from among the dark trees. Warplanes training for the coming battle for Iraqi oil scream over, deafening us. We sit by the pillar and eat and drink, the day crystalline. Three bikers, gaudily dressed, arrive from the east, carrying their mounts. Their leader, a plump and friendly man from Bishop's Castle, asks if we'd like to be told what's what around the horizons, and when we politely demur, telling him that we're of this country, he proceeds to tell us anyway, using names we don't recognize. I find my gaze resting on the faint skyline that is Mynydd Epynt: 'Gwybedog, Blaen Talar, Gilfach yr Haidd and Pant y Blodau' are gone. In their place came 'Dixie's Corner and Piccadilly Circus, Canada Corner and Gallows Hill'. Gallows Hill for the Hollow of the Flowers – not even some Tarpeian story to give a charge of meaning to the change. How easily landcape can be robbed of memory...

We wander on, freed. Cribin Fawr, peat-hagged, is like some miniature version of Kinder Scout, the cotton-grass in its last ragged bloom, swirls of gravel light-hued among heather and umber, the sun's descent giving fresh accent to the slopes all around, allowing us to turn these faceted jewel-hills around in our memories, in the glory of light. From Craig Portas, peregrines scream. We sit on the end of the igneous intrusion from behind which the fall of Maesglasau jets out, a slender thread of silver against dark blues and vivid greens, to plunge on down for 500 feet in its secret gorge to the valley floor. '*O! Tyn y gorchudd!*' Always there will be these small and secret places as recompense, always we will be able to turn our attentions to the within of nature, like children who retreat into themselves for fear of the abuse without, and who plead silently meanwhile to some unknown authority beyond for it to stop. Our land...

So we descend – a gruelling long slope, national park footpath arrows sporadic and misdirecting along it – through the bracken and the rhododendron thickets to Dinas again, and a table still standing in the sun, and refreshing hoppy beer and the solace of company and more added to memory's store.

(2003)

PART FIVE

Around Dyffryn Tanat

One of the places in which I've most enjoyed living was Dyffryn Tanat, beneath the southern scarp of Y Berwyn ('the White Barrier'), the great moorland bulwark between Hirnant and Y Waun where snow falls earliest and often lingers longest. Away from main thoroughfares and large centres of population, it had a traditional rural community that cared for its land and observed the old festivals like Plygain in small, remote churches of ancient foundation. This first piece recounts how I first arrived there.

'THE LOST TRAVELLER'S DREAM UNDER THE HILL'

Of late I've been taking my evening walk up Paddy's Dingle. It's good exertion at the end of a sedentary day, slanting up a thousand feet in not much over a mile from Llangollen town to reach the Finger Farm on the ridge above. And it's shady and cool in the tunnel of trees, low dappling sunlight streaming in across the valley of the Dee. Here and there the track cuts down to stepped bedrock, and I like to think of George Borrow's boots ringing across these same strata, or the quieter wooden clogs of John Jones the Methodist weaver, who was Borrow's guide, and who often crept down this way, his purse full of money from some commission delivered south of the mountain, his mind tormented with thoughts of being waylaid by the tinkers who encamped here and gave the dingle the name it still bears a century and a half on from that time. Early last week, in mist and a light, blessing rain I climbed up there again. Along the top of the ridge lambs careered about in skipping gangs and the curlews floated and called across the pastures, cloud muffling down their bubbling cadences to a sound soft as water. I paused by a gate looking south into the valley of the Ceiriog, that from this point appears as a steep and tree-lined gorge. Suddenly a breeze caught at a thinning of the mist, rolled it away like a veil, and in the distance, flooded in light from a traversing shaft of sun, a crested hill like some grand animal in recline – a hill that had never troubled my consciousness before, but seized the imagination now and for days after would not let it go.

So with this memory and an afternoon to spare, a few days later I parked my car at Pont y Meibion – the children's bridge across the Ceiriog the name of which had caused Borrow and those he questioned such perplexity in 1854 – and with no clear idea of where I was bound or which of the hills of this area might be the one I'd seen in that visionary glimpse, I set off in a direction that I hoped would give clear views to the south. By the first bend in the track bees were busying themselves between their hives and the heavy clumps of blossom on a rowan tree, the flower heads strangely lumpen against the elegance of branch and feathered leaf. Above me two ravens, with something of malicious glee in their flight, were mobbing a buzzard, and a peregrine bearing a pigeon in its talons sheered in to a ledge on the nearby crag. As I stood and watched, a stocky, friendly, importunate piebald pony inspected my pockets with great dexterity, and when I took off my rucksack to look for an apple, took this as an invitation to the nosebag. We performed a little extricating ballet together before he was happily munching away on the apple. 'No such thing as a free lunch,' I told him when he'd finished the second, jumped up on his back and urged him on with my knees, at which he trotted, rather pleased and excited, up to the next gate where I rolled off and we parted company with some apparent regret on either side, and many lingering backward glances. Pheasants called from the depths of the wood, and the spikes of foxglove were spearing through the bracken, the speckle of white circles on their purple bells leading in to brilliant, deep-yellow anthers hidden in rows on the upper side within. The detail of flowers is so miraculously perfect, so consummate. I sat on a rustic bench kindly set in to the trackside and carved with the hopeful text, 'I will lift up mine eyes unto the hills', was surrounded by flowers, and felt blissfully happy and at ease.

The valley I was following, that of the Nant Llechwedd Gwyn, cut steeply into the 1,500-foot-high moorland plateau that stretches, deeply dissected and incised, from here to the northern outskirts of Cardiff. The track skirted the edge of Springhill Wood to join a minor road crossing Pen y Gwely ('the Bedhead'). All the way along it little circular signs nailed to posts advised me that I was on the Ceiriog Trail, and fluorescent blazons from some Pony Club treasure hunt or fundraising charity walk were tacked here and there the better to guide those who might have missed the first set of markers. Grey giants' legs of rain marched the clouds across the landscape. A grass slope opposite on to which the bracken was steadily encroaching was of that incandescent green of June. I reached the junction with the road. In the fork between it and the track, a triangular quartz-speckled boulder above it, was a pool that was surely the spring of the hill. Its surface laced with brilliant white stars, delicately toothed leaves and pale stems of water-crowfoot, so lovely that I sat there maybe half an hour in contemplation, aware of the jewelled rock, the atmosphere of long knowledge that hung about the place, and gathering strength from them.

Eventually I stirred myself, my hill objective visible now in the distance, and set off through prairie fields of Euro-grass where once the high, natural pastures would have spread, the eyebright and the cowslip gleaming among them. Where a path was marked on the map there was none on the ground, nor stile either, so I left a trail of crushed olive blades across to the bridleway traversing the moor, to jag south then east where I met it and dawdled through flocks of sturdy, springy lambs with sticky-out ears that crowded round as I walked, their mothers bawling raucously at a distance.

The way descended, came to a barbed-wire enclosure where black shreds of ripped polythene bale-wrapping that are so ubiquitous in our countryside now clattered in the wind like baleful prayer-flags for some corrupt and corrupting ceremony. Beyond the enclosure a forestry plantation had been clear-felled, a sign standing out there from the ruin of the good land. I crossed over to read it. '218.352' it read – a cipher as incomprehensible to me as the Welsh names given to the features of this landscape over centuries or even millennia would be to those who have drawn their profits from here at the expense of the land's despoliation – a reductive cipher, a number, a small god to those who worship material things. I passed down rather sadly through the dark forest that spreads now across the flank of the Crag of the Sow, the territorial disputes of ravens chorusing me along, and came to a reservoir, where laburnum in flower by the stream flowing into it and beech in its June glory reminded me that the alien need not be the ugly. But as I sat by the dam, opened my flask and plotted my way on, an aspect of what had happened in this place took me with peculiar force: the uniformity of dark trees, black water – we have taken away colour and light and variety. A place where now and again a passer-by, looking on the morning light across a hill-slope, at the glint of a stream coursing down its tiny falls like liquid silver, at the flocks of small birds swirling over the meadows, might have been, in the perfectly-realized expression of Simone Weil's, 'annihilated by the plenitude of being', has been extinguished, robbed of light: and thus also thereby our experience and understanding of the world, and all that is numinous in it.

I came down to the road, crossed it and followed an old sunken way round the shoulder of Mynydd Lledrod, nettle-grown, avenued with gnarled and aged thorns from the time of the Enclosure Acts on which hung the last discoloured blossoms of may. '*Blodau marw mam*' the blossom's called in Welsh ('the Flowers of Mother's Death'). In its first pure shimmer across the hillsides and along the old field-boundaries in the May month its scent is rich and warm and musky, like a woman fresh from love-making. But as it fades, an element from within that fragrance intensifies to the exclusion of all pleasure and takes on a shocking stench of decay. I pushed through the thickets into more salubrious air and saw ahead the long ridge for which I was making, clear for the first time, and identifiable on the map now: Gyrn Moelfre ('the Horn of the Bare Hill'). It was elegant, desirable, still a couple of miles distant so I paced on quickly to the bridleway along its southern flank and started the gradual ascent. At a farm an affable sheepdog came out to rub against my leg and turn up its muzzle to be petted. A mile beyond, the track curved back round to gain the ridge of the mountain, and I followed that by the boundary wire to the summit.

I call it a mountain and you may laugh, for this is no high hill – but somehow, it feels like one, it has presence disproportionate to its height, is lonely, quiet, untrodden, aloof. By the Ordnance Survey pillar, around which spread the light new green of the bilberry, the view – particularly to south and east, for to the north the Berwyn was boiling with cloud – was long and rich in detail and texture. There was a strange bas-relief design – perhaps military, but worn down by wind and rain – in the concrete of the pillar, and the summit was singular and uptilted, crags rimming the hill to the south. I wanted to linger, but I had started late and it was already well after eight, rain in the wind and the car miles away. In the valley beneath to the north a small building drew my eye whenever I looked that way. I plunged down the steep hillside and through good and tended land towards it.

It was a church – very small, very simple, completely unadorned, and mid-Victorian. It was open. I went in and looked around. Diamond-paned windows with gentle tints of blue and green let in a soft light. Hanging oil-lamps had been converted to electricity. In front of the pulpit a single-barred fire perched across a pew-corner. The great Welsh Bible was open at John XXI:

> … when thou wast young, thou girdedst thyself, and walkedst whither thou wouldest; but when thou shalt be old, thou shalt stretch forth thy hands, and another shall gird thee, and carry thee where thou wouldest not.

I went outside and sat on the ancient earth within a circular churchyard beneath a dozen yews maybe a thousand years old. In the wrought iron of the gate by where I sat, enigmatically, there were figures of birds and a sun-disk that could have come from La Tene or Gundestrup, could have illustrated the *Tain bo Cuailnge*: 'With the passage of time, and with the influx of new ideas and techniques, the preoccupation with solar phenomena must have lessened, and the sun bark, with its swan terminals, and the entire solar symbolism of the early period degenerated into a set of artistic motifs in which the various distinctive elements of the sun cultus become blurred and confused.' (Ann Ross, *Pagan Celtic Britain*). A sweet scent of honeysuckle filled the air. This ancient earth, this quiet, secret churchyard dedicated to Cadwaladr, the last High King of the Britons, who died of the plague in 664 – Cadwaladr the Wise, whose name means 'battle-shunner', whose saying ran, 'the best crooked thing is the crooked handle of a plough...'

As I sat there in the twilit churchyard, a farmer who'd been separating out sheep to treat against blowfly puttered along the road on a quad bike. His dog leapt down from the carrier and they came into the churchyard. With shadows lengthening, deepening under the yews, the scents of honeysuckle and haymaking all around us, we shared the remnants of my flask and talked: of his grandfather's sacking and eviction from his tied cottage on the Nannau estate for taking a pheasant, so his family had moved here a hundred years ago – there was his grandfather's grave, he gestured, and there his parents, and by them his, in time. I told him about Ernanno Olmi's grave, quiet masterpiece, *The Tree of the Wooden Clogs*. We spoke of dogs, and farmers he knew who I'd worked for years before, and of sheep country and its long traditions. A quarter-moon was stalking through the clouds as we parted – he for his home close by, me to the long miles by the bridleway over the hill in the fading light, the firing of the engine, the pointing of the car down a dark road...

(2002)

COTTON WOOL WORLD

In the grey forenoon I set off for the estimable little peak of Mynydd Mawr. The wild scarp of heath northerly and westerly wraps itself round this miniature, shapely mountain, creating a sheltered climate more akin to the soft shires of the Marches than the high country of Wales. But not today.

Within minutes, the first trailings of mist crept across roughening slopes. I kept on, veering this way and that to examine a late heath orchid, or the site of a snipe's nest, or the still-warm form among the sedge that the brown hare – which looked back momentarily, ears swivelling, before loping on out of sight – had just quit. Ahead was nothing but the soft white-grey overall, every horizon blanked out from view.

By now, strictly speaking, I was lost, had been zigzagging around in the cloud for half an hour, carried no GPS device nor mobile phone – but how enviable a state that is in a country tyrannized by considerations of Health & Safety. In my view, we should all get lost more often. It brings gifts. The little yellow stars of the tormentil that braid the mountain turf stood out as they seldom stand out, like sown jewels. When I almost stumbled into a miniature quagmire, orangey-yellow spikes of bog asphodel were incandescent in their warning – and in their turn called in all the long memory of the shepherds with whom I had worked and walked the hills of Eifionydd years ago, who had held this beautiful mountain flower to be poisonous to their livestock, though in fact it's merely a sign of acid, meagre land.

As I wove my way on through brief shaly crags, suddenly I came at the Ordnance Survey pillar on the summit. I wish I could say that the clouds parted, the sun shone, and I could see clear down the Severn Plain and beyond the long wave of Wenlock Edge to the Malvern Hills rising in a blue distance. But this was Wales and our present summer, so it only remained to descend back into the damp and cotton wool world.

(2003)

THE BARRIER

Certain groups of hills define our outdoor lives. Our first interest in or affection for the outdoors grows into a passion upon them. We come back to them recurrently, feelings grounded there acting as touchstones and certainties to our more wayward existence. For me, I suppose, the perpetual places would be Kinder, Cader, Pennant, Berwyn. These are the heights towards which, if exiled, my thoughts would first drift and then focus. Or in the synaesthetic moment, harsh call of a grouse across my local moor will fill my nostrils with high-summer-fragrance of the heather; glimpse of a splintering and serrated ridge in the Pyrenees by some synaptic surge recreates feel of a rickety flake on which I once had fearfully to pull, scrambling high on the Cyfrwy Arête, the world plunging away beneath; or a cold dab of rain drifting under my umbrella as I walk to the local shops transmutes to dark clouds louring over the Berwyn ridge that is so lonely, spacious and apart, blanking off its distances, reminding that this, down the centuries, has been bulwark and harsh barrier for the lovely hill-country of Wales.

I've known the Berwyn for as long, almost, as I've been coming to the outdoors. There was for me always a kind of magic about its name. The library of my grammar school was a version of safe and quiet heaven, from which glimpses of the Derbyshire hills. And it had an outdoor section, with a few mountain books that I devoured time and again, avidly: Charles Evans's *On Climbing*, Colin Kirkus's *Let's Go Climbing*. Both of them recounted outdoor odysseys that started on the Berwyn. The latter, little prelapsarian hill-classic that it is, had, between pages 40 and 41, an idiosyncratic Bartholomew's one-inch-to-the-mile map – the only one in the book – of the Berwyn high tops, contour-shaded in fawns and umbers and russets at strangely irregular intervals, its summits white in unconscious cartographic homage to the meaning of the name (Ifor Williams, in *Enwau Lleoedd* – the foundation text to anyone interested in Welsh nomenclature – explains *Berwyn* as deriving from *bargwyn* ['white-headed'], '*bar*' having the same meaning as '*pen*'). I was transfixed by this map, at the age of twelve knew its every name and hill and detail, their position and their meaning by heart. So inevitably I made my way to the Berwyn very early in my own outdoor journey, and have periodically been doing so ever since.

But where, you might reasonably ask, and what is the Berwyn? '*Anial chwith y Berwyn*' ('the forlorn wilderness of the Berwyn') is how the Welsh essayist Tecwyn Lloyd, from Corwen, described the moorland rampart between the river-valleys of Ceiriog and Dyfrdwy. The Berwyn is high, bare moorland, from the lofty and windswept crest of which what would seem to an invader the endless deterrent ridges and peaks of the north are visible beyond. It stretches for well over twenty miles from Y Waun on the English border to the Hirnant pass above Bala, reaches its highest points along the ridge between Cadair Berwyn (827 metres) and Moel Sych (also 827 metres), and rarely falls much below 600 metres in its whole length. The eastern face of its highest section tumbles precipitously down in shaly crags to the fine corrie-lake of Llyn Lluncaws. A little farther down its southern flank is Pistyll Rhaiadr, highest waterfall in Wales. All of this is exquisite country, crossed by old trackways – Ffordd Saeson, Ffordd Gam Elin, 'The Maids' Path' along the Nant Rhydwilym – and chorused by curlew and buzzard. It is a country of contrasts. The valleys of Tanat and Ceiriog beneath lead away eastwards to the patchwork field-and-tree-and-magpie-houses landscape of the Welsh Marches. Curving round to the north and west is the valley of the Afon Dyfrdwy – the Dee, loveliest of British rivers. With its immemorial passes and stone circles and mountain-top burial cairns, its stories of military operation and brutality, of continual movement across the borders of time and land, the Berwyn feels as redolent, enduring and resistant as anywhere in the ancient, small country of Wales.

Habitually I've approached these hills from the north and west – a habit that grew in my early teens when I used often to stay at the simple youth hostel in an old mill on the Afon Trystion that runs through Cynwyd. Throughout the years I lived in Snowdonia, that was the easiest approach too. And it has attractions and advantages. The sense of remoteness and distance from this side is marked. But the drama of these hills is reserved for their eastern flank, and the best centre for their exploration is the captivating little village of Llanarmon Dyffryn Ceiriog, in its wide strath at the head of that turbulent, brief and lovely river. So on a March morning of fitful sunshine I set off to idle along Cefn Hir Fynydd into Cwm Maen Gwynedd, which leads straight to the heart of these hills.

I had a plan, however, and it didn't involve a direct approach. I had it in mind to slip round the shoulder of Godol and descend to the café at Tan y Pistyll. It was a pretty good plan in theory, and started well enough. The air was loud with larksong, the track leading up from the valley of the Afon Iwrch ('the Roebuck Stream') was smooth and easy. But there was a sadness somehow about the land. The decades-long effects of the Common Agricultural Policy, the barbarism of the handling of the recent foot and mouth crisis, lay heavy upon it. That recurrent modern feature of Welsh hill-country, the monstrous corrugated-iron wintering shed alongside the derelict old farmstead, was studded across its hopeful green, and no lambs played. Frank Price Jones, in the volume he wrote for the classic Welsh-language topographical series, *Crwydro* ('*Wandering*'– the book in question is *Crwydro Dwyrain Dinbych*, Llyfrau'r Dryw, 1961) describes the conversations, the community, the mountain flocks, the chapel, the school here. Now they're all gone. *'Gwlad i fugail yw hon, wrth gwrs'* ('Shepherd's country that is, of course'). Not any more! Regional identity and richness has been wiped away, subsumed into agri-industry at first, and then that too destroyed. The land will recover, but its hedged and footpath-traced and peopled friendly character will not come again. It is merely property or amenity now, and embittered somehow in its human dimension. I descended into Cwm Blowty, refreshed by the untouched miniature splendour of a moss-covered wall by a wood of boulders and anemones, and trailed along the road for a long mile to Tan y Pistyll, below Pistyll Rhaiadr.

Snowdon summit aside, I doubt if there's a more dramatically situated café in Britain than this. It has a terrace looking up to the waterfall, which is the highest in England and Wales, so I sat there over tea and toast and in the company of sociable chaffinches to watch its flow. When George Borrow came here in 1854, he described it as like the 'long tail of a grey courser at furious speed'. It's a good impressionistic description, but fails to capture the structural complexity of the fall. A stream of no great volume spills in three columns that pulse and mingle down a blocky, dark cliff of perhaps a hundred and twenty feet, efflorescing on the strata, rosetting white against the black rock before a right-hand mossy ridge obscures the water from view and it tumbles into an unseen pool, from which it jets out sideways again through a remarkable round hole in the foot of the ridge to a series of lesser cascades beneath, the general impression being of less than the two hundred and forty feet that is the fall's total height. It is the hole and the strange spirit-bridge spanning it that Borrow, as a critic of scenery, deplored, that gives Pistyll Rhaeadr its uniqueness and oddly disquieting atmosphere. People are drawn into it, watch from its foot, drift away entranced.

The day was passing and the tops for which I was bound lay the best part of two thousand feet above. I'd climbed to the summit of Moel Sych from this direction twice before: once by the valley above the fall, in order to see the stone circle and alignment there; and once by the southern shoulder of Trum Felen. I remembered from those occasions black grouse calling along the Afon Disgynfa, a peregrine chasing a skylark, the immediate texture of crystalled, frondy tussocks, red-bladed moor grass and quartz pebbles among the peat as I navigated by compass in thick mist to the cairn. But chiefly I remembered the heathery brutality of these ascents and did not wish to re-experience it. There was a clear alternative, a green track rising evenly along the eastern slope above the Nant y Llyn to Llyn Lluncaws, with hobbies screaming from rocky bluffs above, so I took that instead, leaving behind the waterfall crowds. Its soft and unworn turf takes you up a thousand feet gently in the space of a mile, ring ouzels chasing and dipping through the heather below, fox scats and owl pellets littering the cropped grass, before curving in to Llyn Lluncaws ('the Cheese-shaped Lake') – a perfect round disk of water framed in fine, broad ridges. A fisherman was leaving as we arrived, the only other person I saw away from the waterfall and its road all day.

'Much luck?' I asked.

'Half-a-dozen,' he replied.

'So you'll be alright for breakfast, then?'

'Well, they're only small out of here. Mostly I throw them back. Half-a-pound's a good fish. There are too many, you see, so they don't get the chance to grow...'

'Better import a couple of herons...'

'Oh, I don't think so,' he laughed, 'there'll be none at all then.'

I left him behind and climbed a steep path, disgorged pellets of beetles' wing-cases scattered across it and the ravens hovering, round the rim of the cwm above Craig y Llyn to the cairn on top of Moel Sych, which the modern map no longer informs you to be highest of the Berwyn tops (the old Imperial measurement gave it as a foot higher than its neighbour, Cadair Berwyn, a kilometre to the north, but now they are both 827 metres). I've always had the suspicion that neither Moel Sych nor Cadair Berwyn in fact are the highest point, and they certainly don't deserve to be in terms of prominence or character. The real landmark on this ridge is the spikey and geologically rather doleritic-looking top of Moel yr Ewig ('the Hill of the Hind') and on the latest map a tiny contour-circle without a spot height marks it as over 830 metres. I raced along towards it, halting momentarily by a recent monument, in alien black marble with a coloured design, to 'Fiona McWilliam, 1965-1999'. Who she was and what happened to her I don't know, and it's hard to deplore something so heartfelt. Her monument's only yards away from where four members of the Rucksack Club were involved in an accident in the winter of 1962, one of them, Vin Desmond, being killed. Forty years ago monuments in the hills would have been considered an intrusion. Now, in an age when every road accident or street fatality calls forth its instant floral tribute, I think we will see far more of them. If we do, let them be of the rocks of the mountain, as the Bronze Age tumuli were.

A cold mist was rolling in now from the east and the clouds darkening towards evening, horizons closing in. It's an odd reflection that I do not recall ever having been on the Berwyn in entirely good weather, and today was no exception. I've had wonderful bad weather up here, but await my first sunlit, cloudless day. I huddled among the rocks of Moel yr Ewig and in the rising wind listened for the locally celebrated phenomenon of the *Swn ym Merwyn* ('the Sound on the Berwyn') – a 'sort of plaintive blast... as if the mountain itself is groaning as the frostbite struggles out of its shins'. Out came the flask and I drank in tea and atmosphere before hurrying on towards Bwlch Maen Gwynedd.

The last time I was here, five or six years ago, this hill-spine had been rendered a quagmire by mountain-bikers. Before that, twenty years ago, the activities of scrambles-riders were carving up the unfenced hill. Judicious fencing and stiling seems to be letting the ground recover. The old scars are visible, but they are not widening, and the path along the ridge for the most part is firm underfoot, and less recently trodden, I felt, than I'd ever known it. But what optimism that induced was soon dispelled when we came to Bwlch Maen Gwynedd, for thousands of years a thoroughfare for walkers and riders travelling between the mountains and the lowlands. It was marked by a great fingerstone, almost certainly Bronze Age in origin, that gave the pass its local name of *Y Garreg* ('The Rock'). The Welsh poet Ceiriog (John Ceiriog Hughes of Llanarmon, who lived from 1832 to 1837) has a lyric called '*Tros y Garreg*' that refers to it. The stone now lies prone, broken off at its base...

And so to the descent into Cwm Maen Gwynedd, late fieldfares flitting in front, pheasants calling from the conifer plantations, a sense of the bittersweet nature of existence upon me, the human harshness of which we hope to leave behind us, and not be reminded of, on the heights. But in the West Arms at Llanarmon, welcoming to walkers, in front of a log fire in the back bar, good beer washed something of the disappointments away, brought back into memory's sharp relief unpeopled ridges, wide horizons, peace. These are good hills, wild, apart. Let them be a barrier still to all that's uncivilized beneath.

(2002)

UP HERE, DOWN THERE

The other day, with a rage of suppressed energy upon me and half an afternoon to spare, I burst out of the house and drove down to The Berwyn. Parking the car at Hendwr bridge, my dog and I trotted and panted up the lane and muddy track that led past the stone circle and out on to the heathery spur of Cadair Bronwen called Trawsnant. There was a blustery wind in our faces from the south-east which carried with it a thin, niggling rain. Just beyond the ring of ancient stones, we branched off from the path and rested in the lee of a forestry plantation. It was four o'clock on an early December afternoon.

Off from my back came the rucksack, out came the flask, and with my dog nestling close for shelter and warmth – wearing her alert expression, ears cocked to denote expectation of food – I sat and looked out over Dyffryn Edeyrnion to see the little lake of Mynllod on the opposite ridge glinting in the pewter light. Clouds were massing over Y Bala and by Foel Goch. I felt ridiculously, inexplicably happy.

Why?

The place was beautiful, but not excessively or dramatically so. The weather was foul with every sign of becoming filthy later. Down there the dreary grind of repetitive, bill-paying hack-work awaited me when I returned to my desk that night. So whence the sudden elation?

Thomas Hardy, who for this one piece alone lays claim to be considered one of the great hill-poets, encapsulates the mood exactly in 'Wessex Heights':

> ... mind-chains do not clank where one's next neighbour is
> the sky.

I repeated the line over and over to myself as my dog and I sat in the shelter of this buffeted copse, me sipping coffee and rubbing my dog's ears till she groaned with pleasure and rolled over to offer up her muddy belly for the same attention. As I have said, it was 4pm in December, coming on to rain, and though I had neither map, compass nor torch and at best half an hour of daylight left, I felt disinclined to go back 'down there'. After all, I had made good my escape and the hill reared up behind me. So away went the flask, I buttoned up my coat, pulled my hat firmly down over my ears whilst Kigfa danced in approval, we turned into the wind and set our faces to the ridge.

There is a sensuality to be derived from all motions of the flesh, and walking uphill into a gusting, chill wind is no exception. If you detach yourself and observe it, so much is added to the enjoyment of a day out. I love the counterpointed rhythms of a rough walk, the strange calms in the wind's onslaught which cause you to lurch forwards from your braced stride, the piquant crackling wobbliness of joints scourged and ruined in a thousand jumps from boulder problems or the starts of difficult climbs. On we went, the path a serpentine allurement, a siren song of distance, Kigfa mincing along in front, round-rumped and cow-hocked, her ears flapping in the gusts. Out on the moor we skirted a mire and ensnared ourselves thus in deep heather, from which we struggled back urgently on to the path. At the gate where the track up from Clochnant joined in, we were in the mist and it was thickening down to darkness, with sleet now sticking against the wet green of my jacket. My heart by now was definitely racing, and not just from the exertion. You surely know the feeling – that sudden access of fierce joy when a challenge emerges to confront the prudent choice. I had intended a short stroll, perhaps at most up to Bwlch Maen Gwynedd and down again. But somewhere up there in the mist and sleet, in the wild wind, were Cadair Bronwen, Arthur's Table, the couple of miles of splashy high ridge on the two-and-a-half-thousand-foot contour over to Blaen Llynor and the Nant Rhydwilym. How the wind rouses an exulting passion of opposition – what option is there ever but to go on, to seek out the bare, wild places in all their purity and obscure, howling loss? Set your shoulder, turn your stinging cheek, and press on, 'for the desire of the heart always exhorts to venture forth'. To be up there, in the night, in the storm, is an assumption into that elevated, elemental consciousness that the early Welsh and Anglo-Saxon poets knew. Man may be doomed to loss, sorrow, desolation, but if he tries his strength and will, however briefly, upon the indifferent vast hostility of the elements, he rages against futility and asserts his right of being. The code of the warrior is at the heart of the mountaineer.

So Kigfa and I laughed and bounced and scurried along, taking decisions by instinct and confident in facing up to whatever their outcome might be. This way or that? The cairn loomed up, snow packing its crevices, but we did not stop, ran stumbling on, the path downhill now, no light beyond the faint grey glow of wet snow. The wrenching plunges into bog-holes, the slippery peat, the dips and rises of dark ground were seemingly endless, before the uproarious relief of coming out of the mist and hitting upon the track by the Wayfarer Plaque at the Nant Rhydwilym, down which we turned towards home.

With the pressure off, and it being full dark now, we did lose our way on the descent. I wanted to keep on the right bank of the Afon Llynor but missed the fork in the pitch-blackness and crossed the stream by a bridge above the forestry. Seeking to remedy the error, we took the first track we came across down through the trees, losing height rapidly and pleased that it was heading in the right direction. A mile later we rounded a bend and saw our track stop short at the bank of a swollen and substantial Afon Llynor.

We could have gone wearily back up the hill and taken the other track, on which was a bridge. We didn't need to wade this frightening rush of black water. But I put Kigfa on a lead and in we went, thigh deep into its chill shock. Another six inches and the current would have been too strong for wading. Once out it was bouncing and barking, frisking and gambolling all the way down past Blaen y Glyn, the moon now showing through gaps in the cloud, brilliantly edging the fretwork of trees, an owl dropping in hushed white silence over us to glide on across the stream.

Back down in the valley the elation remained as a spiritual presence, and a physical one too in the body's tingling weariness. It is a washing of body and soul to get out into the simplicity of these hills.

(1985)

DIAMOND INSTANTS ON THE MOOR OF THE GRAVES

Maybe as the year stops down to the smallest apertures of light, in the darkening days before the feast of St. Lucy, so too do the perspectives lengthen, and the depth of field stretches out through the dimensions of time, linking us to our losses. These December days before the winter solstice, though they seem devoid of light as our attuned rhythms still down within the natural cycle, carry with them awareness of process and the promise of light's returning. And hence, then, expectantly we seek out the glimmers.

In drenching weather and under dark clouds I made my way south of the Berwyn to Pistyll Rhaeadr, highest of Welsh waterfalls and the most positively atmospheric. The little river, the Afon Disgynfa, that plunges over the lip to become in that point of departure the Afon Rhaeadr, was in spate, jets of water mingling to plunge directly on to the mysterious natural bridge below the main fall, through which a further torrent gouted forth, braiding in to the cascade, which was tinged with peat so that the whole fall became like heavy flaxen hair that was turning to white, became like some emanation of the goddess, and made me think of standing on the footbridge below at Beltane years ago, with my lover before her last illness, the *pistyll* then in equal spate. There are places of power in the natural world, and this for me is one of them. I stood here in remembrance on this shortest day, the spray beading my hair, reciting John Donne's verses for what there was in them that aligned with season, history, mood:

> Study me then, you who shall lovers bee
> At the next world, that is, at the next spring:
> For I am every dead thing,
> In whom love wrought new Alchimie.
> For his art did expresse
> A quintessence even from nothingnesse,
> From dull privations, and leane emptinesse:
> He ruin'd mee, and I am re-begot
> Of absence, darknesse, death: things which are not.

Like sodden hanks of fleece the grasses on either side of the fall hung lankly down, their texture somehow predominating within the scene, as though all the flooding rush of time were somehow subsumed into the fixed and subdued. I turned from all that fall to the path through the wood. Chaffinches flitted around, and the leaves of beech and birch, throughout this autumn still surprisingly thick on the boughs, were pale lemon, burnt orange, even a crinkled and glossy green. As I climbed higher, away from the intensely concentrated interest around the cataract, it seemed to me that some transfiguring force was at work in the landscape. Wherever I looked, what my eye came to dwell upon was a rich, saturated, mature intensity of colour which owed nothing to spring's vivacity or summer's fullness. Over by Cerrig Poethion across the Nant y Llyn the bracken was umber; over by Braich y Gawres ('the Arm of the Giantess') it was a dense maroon, magical, resonant. I looked at it in wonderment. For all that it's considered a menace, bracken is also beautiful, adds immeasurably to the shading and coloration of our home hills, and has been around, it would seem, for millennia. As I walked past the first of the ancient cairns in the long valley above the waterfall, I was on the one hand feeling glad that it was winter, and therefore the time when the bracken has fallen and died back, revealing the features of the landscape; but on the other hand fixing my attention in a kind of ecstasy on what it added to the scene.

A harsh, insistent wind from the north whipped the cutting rain into my face, and allowed no comfort here. I was heading for the stone circles on Rhos y Beddau ('the Moor of the Graves'). Up there, splashing along the rushy, miry path across the cold heath, it was a vile day that precluded any pleasure or ease in the prospect of making for the summits. I slipped down out of the wind into Cwm Rhiwiau, a curlew gliding song-less away from me along the course of the Nant y Cerrig Duon ('the Stream of the Black Stones') that joins the Afon Disgynfa at the sheepfolds by Rhyd y Cwrliwns – leapt the stream at Cerrig Beddau ('the Stones of the Graves') and as I traversed the hillside beyond, felt the forces of landscape gathering around me.

I crossed the bracken hillside to the cairn which marks a point of entry to a ritual landscape, hidden behind an outcrop, secret, and from it took my bearings to the inner sanctum of this place, where the sense of its wholeness is expressed. Under a louring sky, I scanned among reeds for the rocks, and there, slowly emergent to the attentive senses, the stone row that leads to stone circle, like birth-canal to goddess-womb, made pregnant by our reverence. What was this place? Of which only bare and sunken stones remain. What decoration, what sacrifice, what celebration, what ritual here? Not the faintest echo comes back to us from the bowl of the surrounding hills; we do not know; and yet there is a cumulative energy about the whole. This place has signified, for those who have gone beyond. As if to measure that, from the north as I stepped within the circle, magically, coincidentally, synchronously, a clearing of the clouds, a shaft of sun that seeded all the rushes with diamonds.

As I walked back down that long valley, the sun itself rolled along the ridge westerly, freed of mist, and its light transfigured all, arched over me a double rainbow. Above the waterfall once more, a dark dog fox loped towards me, leapt the wall, made for the stream and turned to wade downwater for maybe twenty yards before slipping across to the crest of the crags and disappearing down them. Seconds later a pack of baying hounds poured over the wall, splashed straight through the water and streamed over the hill, aimless, urgent, off the scent.

But He had padded soft along the perilous ledge beneath, and scentless now squatted on his haunches, tongue lolling, panting, his pelt beaded with diamonds, time indistinct and the water falling in front of him, protective, transfiguring, like a goddess veil.

(2005)

THE APPROACH

This ridge – it had slipped into my notice, registered like a friend's enigmatic smile in the forty or more years I'd haphazarded this way. Y Gribin, it's called, in plain Welsh ('The Ridge'). Then one evening, May-time maybe and the blackthorn blossom puffed across its lower slopes, a breach in the clouds and slant western light caught it, reared it up and imprinted it into my consciousness as I stood in the village beneath. *The Ridge.* It was elegant, sharply defined, appealing. So that I had to come back, and would not rest until I knew it. There was some scant information to be explored, my own knowledge to be quantified. None of this amounted to much, beyond the suggestions, the enticements of the map (which to your imagination are many). It was an unwritten page in the book of experience – from the great barren of the western Berwyn, roughest and most intractable of Welsh landscapes, between the extravagantly lovely valleys of Pennant and Rhiwarth an elegant spur thrown south and east: Hafod Hir, Waun Bwlch y Mynydd, Merddyn Ficar, *Y Gribin*.

Hafod Hir I had traversed half a lifetime ago, in the course of writing about a grand traverse of Berwyn and Aran for one of those outdoor picture books. Back then, I'd been on my way to Cyrniau Nod, which those few people who had ever visited seem agreed was one of the most desolate and inaccessible two-thousand-foot summits of the Welsh hills (new tracks from forest to the west have changed all that). When I think back to the rain-sodden September afternoon of my own encounter with it, struggling against the lash of the wind up pathless slopes of knee-deep or thigh-deep heather, with my old labrador bitch following forlornly in my wake, the phrase through which I tried to express it, distil the sense of it into the subsequent essay I wrote, runs insistently through my mind: 'the archetype of suffering under a louring heaven'. Regardless of the map's beguilements and knowing something of what might come in the place beyond, when I came back to make its acquaintance, my objective was the ridge – no more than that.

Out of Llangynog I walked on a sweltering afternoon at the beginning of July, turning sharply uphill just beyond the chapel along a footpath through fields where great oak trees and beech trees bore the lush foliage of summer, and the rowan branches were already rusted with promise of coming fruit. No onward ascent up the ridge being marked on the map, I quested left along a hawthorn bank under a slope of chest-high bracken and came upon the hidden key. The ferns to either side exuded their strong aniseed-disinfectanty scent, a narrow and hidden green way curved through them up the lower slope, and gave out on to a narrow crest where the path held true. Slaty strata veined with bold quartz shelved amenably, starred with stonecrop and brilliant with parsley fern, as though to signify that this small and perfect feature was perfectly of the mountains, partaking of their character, clothed in their distinctive plants.

In a brief half-mile it took me a thousand feet up, into an entirely different place of thrilling breadth and rich tonality. Far below me was the wide strath of the Tanat valley, surrounded by hills where a remnant terracotta of last year's bracken was a pale wash behind the intense, emergent green. The valley is patchwork-fielded, woody, scattered with hamlets, its river fed by streams flowing off the high Berwyn, and it leads down to the Severn Plain and the English shires. From up here, the village immediately beneath stands revealed in its human design: its houses and caravan parks are drawn up in circles, as though they were wagon trains awaiting marauders who might descend from the hills. Among them, in inexorable progression and proximity, school, five-a-side-football pitch, bowling green and graveyard. Weekend convoys of those modern recreational Behemoths, the Sports Utility Vehicles, crawl through the village. High above, beyond the crags, I could see across to the hilltop of Craig Rhiwarth, could register the dimplings there which were the strategically crucial Iron Age defensive site of Craig Rhiwarth. And in my imagination I could understand how the owners of the 4WD vehicles that are draining the resources and threatening the future of our planet are a modern manifestation, infinitely more corrupting, of the age-old insecurities of humanity.

Up here, the Gribin had given out to a broad plateau-ridge undulating north and west. The peaks of Aran broke the horizon westwards, a wind glanced across the nose of the spur and blustered briefly at my presence. I meandered along the rim above Pennant and sat among silken grasses to study what lay all around. This land – even where it is new in my experience of it – gives me a feeling of old, long familiarity. In plan, there is something about it that is always the same. The long, level skylines of Wales, deeply indented and stretching for a hundred or more miles to the south are where I have spent much of my life wandering. The detail and the specific distinguish one place from another, but the pattern is always as recognizable as that of human psychology in an individual's behaviour. The moor itself reinforces the perception. Brief outcrops of grey rock, the bright star of a single tormentil flower among the bilberry's spreading green discharge all sense of monotone there, and remind me of Boswell's admiring exclamation upon the portraits of Sir Joshua Reynolds: 'By how small a speck does the painter give life to an eye!'

In the dark forest opposite I caught at a flash of movement. A large bird, pale against the sombre backdrop, was angling its wings to the thermals, spiralling in great circles above the moor. I took out my spy-glass and focused on it, thinking it would be a red kite, but instead found myself looking at the rarest and most beautiful of our great raptors, a hen harrier. Whenever I had seen one previously, it had been gliding low over moorland, causing consternation among all the small birds. Here it soared. I thought of the two males that had been shot recently on the grouse moors of the Peak District – the mindset of the 'sporting' fraternity has scarcely advanced from the time, a hundred years ago, when

W.H. Hudson could record the conversation of the gamekeeper who boasted of having shot nightingales in a wood because they disturbed the sleep of his pheasants – and I feared for the safety of this marvellous bird, a sighting of which is one of the defining experiences of wild country, and which has been persecuted to the brink of extinction over the last century-and-a-half by the agents of those who preserve easy targets to kill for pleasure. A landowner in the High Peak of Derbyshire, when cautioned recently by the police about his record of killing protected species – among which the hen harrier ranks high – retorted that if it has a hooked bill and is on 'his' land, his orders to his keepers are that it be shot, simple as that. The old arrogances of the aristocracy, its flauntings of law it knows to be ineffectual against power, privilege and wealth, live on.

I walked on, the moor beckoning, the world of humanity behind and below. Meadow pipits in bounding groups of four or five flitted around and pairs of wheatears scudded away. Already there was a faint bloom on the hillsides ahead that would soon glow into the heather's August glories of scent and hue. The tousled white globes of bog-cotton, forever waving, shimmered, and here and there an emerald *fign* – a marsh-pool – of brilliant sphagnum shone out from the hillside. From Hafod Hir I looked across to the lonely stand of pine where I'd sought shelter after crossing Milltir Gerrig years ago, and I remembered the roar of the primus against the soughing of the wind through the branches, the gratitude for the warmth of scalding tea.

From the edge looking down into Cwm Rhiwarth, stones set like arrowheads aimed skywards marked one of the old ways. My way ahead lay through fields of rushes gilded here and there with clumps of shrubby cinquefoil in flower, across slopes of feathery lilac grasses riffling in the wind, as achingly beautiful as they will be to every blessing and grateful consciousness that here attunes in millennia to come. Remembered words of a wise artist-friend whispered to me: 'The scale of colour is held by the sunlight, forever changing'. Little russet butterflies with intense patterns of black spots danced across my vision, and red grouse with a harsh, emphysemic chirrup and hack took heavy flight from my intrusion. Across to my left a salient ridge of the moor, humped and domed like the head of an elephant, pushed down towards Pennant Melangell, illuminated so that it stood out in bright relief from the shadowy hillside beyond. As though a wrinkle in its flank, an old green way seamed across it and I circled wide to reach the point where it entered the moor, and descended by it into the valley through pastures where tail-less bright pheasants scuttled and rollicked and ravens called. Beyond a house where the owners threaten users of the footpath with notices warning of aggressive dogs – how often do we find such ill and possessive intent proximous to sacred sites! – I come suddenly upon the little, belfried, reverently-restored church of Pennant Melangell, and enter the *temenos*.

The ancient yew trees, the circular churchyard, alert you to the fact that this, in origin, is a Bronze Age site. There is a story attaches here, which comes down to us in a seventeenth-century redaction but is undoubtedly much older. Melangell, who may or may not have been a noblewoman of Irish descent, gives refuge to a hare being hunted by the dogs of Prince Brochweil. Certain magical events convince him of her sanctity, and he grants to her land for a religious retreat. Anyone acquainted with medieval hagiography will recognize the motifs here: reverence for all life as being at the heart of the religious experience; the hunter's change of heart; the nature of magic and its redemptive power. You find it in sources as disparate as *La Légende Dorée*, early lives of Saint Francis of Assisi and the Northumbrian story of Saint Godric and the stag. The belief implicit here is allied to, and a refinement of, the respectful and propitiatory impulse of the hunter towards the quarry by which he survives, the eschewing of greed and needless slaughter and recognition of kinship with the tutelary presences of the land, that is evident in prehistoric cave art and First Nations ritual alike. For at least a thousand years in the Western tradition the lesson has been read to us, and still we have not heard.

Twilight thickening, I went in to the open church, sat for a while in thought by the earliest Romanesque shrine in northern Europe; and then, closing the door behind me, ambled back along lanes where the last bloom of the dog rose coincided with campion in its summer profusion, and the sweet fragrance of the meadowsweet frothing into flower on all the wayside banks; which are riches enough for me.

(2006)

'FOR ONCE, THEN, SOMETHING...'

... What was that whiteness?
Truth? A pebble of quartz? For once, then, something.

Robert Frost

Crossing the mountain above Montreal, stopping by woods on a snowy evening, a bitter and unimpeded wind down from the Arctic creaking through the birch trees, suddenly I was overcome by longing for my home place, and by a feeling that Jan Morris describes with perfect weight and precision in her self-proclaimed last book, her exquisite meditation on *Trieste and the Meaning of Nowhere*:

I am homesick, I am thinking sad thoughts about age, doubt and disillusion, but I am not unhappy. I feel there are good people around, and an unspecified yearning steals narcotically over me – what the Welsh call *hiraeth*.

What fixes in my mind, disjunctively, in this cold Canadian twilight is what I see each morning when I look out to view the world from the skylight in the loft where I sleep. Across a roofscape to which the warping of timbers over centuries has imparted a sense of wave-motion, beyond the old and moss-grown church tower that stands foursquare to all weathers, rising steeply above the banks of the swift-flowing, alder-shaded river there is a hill the hoving-into-view of which, as I journey up the long valley after each absence, tells me that I am home.

I love the sight of this hill. It is barely a thousand feet high, and the summits that rise to the north are almost three times that elevation. It's not on any recreational footpath. There isn't even a public right-of-way to its summit, though the farmers in these parts raise no objections and show no discourtesies to those who pass quietly and responsibly over the footpaths and open pastures of land they tend. I would think that very few reach its summit from one year's end to the next. It doesn't attract attention somehow. Those hastening from one place to another would not be drawn here. From down-valley a lower, conifer-planted bluff obscures it from view. If you approach from the west, again it somehow eludes you unless foreknowledge has alerted you to its presence.

It is a low, bracken-clad hill, its southerly slope shaggy with small outcrops of rock, and all around it there are other, shapelier, grander hills that more stridently claim our gaze and admiration. Yet I have come to be charmed and enamoured and contented with this hill, in the way that a rare and lucky man or woman might find in their domestic companion someone whom a world that is bent and fixated on appearance and achievement might not celebrate, but whose imperturbable modesty, constancy, good humour are sources of quiet delight.

It has a name, of which I'll give you a version – 'high place of three fountains' – and a presiding quality, which latter is that of a repository of light. With a low, bright sun on evenings before the equinox I have seen it aflame. On winter mornings it rises above valley mist and frost as a shimmering presence, its bracken a sodden, heavy terracotta against the sky's wan blue. This afternoon, the light westering, it seemed to stretch itself, elongate, become a dragon-like form emerging from wooded ground behind, and above it a crescent moon sailed into evening brilliance and solitary ravens made for home.

So, on a hilltop of Quebec lower even than this modest one of Wales, sense of home place pervaded my mind, and also, memory of an account I'd read of time spent by the poets Gary Snyder and Philip Whalen, and the spontaneous bebop prose-writer Jack Kerouac, fire-watching during summers of the 1950s in the Northern Cascades along the borders of Oregon and Washington State in America's Pacific Northwest. Something Snyder had written resonated with me:

> Aldo Leopold uses the phrase 'Think like a mountain' – I didn't hear that until later, but mountain watching is like mountain being or mountain sitting. How do you watch a mountain? Nothing's going to happen in any time frame you can consider – except the light changes on it. And so that was my mountain watching. The changing light on the mountain was like the changing thoughts in my mind, just these little shifting shadows, that's all it is.

There is, I think, something quite simple and most profound in this – what we take from the mountain is so clearly related in essence to what we bring to it. I read in an outdoor magazine recently, lavishly spread over six pages, an account of a walk around the valley where, years ago, I spent four idyllic, harsh years in my own phase of 'mountain watching'. My attention had been drawn to this account by a friend, who'd written to me about its 'tired use of cliché – "delectable", "impressive", "spectacular", "breathtaking", "big dipper skyline" (oh, dear!) – and lack of any real engagement with the landscape'.

What struck me most forcibly about the article was a kind of breezy prescriptivism in describing route that was allied to trite and vacuous description and the briefest of nods to the crucial dimensions in this particular valley of culture and history. It is not that the writer had brought no knowledge with him – many of us go to places of which we know little or nothing, and yet come away with clear observation, empathic impression, quizzical curiosity – but rather that he had tramped round his circuit and been content to impose on it his own small stock, unleavened by attention, as though that were the sum of the place, a few common adjectives applied thereafter in order to give it rank in the world's eye. We see in a place what we bring to it?

As the light increased I discovered around me an ocean of mist, which by chance reached up exactly to the base of the tower, and shut out every vestige of the earth, while I was left floating on this fragment of the wreck of the world, on my carved plank, in cloudland... All around beneath me was spread for a hundred miles on every side, as far as the eye could reach, an undulating country of clouds, answering in the varied swell of its surface to the terrestrial world it veiled. It was such a country as we might see in dreams, with all the delights of paradise.

That's Thoreau on Mount Greylock, from *A Week on the Concord and Merrimack Rivers*. You could perfectly reasonably say that there's almost nothing here. In terms of facts, specifics, all else but general impression of the scene, you'd be perfectly right: except for the way in which the personality of the writer is caught up in what he describes – the increasing vision, the urgent rhythm, the final rapture:

> Little shifting shadows, that's all it is…

Or is it perhaps more akin to this?

> If, when there is quiet, the spirit has continuously and uninterruptedly a sense of great joy as if intoxicated or freshly bathed, it is a sign that the light-principle is harmonious in the whole body; then the Golden Flower begins to bud. When, furthermore, all openings are quiet, and the silver moon stands in the middle of heaven, and one has the feeling that this great earth is a world of light and brightness, that is a sign that the body of the heart opens itself to clarity.

By way of the golden glade (this, in the language of its own region, is the name of it, just as the name of the hill is as I have given it to you, and why they should be called thus is a question to which the drifting shadows of your mind can supply answers as good as any I might provide) and with an old dog I look after from time to time for company, I set my face to the ascent.

Of my home hill.

The Way, under a grey sky, in a bitter wind, was mired and despoiled, all the detritus of impoverished upland farming strewn about – galvanised rusted sheeting, black polythene, ankle-deep mud. Yet the farmer here is civil, cares for his animals well. The path beyond his farmhouse veers sharply west to contour the hill and an old fallen boundary heads up from it towards the hill's summit. Here, spaced by outcropping strata, are the three fountains. Should I describe them as possessing any degree of 'romantic' charm (and hence dissemble to you)?

At best in this season you might find a small, gravelly pool among a litter of fallen bracken, a runnel seeping downhill from it. That's all there is: water, vegetable decay, the unremarkable, that at such distance I had longed for. But don't doubt that this apparently insignificant landscape can somehow signify, through those fleeting shadows, sudden surges of illumination, that traverse the country of the mind. The hillocks in city park or stretch of wasteland that were mountains to the sportive and imaginative child are indiscernible to the returning adult. Whose perception most imbues with life? Is the dimension landscape haunts only that of the physical, tangible world?

What affect inhabits here?

The first pool I find – perhaps there is turf around it starred with eyebright, in early summer before the bracken unfurls its croziers to obscure the slope. Perhaps there is a clear spring bubbling through shingle. It is called 'attentiveness', and as I look down and consider its particular nature I recall my dear late friend Bill Condry examining minutely the leaf of a saxifrage in January on Cader Idris, his face gleaming with what he gave of himself to the task, describing to me the information it brought him, who had trained both eye and mind to notice such things. His hymn of praise to this tiniest plant in its hostile setting echoing, harmonizing in my ear, I climb beyond to the next pool, which is called 'celebration'.

> I discerned, as I thought, beyond the picture,
> Through the picture, a something white, uncertain,
> Something more of the depths – and then I lost it.
> Water came to rebuke the too clear water.
> One drop fell from a fern, and lo, a ripple
> Shook whatever it was lay there at bottom,
> Blurred it, blotted it out. What was that whiteness?

A rowan tree grows above it, clusters of berries darkened from the first frosts. A flock of fieldfares, chattering and squeaking, dapperly marked, wings flashing white, descends upon it and in minutes strips it bare before swirling away in the wind. Visitants, they know beauty as sustenance. The pebble in the depths clarifies. I make my way to the last and highest spring, which is called 'love' and wells from solid rock. Those who would only slake their thirst cannot trample and cloud it. To find it and to drink from it is to take the sacrament of our union with the earth, of our oneness. I wet my lips from the source. The old dog laps at the rivulet. We climb on to the summit. A spine of ribbed, volcanic rock stands proud of the hill's dome, pointer to this region's geological complexities. The wind drops. All this typological landscape becomes uncannily quiet. The surrounding hills shade down into encroaching night. Did I pass this way? Should you? What I have lived for. My mind drifts back over oceans to that other evening:

> The woods are lovely, dark and deep.
> But I have promises to keep
> And miles to go before I sleep,
> And miles to go before I sleep.

(2003)

PART SIX

The Middle March

Time in this section to reverse the colonialist process and reclaim for Welsh hill country terrain that traditionally, atmospherically and geographically belongs with it? This is border country, and the border in these parts wriggles like a live thing! The first summit we traverse in this errant enterprise is still a part of Wales, and a very visible one too. For the rest, well – if they're not in still in Wales, they feel as though they should be. Besides, how can Caer Caradog not be a Welsh hill?

STONE CIRCLE, SICKLE MOON

On a bright January morning, hard frost on the ground, I drive down to the west Shropshire hill-country that is one of the supreme delights of the British landscape. It's a region defined by its mood, which is one that I've known since my earliest consciousness of the outdoors: primitive, superstitious, even darkly elemental. There was an economic factor at work in how I was introduced to it. As a solitary, bookish child in late 1950s Manchester, a brief walk from where I lived was a second-hand bookshop, with shelves outside that sold volumes for as little as threepence or fourpence – novelists mostly who'd been popular thirty or forty years before: Ernest Raymond, Rider Haggard, A.E.W. Mason, Mrs Belloc Lowndes and the rest. The old man who ran it liked outdoor literature, was a friend of Paddy Monkhouse's, let me pore endlessly over volumes like E.A. Baker's *Moors, Crags and Caves of the High Peak*, that at fifteen shillings I certainly couldn't afford. He directed me to Mary Webb's novels. In the 1920s she'd been the fashionable fiction-writer of the time, her bleak and tortured tales of women victims in cruel emotional landscapes tuning in somehow to the *zeitgeist*. The feminist publisher Virago gave her a second run in the 1980s, but her austere settings, passive heroines and lack of explicit sex and shopping failed to stir much interest then among a metropolitan readership. Bruce Chatwin plagiarized her (as well as Hardy and D.H. Lawrence) extensively in his novel *On the Black Hill*. I read her because the bookseller suggested I should, because you couldn't pick up a volume of Hardy for threepence, and because there is, in her communicated sense of place and its effect on peoples' lives, an economical literary mastery that I can still re-read with pleasure. The area in which each of her novels is set is Shropshire, and more particularly this hill-country to which I was bound. The first I came across, *The Golden Arrow*, has its climactic scene up on The Stiperstones by the Devil's Chair, brings in all the legendary texture of Wild Edric and The Hunt. In those waiting days before Epiphany and the return of the light, it seemed an appropriate place to go.

From Chirbury, through Priest Weston by way of Whittery Bridge across the Camlad gorge – the names in this part of Shropshire, in their mingling of the Celtic and the Saxon, are an unending source of delight – I drove to park on the broad heath saddle between Corndon and Stapeley Hills. The former is one of those dominant and detached peaks the presence of which broods for miles around. I'd seen it often from the Long Mynd, from The Stiperstones, from the hills above Trefaldwyn, admired its shape, thought some day to climb to its 513-metre summit. To take the steepest ascent of the day first lies somewhere between masochism and sound policy I mused, toiling up the snow-covered flank. The top's an extensive plateau, its spaciousness marred only by an ugly square block of old conifers to the west, alongside which I'd climbed. The 'concessionary' (apparently the hill 'belongs' to the Powis Castle Estate, which graciously allows members of the public the privilege of climbing it) footpath arrives very suddenly at the Ordnance Survey pillar and Bronze Age cairn, of which latter there are five in total around the perimeter of the plateau, the north-easternmost an extraordinary triple-chambered construction into which I clambered to shelter from the wind – a sharp-toothed bitter assassin from the east that has a wonderfully poetic name in Welsh: *Gwynt y Dwyrain, gwynt traed y meirw* ('East wind, wind from the feet of the dead.') Along the horizon to the west as I sipped tea from my flask were the ridges of Pumlumon, Cader Idris, Aran and Berwyn, rising from haze into crystal air. Arenig asserted itself north-westerly, nodding as if in shared pleasure at the sighting of old acquaintances from a new point of vantage. North and east, close observation revealed evidence of the old lead-mining industry. A century and a half ago the valley beneath, from Appletree and Hyssington down to Pennerley and Shelve, would have been intensely industrialized. Now it is quiet and pastoral, the few old winding-houses and spoil-heaps subsumed, absorbed. The shafts down to forgotten levels, where pick-marks are fresh and unweathered as if made yesterday and water drips relentlessly on to trucks that rust and rot, are fenced about. The wealth has been extracted, taken away, processed, used – bullets, church-roofs, plumbing, all milked from the earth, that is then left to repair itself as best it can. I plunged down the craggy slope of Corndon, through White Grit to Squilver Farm and over the ridge to Berth House, where an elegant, powerful German Shepherd dog with a loud bark kept pace with me behind a fence bordering the footpath, baying in proprietorial aggression and then happily waving its tail when spoken to gently, and placing huge paws on the wire as it panted to be stroked. More interlinking footpaths through pretty, sylvan dingles where the primroses soon will flower led over the infant West Onny River and round Brook Hill into what sounded like a battle zone. Echoes of gunfire ripped across the trees. Below me, at Brookhill Farm, in a series of earth bunkers World War Three seemed to be breaking out. But it was only men with rifles and pistols at their target shooting, and the heavy, slow pheasants whirring among the trees were safe from their depredations. For all their noise, I was thankful for shooters who do not choose to set their sights on living creatures.

Not that this sentiment stopped the retired nurse from Bishop's Castle, whom I met striding out towards Nipstone Rock on the Stiperstones, bemoaning the loss of tranquility hereabouts. 'I expect they're practising for Iraq,' she commented tartly, her cropped blond hair bristling, 'though I don't suppose many of that lot will be heading out there, more's the pity!' With a final sniff, she trotted down into the woods and left me to continue along this strangest of English hills.

The founding fathers of British geology – Darwin, Murchison and Sedgwick – puzzled long over the rocks of Shropshire, and we can still wonder at their physical presence. The hills all around – The Wrekin, Caer Caradog, Breidden to the north – rear up like miniature Mamores, mountains in all but height. The long ridge of The Stiperstones, from Heath Mynd to Pontesbury, is capped and crested along its most dramatic section by shattered tors of quartzite, their faces black-crannied, sightless eyes on the road to Basra, blocks and shards lying everywhere about like innumerable white jagged tombstones among the cowberry and the heather. Even the popular ridgeway is a hard and stumbling track to follow; the weekend strollers limp slowly along it and seek relief from their labour by scrambling up steep rock to the 1,762-foot high point of The Devil's Chair. Here's Mary Webb's description:

> ... a mass of quartzite, blackened and hardened by unaccountable ages. The scattered rocks, the rugged holly-brakes on the lower slopes were like small carved lions beside the marble steps of a stupendous throne. Nothing ever altered its look. Dawn quickened over it in pearl and emerald; summer sent the armies of heather to its very foot; snow rested there as doves nest in cliffs. It remained inviolable, taciturn, evil. It glowered darkly on the dawn; it came through the snow like jagged bones through flesh; before its hardness even the venturesome cranberries were discouraged. For miles around in the plains, the valleys, the mountain dwellings it was feared. It drew the thunder, people said. Storms broke round it suddenly out of a clear sky; it seemed almost as if it created storm. No one cared to cross the range near it after dark – when the black grouse laughed sardonically and the cry of a passing curlew shivered like broken glass.

The uneasy mood of the place finds further expression in Shropshire's own version of the European folk-tale motif of The Wild Hunt – led in its incarnation here by an eleventh-century Mercian thane who has transmuted into Wild Edric. With his scaly-tailed demon-band, to view which is to die, he shrieks, howls, swarms and swoops over The Stiperstones to signify impending war. Not wishing to encounter this despairing vision, the sun westering and making all the miniature globes of ice embroidered into the heather glint like pearls (what riches, blessings of ethereal beauty, in the miniature world!), I slipped by icy paths down into Mytton Dingle, jogged along footpaths through spinneys of holly, and oak from which the trailing mistletoe hung down, into the old mining region and over to Shelve. The Hope Valley, into which I descended, was deeply shadowed now, and the Bronze Age circle of The Hoarstones barely discernible against the dark hill. Through boggy conifer plantations that squeeze more wealth for investors out of soured ground, I gained the bridleway along Stapeley Hill. Frost diamonds feathered the quiffs of blond grass and caught at the afterlight. The day was fading fast, the snowy track a glimmer. Corndon Hill's great bulk ahead, I raced along in gathering night, hill-shapes and the creak of my footsteps across the snow for company, skated across frozen flashes, and came to the dip in the hill called Mitchell's Fold.

In it is a stone circle dating perhaps as far back as 2000 BC. Maybe once there were as many as thirty uprights here. Now there are fifteen, the largest of them the height of a tall man. Other monuments from the same era are situated round about at no great distance – The Whetstone, The Druids' Castle, the great cairns on Corndon above. To arrive at a place like this, alone in the snowy dark, is to lay yourself open to the temptation of joining those labelled by Glyn Daniel as the 'off-archaeologists', with all their speculation about what these sites were for. Astronomical alignment? Astronauts' landing places? Druidic temples? The impedimenta of an 'ancient science that marked, perhaps even manipulated, some mysterious form of natural energy'? There have even been projects to measure this 'energy' using ultrasound scanning and control sites for comparison, which have produced significantly odd and remarkable results. Who knows? The stones tell a story. A story is told about the stones. It runs thus: in bad times long ago, people were hungry and all they had to depend on was a fairy cow who came here night and morning to be milked. There was always enough for all, so long as everyone only took one pail. Never more than one pail for each – on that the story is quite clear. But a witch came and milked the cow into a sieve until she ran dry, went away, and was never seen again...

You scarcely need a working knowledge of the role of the cow in Celtic mythology to deconstruct this story. Shadows of the old gods are here. As Alan Garner wrote of a similar Cheshire folk-tale in one of his essays: 'It is in its present manifestation a Celtic cosmos, not an English one. It is old, and it is alive.' In other words, it has a continuing relevance. As in: 'George the oil billionaire wants all his pails filling till the well runs dry, and his pal Tony's adding a few to the queue.'

Oh yes! 'Let none admire/That riches grow in Hell...'

In the folk-tale, a giant owned the cow, and he was so angry at her loss he turned the witch into a stone, and all the other stones were put up round her to keep her in place. In years to come, if we don't rediscover our reverence for the land, there'll be more stones in the circle. Name them for yourselves. And I just stood there in the night, leaning against a restraining upright, looking up at the stars. To the south, silvery, rose the thinnest sickle moon. Despite everything, it filled me with joy.

(2003)

ON LLANYMYNECH HILL

(for Hilda Murrell, rose-grower)

An excited shrill chatter bounces and amplifies off the amphitheatre's great walls, syncopated with screech and grate of trekking poles on hard rock-pavement. This nature reserve in vast old quarries that straddle the Wales/England border at the southern end of Llanymynech Hill is seldom left to the accomplished silence – *y llonydd gorffenedig* – that characterizes most abandoned industrial sites in Wales. Traffic-roar from the busy trunk road between Y Trallwng and Croesoswallt below reverberates from vertical plane surfaces of pale grey limestone, rolls away like a low threat of thunder into the flat mere country of north Shropshire. I walk from a lane where dog rose is still in brief, frail bloom, take a gravelly path past a plethora of official do-not signs, and investigate from what cause this sharp susurrus might derive.

The answer's soon accosting me with gusto and levity – ladies of a certain age on a weekly botanical outing, a score of them at least laughing and pointing their way among old spoil heaps, all of them ready to lance inquisitorial comments at this solitary male who's intruded on their temporary domain. 'Have you seen the pyramidals – glorious this year! – and the twayblades too..?' they enquire gaily, waving those carborundum-tipped poles, at grave risk to person, in relevant directions. I duck under the trajectories, wander off to inspect.

They're right – the quarry floor's a shimmer of purest pink, these late-flowering pyramidal orchids prolifically scattered across it. I kneel with a hand-lens to look more closely at the intricacy of what Darwin, for whom orchids were an early love, called 'a very beautiful example of perfect adjustment in all respects to pollination by butterflies and moths'. In doing so, their delicate fragrance greets me. On the grass nearby, grizzled skipper butterflies bask in the sun, wings wide open, and clouded yellows fly past swift and low. The spoil-heaps behind hold a memory. 'There is perhaps no greater thrill than that experienced by the nature-lover when he sees his first bee orchid,' wrote V.S. Summerhayes in his standard work on British wild orchids. Will I be lucky enough to find these capricious, startling flowers here today? No! Trowel marks in the turf reveal where some collector's dug them up...

Later, I meet the alpha-female of the botanical group, sitting pensively on a bench at the belvedere, close to tears. With growing them on a near-impossibility, the theft of these orchids is an act of wanton destruction: as senseless and brutal as the wildfowlers' shooting of golden plovers; worse even than Victorian fern-collecting, where at least the plea of ignorance could be entered. When will we quit our murderous acquisitive habit, and learn simply to take delight?

(2015)

CAER CARADOG

I left Saxon-named and suburban-acacia-avenued Church Stretton for a hill as disconsonant with its surroundings as that Welsh name is at this distance to the east of Offa's Dyke. East and west, its neighbouring hill-forms are the polite and rolling ones of the Long Mynd and Wenlock Edge, that seem to recoil a little from its eruptive upthrust of Uriconium lava, its dragon's crest of cooled magma. The little town at its foot is tea-shopped, churchy, its streets crowding under rounded slopes, which:

> On gloomy days
> ...redouble the sombre heaviness of the sky
> And nurse the thunder. Their dense growth shuts the narrow ways
> Between the hills and draws
> Closer the wide valleys' jaws.
>   (Hugh MacDiarmid, 'Bracken Hills in Autumn')

Caer Caradog doesn't do that. It causes sight to lift and soar. You leave Church Stretton by plashy lanes and cow-patted, meadow-skirting paths, brocaded hangers of autumn all around Helmeth Hill lending richness and texture to the scene, cross a footbridge over a trickle of a stream barely a mile from town, and above you, the Three Fingers Rock springing from it challenging as a lowered portcullis, rises the southern bastion of the hill. The climb at first is through open woods of ash and scattered, aged hawthorns. It rears up, leaves them behind, the slope of greensward foot-scarred and steep. Outcrops of lava, weathered, buttress the gables of the hill; the path mounts unremittingly.

But not for long. Soon you can rock back on your heels and admire the spreading view. Soon you can see the quartzite crags along the Stiperstones ridge peep out northerly from behind the Long Mynd. Soon Wenlock Edge, its twenty-mile wave of limestone held through aeons at the point of breaking, rolls into view round the shoulder of Hope Bowdler Hill. Soon enough you enter the double ramparts of the great Iron Age hillfort that surrounds its summit, with the Wrekin hanging in misty air to the north-east and banks of cloud westerly breaking and streaming away from the distant hills of Wales. I meet a family with a golden retriever descending, the father pausing to talk whilst the daughters skip light-heartedly on down.

'Good little hill!' he enthuses.

'Shapely. Craggy,' I respond.

'Craggy enough,' he counters, appreciatively. The lift of our situation above the defining valleys has a like effect on our mood – two co-conspirators grinning into the wind. He lopes off, satisfied that the interloper he's met is sympathetic, and no hostile invader.

After a time on the summit, I follow on down. The light of evening is filmy, moisture-laden. It is streaming through Lightspout Hollow and Ashes Hollow and Devilsmouth Hollow on the prime bracken hill of the Long Mynd opposite. There is an ancient, decrepit hawthorn across the slope to my left, leafless, stark. Suddenly the flooding sun reaches it. Its lichened angles glow emerald, the sparse haws on its branches brilliant as garnets. 'Blood of the hosts' the stones are called in Gaelic; their gift is the mystical communion, the moment of knowledge that the unity of life can only be forged by love.

(2006)

TUTELARY SPIRITS AT GUILDEN DOWN

On either side of the track ploughed fields wait for the harrow, give the land a corduroy texture accentuated by late sunlight. Each foot-deep furrow's walled with gleaming slabs of clay too late now for frosts to break down. I walked into the forest beyond. Dawn, dusk, solitude (or at least companionable silence) are the prerequisites for nature-watching. The liminal times between light and dark are when the natural world is most alive. Yet by the still woodland pool small birds were notably silent. I caught a glimpse of barred white among sunlit cinnamon of larches on the hanger beyond, focused my glass and a pale, barred presence leapt into view. A goshawk in adult plumage, massive in its hunched stillness, silencing the world with threat.

From earthworks of Bury Ditches atop the hill, I scanned round before turning back into green and thickening light. The air was filled with thin wheezing of goldcrests. Suddenly their call-sequences simplified and sharpened. Plaintive melodies of willow tits also modulated into hoarse alarm calls. By a stack of felled logs at the first forestry bend nematode form of a stoat, its tail-tip a thrashing epicentre of darkness, described flick-flacks, intent on luring down its prey. Crossbills clipped away regardless from the tops of spruce. The performance was more than my terrier cou ld bear. With projectile swiftness she sped after the stoat. It disappeared among the logs. At a stern word she slunk guiltily to heel. Round the next bend two roe deer capered and kicked up their heels, white rumps flashing in the twilight. Klaxon cucketing of a cock pheasant sounded the alarm, the roe dematerialized, the bird crashed through branches – and was suddenly grasped and borne away in steel-strong talons.

Stillness, followed by a piercing cackle – 'kee-arr, kee-arr'. Tutelary spirits! No hanging-to-rot for this pheasant, no imprisonment for these hawks. A slender moon enfolds the evening star. Great Pan lives, in dark freedom lays out his gifts.

(2015)

IRELAND, RADNOR

On a fine September evening I walked up to Ireland. It's east of the high point on Llanbedr Hill between Painscastle and Rhulen, among the rounded heather hills of Radnorshire. We all have places that are resonant in our lives. This ruined house is that for me. I first came here on a solitary walking tour of Wales when I was fourteen. Then it was sound-walled, roofed, windowed, abandoned. I pushed open the door, explored inside, fetched water from a cold and cress-lined spring, lit a fire of ash-twigs in the hearth, swept the wooden boards, spread my sleeping bag across them, sat on the doorstep to watch the shades thicken and hear the owls.

I sat there again next morning, cradling my tea as the sun rose through a gap in the hills above Colva. This was more than fifty years ago. All that's left now to maintain some pretence of uprightness are a few feet of cracked chimney-breast, and a mound of rubble nettle-girt beneath the trees.

For half-a-century I'd wondered who had lived here. Last week, reading a delightful book called *An Idler on the Shropshire Borders* that recounts the adventures and encounters of Ida Gandy who lived in Clunbury from 1930 to 1945, suddenly there was a glimpse of Ireland's former life. This was the keeper's house, Mrs. Gandy tells us, 'a really kind and friendly man, interested in other birds beside his own game. He showed us where a ring ouzel was nesting in the heather, and a pet raven whom he'd rescued when it had fallen from its nest.' She tells further of how the keeper's wife spoiled the bird disgracefully, feeding him biscuit meal from a spoon.

At Ireland once more, on a glowing evening with heather and gorse in bloom and the air fragrant with their honeyed and coconut scents, it seemed this couple's kindliness had long imbued the place, was what had drawn me back time and again over decades. As I left a curlew flew soundlessly through the ash grove. I felt so grateful to Ida Gandy for the good things I'd learned.

(2015)

PART SEVEN

Elenydd

The name 'Elenit' occurs in both the Pedair Cainc y Mabinogi, *the complex story-cycle transcribed in the fourteenth century but undoubtedly of much earlier origin, and in Giraldus Cambrensis. That nobody's quite sure which tract of land Yr Elenydd encompasses adds to its charm. For the purposes of this book I'm including all the upland generally referred to as the 'Cambrian Mountains' that stretches between Ystrad Tywi and Glan Wysg, and as far east as Radnor and Clun forests. Conifer-despoiled, turbine-trashed, reservoir-drowned, these heights and valleys between Pumlumon and Mynydd Epynt still, at their best, have an austere and lonely soul-restorative beauty, and an intimate sylvan charm.*

A PUMLUMON QUARTET

1: The Shepherds' Lake

The sky-inflected, wind-impastoed lake of Glaslyn lies to the west of the old gibbet-site on the mountain road from Machynlleth to Dylife. From it a track leads to Bugeilyn, the shepherd's lake that hunkers down to gleam among dark folds of peat moorland north and east of Pumlumon. This northerly approach to Pumlumon is one of the most arduous and desolate treks in Wales, and the ruinous old *tyddyn* at Bugeilyn, crumbling away alongside functional modern agricultural building, seems perfectly to express its atmosphere – one of those crack-walled sagging shells scattered throughout the Welsh uplands that have the echo of this small country's long and violent history about them. This area around Bugeilyn and Pumlumon was called Arwystli – the name preserved in the cairned summit of Pen Pumlumon Arwystli, the eastern gable of this great moorland eminence's summit ridge. It was a by-word for the meagre and the impoverished in early medieval Wales. There is an early Welsh text, *Breudwyt Rhonabwy* ('Rhonabwy's Dream') in which the story comes to the eponymous narrator as he sleeps in a vile hut on a threadbare yellow flea-infested cowhide 'in the uplands of Arwystli'.

The text is a complex and sophisticated political satire, important to students of Arthurian literature as a very early source, written at the dawn of the age of heraldry and mocking the colonial ambitions of Edward Longshanks. To its writer, Arwystli was the epitome of all that was disadvantaged and mean. Less so then, perhaps, than it is now? Make your way beyond Bugeilyn along the miry valley between Carnfachbugeilyn and Llechwedd Crin, where the headwaters of the Afon Hengwm gather in a wide, quaking morass of peat and heather and sphagnum pools, and you see everywhere the blanched trunks of rowan and sessile oak that tell of a warmer Middle Ages climate across these hills. If you cross the already-considerable stream under Foel Uchaf and follow its southern bank, skirting under the dramatic and castellated spur of Craig yr Eglwys that marks the entrance to Cwm Gwerin ('the Folk Valley'), which is one of the loneliest and most impressive pathless places in the Welsh hills – you come to another ruinous *tyddyn*. It is less than three miles from Bugeilyn, and as rough going as you will find anywhere in Britain, the landscape absolutely solitary. It is one of the last necessary places, where the freedoms of peace and solitude are undisturbed. From this old steading at Pantau'r Brwyn ('the Rushy Hollows') a green way brings you by the side of the flooding river to its confluence, just above Nant-y-Moch reservoir, with the Afon Hyddgen. A footbridge stretches above falls that leap into a deep pool, perfect for summer swims, before the confluence. It takes you across Afon Hengwm. A quarter-mile away on the other side of the sedgy bottom gleam two quartz boulders, of middling size, not immediately impressive but visible, drawing the eye, particularly when the bracken has died back. This is the battleground of Hyddgen.

2: *Hyddgen from the north*
Once you climb out of Glaspwll and reach the ridge of Esgair, an easy grass track, acrid with the smell of sheep and undulating through hummocks carries you three swift miles south to where a path, the marking of which across high ground by quartz boulders suggests its age, veers down eastwards to the old *tyddyn* of Hyddgen. Its former house is now a nettle-infested pile of boulders, of fallen roof-trees crumbling to tawny dust. Alongside it is a complex of wintering sheds crowned by a crazy-angled chimney and built of corrugated iron sheets, rust-red, surprisingly mellow and suited to the moorland colouring of grass and moss, stream, mine-spoil and peat all around. As a place to live, it is remote in a way few places are south of the Scottish Border, the nearest habitation perhaps four miles away. But then, no-one has lived here for years. At shearing and dipping, lambing and gathering, the farmers and shepherds converge by Land Rover and scrambles bike. The stove flames and smokes, the kettle sings, sheep protest and the men laugh and curse until the work's done. Their vehicles sway off along the tracks, ash flakes and cools in the grate, a bat flickers from the shed's rafters, solitude

orchestrates its *adagios* again. Thus Hyddgen, but there is another aspect to this name. Here's an account from the manuscript known as *Peniarth 135*, transcribed in the sixteenth century but from its language clearly dating to the first part of the fifteenth century:

> The following summer [i.e.1401] Owain rose with 120 reckless men and robbers and he brought them in warlike fashion to the uplands of Ceredigion; and 1,500 men of the lowlands of Ceredigion and of Rhos and Penfro assembled there and came to the mountain with the intent to seize Owain. The encounter between them was on Hyddgen Mountain, and no sooner did the English troops turn their backs in flight than 200 of them were slain. Owain now won great fame, and a great number of youths and fighting men from every part of Wales rose and joined him, until he had a great host at his back.

Walk the track from Hyddgen with the gleam of Nant-y-Moch in front and you come in a mile or so to a little meadow of tussocky grass where Hengwm and Hyddgen streams join together. Its grass is spear-like, carmine-tipped. On the bank above, perhaps eighty feet apart, are those two white blocks of quartz, the southerly one a four-foot cube, its neighbour a little smaller: *Cerrig Cyfamod Owain Glyndŵr* ('the Covenant Stones of Owain Glyndŵr') perches now for the hawk and the quartering crow.

From outside a tent on the bank of the Afon Hengwm, The Flea and I looked across to them as the gold disc of a full moon rose behind Pumlumon. They glimmered a little, the grass waved in a fitful breeze, a peregrine traversed the dusk, stooped half-heartedly and sheered away. The Flea growled softly. The bare facts recounted above are all we know from contemporary accounts of a day six centuries ago when the longbowmen and spearmen of Glyndŵr prevailed against terrifying odds. What the covenant commemorated in those death-symbolizing stones entailed is obvious: the terrible ferocity of warriors with nothing left to lose but life; the grim determination of their cause's last stand; recognition, slaughter, and the raven's profit.

The vegetable life rises round the stones and my mind, running on this theme, turns to a historical curiosity. There is, in Kentchurch Court on the border between Herefordshire and Wales, a panel painting of an old priest called Siôn Cent. If widely known it would be recognized as one of the finest portraits from its time – the early fifteenth century. The representation of an old man, it is a work of exceptional power, is of an artistry far greater than would have been expended then on a mere parish priest. The house in which it's to be found was that of Glyndŵr's son-in-law, Sir John Scudamore.

Tradition has it that Glyndŵr, whose rebellion ultimately and inevitably was contained by English imperialism but who himself was never captured, came to the Scudamore estates of Herefordshire's Golden Valley in his old age, and died there. I believe he did. I believe 'Siôn Cent' is Glyndŵr, the skin puckered and lined, the hair on his high forehead receding now, the eyes sunk deep within the strong bones of his face. It's the same face as on the Great Seal. You cannot look into those eyes, that face, without understanding how, here, by this upland stream, desperately outnumbered, by force of spirit and will he prevailed. And you cannot but see, beyond his moment's necessity, the suffering endured and the waste of it all too, beneath the unchanging outline of the ridge from which his enemies descended, by the constancy of the stream's flow, among these now-quiet hills.

3: The Ascent of Pumlumon

The high summer sun had sucked the marshes dry, baked quaking bogs into immobility, desiccated even the floating foliage of bogbean as I walked by little pools which bejewel Fainc Ddu above the north-eastern arm of Nant y Moch reservoir – a geological curiosity by which a track curves round to the lake of Llygad Rheidol below Pumlumon's summit. As I rounded the spur into the cwm, two ravens flew overhead, making for a rocky bluff around which they revelled in a pouncing, tumbling, pirouetting aerial dance to the screaming distraction of a peregrine nesting there to whom their play was mischievous taunt. The lake itself glittered beneath sombre, heathery crags. Llygad Rheidol is tucked neatly beneath the dome of Pen Pumlumon Fawr, not much more than a quarter of a mile distant from the summit itself, but almost a thousand feet beneath. In 1854 George Borrow, in the course of his pilgrimage to the springs of the three rivers that have their sources on Pumlumon, descended this slope, and a memorable experience he found it:

> 'Yes, sir,' said my guide; 'that is the ffynnon of the Rheidol.'
> 'Well.' said I, 'is there no getting to it?'
> 'Oh yes! but the path, sir, as you see, is rather steep and dangerous... more fit for sheep or shepherds than gentlefolk.'
> And a truly bad path I found it; so bad indeed that before I had descended twenty yards I almost repented having ventured.

Borrow must have made a very direct descent of the slopes above the lake from the ridge, for a brief detour round their western rim leads to easy slopes. The recurrent theme of these hills of mid-Wales is spaciousness, and Pumlumon expresses it to perfection. The quality derives from a rolling levelness of the mid-Wales plateau, the tucked-awayness into deeply-incised valleys of human habitation, the fewness of the roads, the way soft outlines lead your eye inevitably into distances. Despite cloud to the east and overall haze, I could still see the Long Mynd and Brown Clee, with Cader Idris stretched and reclined along the horizon to the north. Near at hand, little flashes of silver were the Bugeilyn and Glaslyn, around whose margins bog-oak starts from the peat. The Severn and Wye valleys thread away along different routes toward England; I followed mine to the dilapidated Ordnance Survey pillar and shelter cairn.

Borrow's description from 1854 is interesting. He scans round, reporting on the wilderness, the 'waste of russet-coloured hills', the lack of trees, and remarks to his guide that 'This does not seem to be a country of much society.' The guide's reported answer runs thus: 'It is not, sir. The nearest house is the inn we came from, which is now three miles behind us. Straight before you, there is not one for at least ten... Pumlumon is not a sociable country, sir; nothing to be found in it, but here and there a few sheep and a shepherd.'

This is a puzzling exaggeration. There were more farms and shepherds' dwellings in the valleys immediately to the north in Borrow's time than there are now. Hyddgen, for example, at which Borrow drank buttermilk, was inhabited at his time and clearly visible less than three miles to the north. I wonder if, for all his physical prowess and perhaps as a result of his exceptional childhood reading, Borrow was short-sighted? That would explain the clarity of his close description and the extreme vagueness of his accounts of hill-shapes and distant views? If so, he might have found fellow feeling with the son whose conversation with his father I overheard as I sheltered in the cairn: 'So you see, Robert, there to the north is Snowdon and Cader Idris. Out west across the sea are the hills of Ireland. The Preselis are in that direction, and you can just make out the Brecon Beacons to the south.' 'But father,' the boy stated, with phlegmatic emphasis, peering into the haze, 'I can't *see* any of them.'

4: Elenydd, Arwystli, Vastare!

Pumlumon Fawr! I can't bring myself to use that bizarre and meaning-filleted anglicized version, 'Plynlimon', by which the first Ordnance Surveyors and innumerable guidebook writers ever since have referred to this great hill. And I puzzle over its continuing lack of popularity with the hill-going community. Perhaps it's because all guidebook writers who deign to include Pumlumon in their collectable lists direct you to make your ascent from Eisteddfa Gurig to the south. If you come at the hill from that angle you'll experience one of the dreariest and most undistinguished routes to the top of any in Britain. Come at it from the north and you find yourself among a tract of wild country on a scale almost Scottish, with a richness of historical and legendary texture that few other places in these islands possess. Pumlumon Fawr from that direction of approach fully deserves its Welsh appellation: the Great Pumlumon!

If you have a night to spare, take the long road from Talybont to the Nant-y-Moch reservoir, leave your car by the dam and walk three miles to pitch your tent on flat, outcrop-sheltered greensward by the footbridge over the Afon Hengwm. This is big and secret country. Find yourself up here in a sudden blizzard blowing in off the western sea, and the long and sodden miles to safety would imprint a harsh lesson. Black's *Picturesque Guide to North Wales*, back in Victorian times, referred to Pumlumon as 'the most dangerous mountain in Wales' and went on to opine that 'few travellers who make the ascent deem themselves recompensed for the toil and hazard.'

Well, that's a view, and I disagree with it. Pumlumon Fawr to my mind *is* one of the great hills. That little campsite by the

Afon Hengwm has long been one of my favourite places, from which my preferred itinerary for the hill begins. I walk back from here a pleasant mile to where the Afon Maesnant tumbles down in boisterous falls. Forty years ago it flowed down into the valley floor to circle a huge Bronze Age cairn, but that now lies deep beneath the water, along with chapel and homesteads and standing stones. The faintest of paths climbs alongside the falls to reach the new track along Fainc Ddu – a high esplanade, outcrop-frilled, that scores across the hillside north-easterly. Its rock-hollows are filled with water, and the pools as I walk past them today are indigo in colour, hemmed with russet grasses under a pale blue sky and illuminated by the morning sun. Jack snipe jag out of the sedge and a red kite glides round the spur of the hill ahead. I pace on and take a rest before the dam at the corrie lake of Llyn Llygad Rheidol, barely a quarter-mile distant from the summit itself, but almost a thousand feet beneath.

In fact, from the last bend in the track before the dam, another of those barely-suggested paths that abound on Pumlumon, are one of its joys, and elsewhere would be eroded gullies, climbs up to the col between Pumlumon Fach and the main summit, and from there it's a pleasant ascent of a few hundred feet to the Ordnance Survey pillar and ancient cairns of the top, about the views from which I should wax lyrical. The day is clear. I can look right across to Breidden and Caer Caradog to the east. Cader Idris sprawls across the northern horizon, Preseli rises south-westerly and the long arm of the Pembrokeshire peninsula down to Carn Ingli and Penmaen Dewi. I *should* wax lyrical, but I cannot. Because to the south, the east, the north, close and far are hundreds upon hundreds of wind-turbines, utterly destroying the affective value of what was once one of the great wild landscapes of these islands: Yr Elenydd, Arwystli – they have been laid waste. I have no argument with wind-energy proponents' intentions or ideologies, but if they are so dogmatic in their beliefs that they cannot see the inappropriateness of wind technology to Britain's last wild places, then they are as selfish, bigoted and wasteful as those they castigate and oppose. I'm reminded of a passage from Neil Ascherson's fluent and richly suggestive account of the state of Scotland immediately prior to devolution, *Stone Voices: The Search for Scotland* (Granta 2002) in which he describes an evening meeting at Inverness when the vote that would lead to the setting-up of a Scottish Parliament was imminent:

> ...an old man in the front row, grasping his stick, began in a sonorous voice: 'Never again will this chance come. Your fathers and your grandfathers look on at you.' I heard a hiss of indrawn breath all around me. He went on: 'This is a moral and even a spiritual decision. Let politics look after themselves.' And the grave men and women in the room began to clap their hands and to cry out in agreement.

The same point applies to opposition to the inappropriate siting of wind power generation – it is a moral and a spiritual decision too important to be left to the politicians, and nor should we be bamboozled by the unheeding strictures of 'green' zealotry. No-one can be against green energy. Everyone should resist its destructive manifestations...

...and so, I rattled along the breezy whaleback to Pen Pumlumon Arwystli, sat in the shelter of the great cairn there and brooded on that name, taken from a tiny kingdom of medieval Wales – Arwystli, among the members of the ruling family of which in the years 1129-1130 nine first cousins were blinded, castrated or killed by their own kin. Nine hundred years on, we're a little more sophisticated in the pursuit of our vendettas, but the underlying brutality and the lust for power remain, though the wounds are inflicted on our landscapes these days. With that thought I dropped down under Craig y March – a marvellous geological and geomorphological feature – into Cwm Gwerin, which is one of the wildest places in the Welsh hills, hidden, undespoiled, the rocky horns of Craig yr Eglwys above accentuating its drama. Come here and you will immediately be disabused of any notion of Pumlumon as dull. Those two miles back to your tent at Hengwm, alongside the dark and fast-flowing river, will seem like more than that – will seem like the experience of undespoiled wilderness again.

(1995–2010)

DRYGARN FAWR

Beyond Ty'n Rhos the track climbs north of the land ruined by conifers, past the moorland pool of Llyn Gynon the stream from which feeds into the Claerwen reservoir, and on to the long ridge of Esgair Garthen above it to the south. This is truly the great wilderness. The headwaters of the Claerwen drain a vast tract of wild country. The rough traverse of this Elan and Claerwen headwater country is the most satisfying (and arduous) approach to one of the best, strangest and most remote of Welsh hills, the taunting presence of which teases at your topographical sense from miles away. It is centrepoint, focus and definition of the Elenydd, presiding spirit of the once and future wilderness, and its name is Drygarn Fawr.

It's always intrigued me, the way in which some hills have a character out of all proportion to their height. Drygarn Fawr is a mere 2,115 feet above sea level yet it still ranks with the finest hills. Height isn't the primal quality here, and the lift of its ridge above the surrounding moorland is by no means remarkable. It has a rocky spine running north-east and south-west – attractive rock, too; a rough, stony conglomerate with quartz pebbles and seams – that rises just high enough to command. Bronze Age man augmented the feeling of the place by building here two huge burial cairns, perhaps a quarter of a mile apart (the third of the cairn that give the hill its Welsh name is a mile away to the south on the ridge-gable of Drygarn Fach). They are visible for miles around, beckoning, and when you arrive at them, neither of them disappoint. The one on the higher summit is perhaps ten feet tall and sixty in circumference, squat and powerful, dwarfing and looking down on the decayed Ordnance Survey pillar on a tump a few yards away. Beautifully built in dry stone blocks, it's immaculately preserved.

The northern cairn is less well cared for, has an old Brecknock county concrete boundary post stuck into it irreverently, but has one striking feature. Its top is crowned with white, glittering quartz, and the effect is quite magical. To the south and east deeply incised valleys lead off to the lush country. Their sides are blotched with heather and patched with outcrops of pink-tinged scree. Beyond are glimpses of the border hills: villages in a folded landscape, fields of ripening wheat and barley, hedgerows, copses, half-timbered cottages. But this is not the land Drygarn Fawr inhabits. The carpet around its throne is of peat, seamed and cliffed and stratified, dark chocolate against sage, tawny and purple moor-shades. The whole of a ninety-degree arc to the north appears featureless, but the map is rich in names. For ten or fifteen miles there is no sign of habitation or human activity other than the impinging forestry. It *appears* entirely featureless, but if you were to follow these vague long depressions where the streams start, there would be rocks with smooth green turf around them, pools of green or of bright ochre, emerald patches of sphagnum, and the sound of skylark, curlew and grouse. The skyline, lacking in striking individual notation, curves round in a slow, powerful, melodic sweep, very fluid, and across the whole scene there is the constant play of light and shade. As I look, it is khaki, but where the cloud shadow has passed, from amongst it glimmers a burnt-out, faint green that is almost grey. The cliffs above Claerwen are red.

Suddenly, in the heart of the moor, a long streak of sun sketches in the underside of a ridge so that it looks like the belly of a recumbent animal. I'm reminded of prehistoric cave paintings. When the electric light goes out the guide holds a candle to them, your eyes accustom to the dark and because of the primitive artist's use of relief in the rock they flicker into magical life. That thought in turn reminds me that two thousand years ago this moor was inhabited. Five hundred years ago people lived here. Now it is empty. But as Hilaire Belloc wrote of a not far distant hill, it is 'like the continual experience of this life wherein the wise firmly admit vast Presences to stand in what is an apparent emptiness, unperceived by any sense.'

(2006)

DOLGOCH

In the field beyond the Elenydd Wilderness Trust hostel at Dolgoch, a tousled grey mountain pony with a heavy black fringe sidles up to nudge at my rucksack. He gets an apple and departs munching and satisfied. Eastwardly, lonely Drygarn Fawr and its great summit cairns are gauzed in light mist. The Afon Tywi, a peat-inflected moorland river, rattles over its stony bed and an observant carrion crow – sole sleek thing in this still-winter-sodden hill-landscape – hops from one Turk's head to another in optimistic emulation of the pony's quest. I sit on a boulder and toss him a biscuit. He dips and collects, glides away to perch on a ruined wall. The path heading downriver has been churned to a quagmire by trekking ponies' hooves. Like the crow, though without his bounce, I play hopscotch across the tussocks. Saturated peat of the moor above maintains the Nant Cwm Du as torrent. I find a leaping place, hurl myself across, tumbling over into the mud in fits of involuntary laughter. On each side long, dark bulwarks of alien conifers are crowding in, squeezing light from the valley.

On the map is the old sub-text to this occluded landscape: Castell Llygoden ('Mouse Castle'); Nant yr Hwch ('Sow Stream'); Nant y Bleiddast ('She-Wolf Stream'). Each of these names had a story. The land to which they attached is lost. Stolen two centuries ago by those sufficiently privileged to make use of the Enclosure Acts, for the last fifty years, slowly, it has been erased. Here once was open mountain pasture and laughing water. The Tywi slides fast, dark and foam-streaked now over shingle-beds, accelerating between shaley outcrops towards a sombre, concrete-towered weir beyond which the new reservoir awaits its tribute. The mountain pony has leapt a fence and followed me, plunging and whinnying in pleasure along the free river to where it deepens. His ears go back as he looks ahead. Out he climbs, and trails back disconsolate through the mire. I follow him.

(2012)

TO SOAR Y MYNYDD ALONG THE DOETHIE

There is an excitement about this valley of the Doethie. It plays on your anticipation. You see just so far into it, and then a bend obscures, a craggy bluff juts out above the stream and you follow ledges above the falls and pools, the mountain ash, the holly and the small, twisted oaks that cling to their riparian steeps. Beyond, there is the haven to which your curiosity has led: a bushing of sweet ash and oak woodland between these valley thighs, distance too in the sight, that takes beauty beyond its admirers; and there is old memory – in the broken-down walls of those who lived here, in the summer pastures of years ago. The ache of it can be unbearable. Camus wrote of the Aegean that 'If the Greeks knew despair, they did so through beauty and its stifling quality'. Perhaps it's here, in the nexus of emotions when faced with temporal heavens, that you find cause for the developers' urge to destroy the loveliest places. Do we, as human beings, lack the magnanimity to stand back and love? Must we always give in to the urge to possess, and if that proves impossible, through envy to destroy the essential nature of what we cannot possess?

I escaped over the hill to the Nant Llwyd ('the Grey Stream'), the name of which inconsiderable tributary of the Camddwr is taken by a small hill farm where old brothers still follow their sheep on horseback, and from which today they were absent, ponies grazing the in-bye land and oiled saddles hanging in the stable, for there was a service a mile away at Soar y Mynydd. This is one of those places it astonishes you to come across. The whitewashed simplicity of chapel and chapel house are so congruent here with plainness of stream and green hill. Chaste front of the house harmonizes with the chapel's two doors, high windows between them rounded and lancet-framed, three red panes through which the sun shone at the back warming those inside. I went through the gate, and from open doors into the blue brightness of the day, these words of Pantycelyn's:

> Pererin wyf mewn anial dir
> Yn crwydro yma a thraw,
> Ac yn rhyw ddisgwyl bob yr awr
> Fod tŷ fy Nhad gerllaw.
>
> (I am a pilgrim in the wilderness
> Wandering near and wide
> Watching, hoping every hour
> To be at my Father's side.)

A woman came out. She wore a floral print dress and the frames of her glasses swept ornately heavenwards. She offered me an order of service and asked kindly, in high, fluting Welsh, if I would step inside. I excused myself. *'Sgidiau budr,'* I told her, with a shrug ('dirty shoes'). But really, it was because I could not – not even into the fine honesty of that place and company. Because if I had gone inside, what would I have done but gaze out through the high windows, watch the mottled light on the trunks of tall pines and the tree creepers in their intense search across them, and my attention, praise and love would be directed on to them. So instead I sat amongst the small and unremembered graves, the tiny mounds among the tree roots that bespeak a harsh former reality, and watched the house martins' vibrant rhythm of wing-beat, fold and glide. At length I walked a little way from the chapel and sat on the edge of a marsh for some time, very still, with the music permeating the air, and one of those small miracles that come to us only when our being is thus quietened then happened. From the clumps of brown sedge darted a snipe, shyest of birds, slender, long-billed. In a brief flurry of sharp wings, it alighted on my palm, upturned on a knee, its feet a pricking roughness soon lost in moist warmth of its down as it nestled there. I scarcely dared breathe, and have never felt more blessed.

(1996)

YSTAFELL TWM

Hemlock and water forget-me-not are flourishing in the sodden alder swamps below the conical hill of Dinas, up-valley from Rhandirmwyn, and woodland foliage of oak, beech and birch, rich with brocaded tints and textures of autumn, rattles in the bustle of a stern breeze. The flooding river is amber-stained with peat, bright with rapids, but no glance of sunlight jewels them today. There is a strangely deserted atmosphere in the woods. When I last came here in June they were alive with the frenetic, miniature-magpie flick and dip of that most characteristic summer bird of Wales, the pied flycatcher, and loud, too, with his sweet binary call and with the green woodpecker's manic laughter. Today, beyond the sound of leaves in the wind and the river's rush, all's silent. I follow the bank round above swift, deep water to the confluence pool of the Tywi and the Doethie.

In the dry seasons its depth and bouldered banks invite the dive – wild swimming doesn't come better than this. Recent rains have turned it into a maelstrom. I turn away from its tumult with a shudder and climb a faint path into the woods. A flash of yellow catches my eye, but it's no more than the spinning descent of an oak leaf, and not a glimpse of the other summer occupant here, the wood warbler. At the hill's summit is a cleft, a landslip in the Silurian rocks through which you can squeeze to a sky-lit chamber carved with old graffiti. This is Ystafell Twm, the cave of Twm Siôn Cati, 'a wild wag of Wales' according to the sub-title of the 1828 novel written about him. George Borrow was much taken with the story, and questioned closely those he met in the area about him during his 1854 tour of Wales that gave us the greatest of British travel books, *Wild Wales*. I suspect the RSPB, on whose land it lies, rather play down the connection as likely to attract the wrong sort of visitor. Certainly what was named on the map in glorious Gothic script is now tersely notated as a mere cave.

(2012)

ROUND HARLEY DINGLE

So few people come here, yet it is one of the loveliest places – marred, yes, and distressing at certain levels, in certain dimensions; but beautiful and grand, one of the prime regions in the Welsh hills. And unlike any other, self-contained, apart, grouped compactly around its magnificent central valley of Harley Dingle. Radnor Forest! Is it the name that puts you off? This is 'forest' in the sense of a hunting forest, or in one of its still older senses – that of 'a wild, uncultivated waste'. Radnor Forest, despite conifer plantation and grant-aided incursions of farming across its lower slopes, is still that – one of the finest moorland areas south of the Scottish Border, on a par with Kinder or Bleaklow, but quieter, older somehow, isolated and individual, with the circuit of heights surrounding Harley Dingle as good a moorland round as you can walk in Britain.

There were golden eagles here as late as the 1940s. The last wildcats *(felis sylvestris)* in Wales were shot here by 'sportsmen' in the early 1900s. Three hundred years before that, Leland could write of The Forest that 'The air thereof is sharp and cold for that the snow lieth and lasteth long unmelted under those shadowing high hills and overhanging rocks. The soil is hungry, rough and churlish and hardly bettered by painful labour.' As then, as now – this strange and little-known, deeply-incised dome of Silurian shales, much of it over the 2,000-foot contour, has mountain qualities and a mountain atmosphere, and is additionally and most pleasingly one of the loneliest of its country's high places.

On an early April morning I parked in New Radnor – a quiet rural village in a peaceful vale, but a borough once, laid out in plan under its strong castle. A border town of great strategic importance, it had a troubled and vivid history throughout the late middle ages. Archbishop Baldwin of Canterbury, in his 1188 mission to Wales to urge men to take the Cross and give money for the Third Crusade against Saladin, preached the first sermon of his journey here. Llywelyn the Great captured it in 1264 and Owain Glyndŵr, at the beginning of his anti-colonial revolt in 1401, 'caused the whole garrison, to the number of three-score, to be beheaded on the brink of the castle yard' – an account promoted by Leland and given renewed credence by the discovery, reported in the *Illustrated London News* in 1845, of a mass of human bones at one site near the old church then being demolished, and at another nearby a corresponding collection of skulls. All this dismally resonant history seemed suddenly not so far away as I began the long ascent of Mutton Dingle.

Which was a joy, all the insignificant small harbingers telling of spring. The little celandines were open in shafts of sunlight along the banks of the stream, and wood anemones gave off their foxy scent. Bright yellowy-green flower-cups of the wood spurge were vivid against their older, dark foliage. I bent to snuff in the sharp, sweet hyacinth scent of the first bluebells I'd seen this year. Long-tailed tits flitted about restlessly, stripping dry moss from the walls to line hidden and intricately woven nests. By a plantation of larch, lime delicacy of the young sprays opening out along all their graceful, drooping branches (if all forestry plantation was of larch, would we feel so averse?), the lane forked, passed through a gate and became a green track broaching the moor. Sheep bickered and called to their lambs on smooth sward around isolated trees of rowan and birch. A hazed landscape opened up all around. As I climbed higher, lonely thorns and wind-seeded spruce broke up a monotony of heather, sun glistened on the new growth of bilberry, a raven called distantly. No human presence stirring in the landscape, I left my sack by a gate and bustled up the quirky little peak of Whimble. Carved off from the main plateau by post-ice-age glacial meltwaters flooding through Whinyard Gap, it's a conspicuous and alluring landmark, its conical summit capped by a tumulus dating from the Bronze Age.

Skipping back down to the gate, the depths of Harley Dingle were on view beneath, the strange parallel shale gullies called Three Riggles on the flank of Great Rhos leading the eye down into it. The green way curved round above a clough – that of the Nant Ystol Bach – and brought me to Whinyard Rocks, resistant Silurian grits and flags of which, weathered rough and sharp and furred with lichen, were exposed by the same meltwater floods that separated Whimble from the main massif. The bed of the channel through which the waters flowed is now a high and overgrazed pasture, a huge wintering shed sheltered by conifers at its eastern end. No wonder disease takes root. I took a sheep path slanting left across the slope to turn it quickly from view, loped through another high pasture with a flattened tumulus, crossed a stile and followed a narrow and teasing path through deep heather to the summit of Bache Hill.

This easternmost of Forest summits is beautiful both to look at and to look from. The Ordnance Survey pillar's set atop the central of a line of three tumuli, its perfect little mound standing proud of the crowding vegetation, and as good a place to lounge in the sun as exists perhaps in the whole of Wales. All around were the lesser and unpeopled hills – Rhulen and Llanbedr, Glascwm and Gwaunceste, Hergest Ridge and Harley's Mountain, and as backdrop to them the Black Mountains and Brecon Beacons were hinted presences, suggestions of forms barely resolved from the overall haze today. To the north-east, just visible, was the strange, crooked church of Pilleth, its tower dating from the fourteenth century, rusting breastplates and spurs still stacked haphazard on its window-ledges when I last visited there. Above it on the hillside four tall *Wellingtonia* trees mark where many of the dead from the warrior-prince Glyndŵr's bloodiest victory, the battle of Bryn Glas in 1402 – one of the best documented of its time, were buried. There were 1100 of them by the most reliable accounts. Their genitals were cut off and thrust in their mouths by the Welsh women, as warning to the English and early form of psychological warfare.

A mile away to the north-west, a tall telecommunications mast and transmitter station dominate the whaleback ridge. There's an option you can choose to keep it from sight, which is to follow a forestry track through spruce plantation from the col between Bache Hill and Black Mixen. To take it may be to substitute one unsympathetic intrusion, one degradation visited by man on a marvel of natural landscape, for another; but at least it gets the suffering over more quickly, and once you're at Black Mixen's 650-metre summit, the electrical hum ensures there's no temptation to linger. I hurried on by a path close to the rim of Harley Dingle, passed a glossy interpretation board incongruously placed by the Radnorshire Wildlife Trust in its reserve abutting the plantation here, and rested awhile looking down the length of the Dingle. A pair of ravens flew out noisily from their nest on Great Creigiau – this mix of English and Welsh in the place names is very characteristic in Radnorshire – and mobbed a hen harrier that continued to ghost unperturbed down the valley. Fox scats and the grey pellets of short-eared owls, tiny bones of voles and mice obvious within them, were scattered across the turf. Tint and hue of the great valley beneath was exquisitely diverse, peach tones of bracken slopes contrasting with umber of the heather. I felt myself back in the world of nature, and the sense prevailed as I raced along, mast on my blind side, to the summit of Great Rhos, high point of the forest at 660 metres.

The three-mile-long western ridge of the Forest, from Fron Hill in the south to the tumuli above Cwm Bach northerly, is a moorland glory, spacious and aloft. I pondered dropping down Davey Morgan's Dingle to the fall of Water-break-its-neck below the spur of Esgairnantau to the west, and visiting a secretive little cave above where tradition has it that Llywelyn the Last sheltered shortly before his murder at Cilmeri. Thomas Roscoe's nineteenth-century description of the fall was in my mind: 'The rocks form a narrow, high amphitheatre, over which the water is precipitated in scattered portions, and falling into a dark pool, meanders away among the fragments of rock until it gains the more open glen.' Pleasingly-named though it is, for weeks there'd been no rain, and I remembered the disappointment of previous visits there in dry weather, the dullness too of the return to New Radnor through forestry not present in Roscoe's time, and along roads. Instead, I ambled along the ridge to the col before Fron Hill and started to descend the slanting green way that leads from a tiny quarry there into Harley Dingle. In front, Whimble and Great Creigiau glowed with light, majestic from this angle. A cold wind sprang up. Metal signs warned against straying from the path, for most of Harley Dingle is occupied by a munitions testing range – commercial, not M.O.D. – and the signs advise that live shells may be lying around. Gimcrack buildings, targets and brutal roads scarred the ground beneath, untouched now by the sun. I descended into the valley of the shadow of death, wondering where the rounds tested here ended up? I thought, too, of George Bernard Shaw's visit to Radnorshire: 'One day... as he stood gazing at the surrounding hills, so accessible and yet so solitary, with arms outstretched he suddenly exclaimed: "No man ought to be in the government of this land who does not spend three months every year in such country as this."'

Beyond a plank bridge set high above the stream in the dingle, a path branched along the margins of a wood and led back to Newgate Lane in New Radnor. A woman – the first person I'd seen walking all day – and a friendly dog came along it and exchanged greetings. The blackthorn was in blossom, recalling William Cobbett's peerless description from *Rural Rides*:

It is a remarkable fact that there is always, that is every year of our lives, a spell of cold and angry weather just at the time this hardy little tree is in bloom. The country people call it the *Black Thorn winter* and thus it has been called, I dare say, by all the inhabitants of this island, from generation to generation, for a thousand years.

Dear, straightforward, radical old Cobbett, the 'wandering and single-handed champion for those on whom corruption feeds' – what would he have made of our times, of their 'spin', duplicity, ulterior motives? With that thought clouding my spirits, I trailed back into the village under the castle walls where Glyndŵr had lopped the garrison's heads six hundred years ago, bought bread and wine and took them down to a beautiful little river, very quiet and unknown. In its oakwood glen I sat on a shingle bank in the sunset, and this happened, over a space of hours: a dipper worked the stream feet in front of me; the sun set as a great red and rolling orb; a sturdy horse with a white blaze came to the far bank and communed; a little owl alighted on a branch within arm's reach and peered, unperturbed; a bright half-moon shone down, a badger travelled across the field upstream in its gleam and two ducks scolded until it had passed; there was no human sound, no unnatural light; the stream pulsed on, the air very still, and a glimmer of frost settled across the moss and the bladed leaves from which more bluebells will soon rise. Around midnight I left, poured out the last of the wine I'd brought for the spirits of the place, and knew some peace.

(2003)

ON KERRY RIDGEWAY

Bare, cropped hedges of hazel and hawthorn, riddled with glimmering light, bound fields that stretch up to green westerly ridges. I took a path descending from the Ridgeway towards the River Unk. This insignificant stream concertinas its way down a valley too big for its volume, like a scrawny boy in a fat uncle's hand-me-downs. Its quiet surrounding landscape is one of robust spurs and rounded hill flanks. On a mist-smudged day of the year's ending all was still, not a breath of wind to stir last lemony leaves on field maple, last umber hangings of scattered sentinel oaks. Something sulphurous caught at my throat as I reached the margin of Nut Wood – a pungent animal scent, neither stoat nor polecat but surely one of that family? In the same instant my ears were assailed by fingernails-on-a-blackboard screechings of an alarmed wren, that whirred to and fro, in and out of the underbrush, minutely and vociferously indignant. What was it scolding? I stilled myself into the landscape and watched: focusing on the wren's continuing commotion, absurdly loud for so small a creature; recalling how my grandfather would reward me with a farthing coin bearing Humphrey Paget's alert, dumpy 1937 design of the bird whenever I spotted one in the hedges of the Manchester park at the bottom of his street.

As I remembered this, the wren's protests reached a crescendo. Bounding out from under gorse bushes came a weasel – a slender dancing presence in chestnut and white, vibrant, barely a foot long, dark eyes in its arrowhead skull searching for prey. It ignored the wren, scented around, loped over to where a small rabbit crouched immobile under a bank. In a savage flurry of motion it fastened on the back of its neck and bit hard and deep, then disappeared swiftly as it had come, leaving the unresistant rabbit paralysed, trembling: a hedgerow brutality, a survival necessity, savage but not tragic, miniaturized, only the wren's alarm as elegy. I did not interfere.

(2015)

GUN HILL

Twyn y Garth – locally known as Gun Hill; scarcely 1,000 feet high, its top is circled with a fine Bronze Age fortification, the views up the Wye, across to the Beacons and into Epynt majestically wide. It possesses a remarkable oddity – a 25-pounder field gun from the Great War. The story goes that it was bought jointly by the villagers of Erwood and Llanstephan as war memorial and placed on the village green of the former. Night raids and thefts of the gun by the youths of the two villages ensued until the compromise was reached of towing it to the top of the hill that looks down on both of them, and here it still stands, rusting, the wood-spoked wheels rotting away, pointing at the military ranges of Epynt across the Wye. I find it quietly moving, more poignant in its position and decay than all the phallic God-King-and-Country tokens to the same purpose across the land.

A squall of rain drove me from the hill's summit. I made my way down by the farm of Ciliau, curious to see whether this untouched seventeenth-century farmhouse had been gentrified in the quarter-century since I'd last enjoyed summer-evening hospitality here. It had not. A tortoiseshell cat sitting on the doorstep gave me brief hope, but no smoke came from the listing chimneys, no light from the kitchen within. Decayed machinery littered the yard, the cat fled to the barns at my approach. As I looked closely, I saw cracked window-glass and fissured walls. In the orchard, fruit trees grew mossy and unpruned. Round the front, where bean frames still stood in the kitchen garden, the outer course of a gable had fallen away. These shales and mudstones are poor building material, do not long survive neglect. All will be ruin soon, where there was hospitality and warmth of human interest. I had stories here from the old man over a glass of his potent cider. They mingled folk-tale and history: water-sprites on a green rock at Craig Pwll Du, cavaliers jingling two abreast along the Painscastle lanes. Not for the first time in these Welsh travels, I was reminded of the great lament from the ninth-century Heledd cycle:

> Stauell Gyndylan a'm erwan pob awr,
> Gwedy mawr ymgyuyrdan
> A weleis ar dy benntan.

> (Hall of Cynddylan each moment pierces me
> With memory of great talk
> I witnessed at your hearth.)

Had it been restored, over what subjects would the hearth-talk – the dinner-table conversation – range now? Reality television programmes? Property prices? The National Lottery? Serial murderers? The Cardiff Opera House? I'm glad I knew it in a former time...

(1996)

MYNYDD EPYNT

Opposite the inn at Erwood, steps lead to a steep green lane, sunken and celandine-carpeted beneath its sheltering oaks, that climbs out of the Wye valley on to the long ridge called Twmpath. There was spring sunlight flickering fitfully across the bark of an oak trunk, the grains of apple-green lichen luminous upon it and a drift of crisp leaves around its foot. Resting my back against it, I relaxed down into the lane's repose to catch at its former usage. The beef cattle from the green straths of Cothi and Tywi, from Llanddewi Brefi and Llanybydder, from all the rich pastureland between the Elenydd and Cardigan Bay once streamed and funnelled this way, bullocks bellowing, tar-shod geese hissing, boys yelling, dogs snarling and yapping, drovers hallooing 'Buwch! buwch!' as the whole furious precipitate tribe plunged and slithered down towards the crossing of the Wye and the tracks out to the smithfields of England. This was one of the main trade routes, one of the arteries of the west Wales economy for perhaps four hundred years, its livestock heading out by tens of thousands from the soft fields of their rearing to sharp steel and the town's appetite. Here's how one regional historian from the early years of the century, looking back on a way of life only recently defunct, pictured the scene:

> The track was ploughed by the hoofs of the cattle in the damp weather, and manured by the cattle as they passed over it. In the dry weather it would be harrowed by the hoofs of the cattle again. No bracken or fern has grown on it since and it is still today a green sward which has not been used since the black cattle went over it.

The echoes of the last beasts' bellowings have long since dissipated across these long horizons. You breast the ridge of the Twmpath and come into a subtle-featured country of buzzard-mewed skies below the moors of Epynt. I followed little roads with cropped hedgerows, fields with wattle fencing and fat Kerry sheep, a continual dipping scurry of flycatchers, most characteristic of Welsh birds, in front of me. By way of the Nant yr Offeiriaid ('the Priest's Dingle'), dusty with the spring budding of hazel and willow and a place of so calm and unremarkable a loveliness that it puts you quite at peace (which is as well in view of what's to come) I came to the Griffin Inn at the head of Cwm Owen.

It's twelve hundred feet up, dark-beamed and gas-lit, and I went in for a sandwich and a glass of beer to fortify myself against the next stage of this journey. I remember nights here thirty years ago when the farmers would drink through to the dawn, singing, telling stories, a prickling tension coming from them whenever any brash young soldier chanced this way pining for his lager. Now the landlord talked gratefully of the business from REME last month, the Paras last week. I kept my mouth tight-sealed, acknowledging economic necessity, and all the time sound of gunfire beyond the door. Epynt, since the early years of the last war, has been the largest military range in Wales, the map spatched with red lettering: *Artillery Range, Danger Area, Rifle Range...*

You cannot move anywhere in the Elenydd or the valleys that intersect it without being conscious of Epynt's great hill-barrier to the south. It has presence, its name carrying a talismanic charge, standing almost for the type of these Welsh hills. Its thousand-foot-high slope runs in a long wall from Llanfair ym Muallt almost to Llanymddyfri. I love the lines from Cynddelw Brydydd Mawr's *Rhieingerdd Efa* ('*Maidensong of Efa*') on Epynt:

> Cyfleuer gwawr ddydd pan ddwyre hynt,
> Cyfliw eiry gorwyn Gorwydd Epynt
>
> (Bright like daybreak in the moment of its arriving,
> So bright is the snow-gleam on the wooded scarp of Epynt.)

But you cannot now walk freely along the crest of that scarp. From the brown moors above where Bronze Age man made his burial mounds, among which he placed the mysterious permutations of his stone circles, there comes the thud of howitzer shells, the stutter of automatic weapons, the ragged staccato of rifle fire. There are rights-of-way, of course, used since prehistory, and you may still use them *by the book*. The battle-range ordinances tell you that you may pass here when the red flags are not flying. That's a sour joke. The knots of their lanyards are sealed with moss and algae, the gates' hinges rusted shut. These scarlet prohibitions are never taken down. For the public good, no doubt, but maintained by dishonesty and sleight of hand.

If you imagine that there will ever be any change in this situation, then you are more sanguine than I would ever dare to be. I cannot see the Ministry of Defence ever being prepared to relinquish its tenure here. In the history of its land acquisitions, which generally take place in the heightened emotional climate of wartime, often as not there are promises stated or implied that the land will be returned to its rightful occupants on cessation of hostilities. Invariably, that contract is dishonoured. It is justified, of course, in the interests of national security and defence. Training is necessary, especially as other countries grow increasingly sceptical about our military presence on their soil. Also, you'll be pleased to learn, it's environmentally friendly. All manner of plants, birds, animals, are grateful for the respect accorded them by the army during its training routines, its live firing across these landscapes. The case for this was argued in the MOD's tasteful and persuasive study of its own impact on the landscape published – to near-universal scepticism among concerned bodies – as *Defence and the Environment*. The arguments go back and forth: the *Report of the Defence Lands Committee* (the Nugent Report) of 1973; the Countryside Commission's study of *The Cambrian Mountains Landscape* and the UK Centre for Economic & Environmental Development's extended discussion paper on *Military Live Firing in National Parks*, both from 1990. In all this languishing verbiage, Epynt is the ghost at the feast. It is a huge hill area, and a forgotten one:

'Let's ignore Epynt, and then we can get on with the more

popular and significant campaigns to be fought for access to Dartmoor, to Castlemartin on the Pembrokeshire Coast, to Otterburn in Northumberland,' goes the argument. I'm not inclined to accept it, nor the idea that Epynt is barren, dreary, treeless, insignificant. It is not. It is one of the key places in the Welsh uplands, and if it were not for the surly presence and dishonest prohibitions of the military, it would widely be recognized as such. What I would like to see in the short term, and what I cannot imagine anyone might reasonably oppose, is the reaching of an accommodation with the army: at weekends and holiday periods, in accordance with its own ordinances, the flags are taken down, the public rights-of-way which have existed for millennia opened up, the Drovers' Arms up there on the Upper Chapel to Garth road which the MOD land agent hereabouts, to his credit, has recently restored, turned into a café and perhaps even an exhibition centre on the history of these moors. Let them lease it out to private enterprise, let them put in for lottery money for the project, but above all, *remove the barriers, let the public in.*

I do not believe that individuals within the armed forces are unaware of the amenity value of this land. On the contrary, as I walked across it recently, I came across a touching example of just that. At the Drovers' Arms an old woman and her daughter drew up in a car, climbed out, bunches of snowdrop plants in their hands. We talked. She was the widow of a REME officer who'd driven the first military roads across the ranges on their acquisition in 1940: 'After he'd retired, he often used to say to me, "Let's drive up on to Epynt." He loved it up here. When he died last year we scattered his ashes from that knoll, which is where I'm going to plant the snowdrops now.'

I hope they flourish for her. I hope the army opens its heart a little too, and abandons its harshly exclusive deceits. Meanwhile,

obviously I cannot advise you to trespass there. But let's
conjecture. If, in the course of this journey, I had found myself,
having made a four-mile detour by road down from the Griffin
and back up to the Drovers' Arms, able to sneak round the cordon
of soldiers – Dutch in this case, on a training exercise – and had
managed, furtively, camouflaged, hiding in hollows, hunted by
Land Rovers and buzzed by helicopters, to traverse this great
moor where there was once school, chapel, community, but
where the houses now are blind-windowed shells; if – and I must
stress that this is conjectural, because I don't wish to get anyone
into trouble with the MOD – I'd been able to rise above the fear
and threat to walk this finest of moorland crests along from the
Drovers' Arms to Tri Chrugiau (which cairns, I'm sad to say,
the army have treated with scant respect – how interesting it
would be to have some properly independent archaeological and
environmental studies carried out on the army's impact here),
what would I – or you, whom I cannot possibly recommend to
follow my conjectural example – have found, before dropping
down to that last outpost of empire which is Llangammarch
Wells? I'll tell you: despoiled land; a sad absence of peace and
freedom in a place where those qualities alone are the rightful
inhabitants.

(1996)

PART EIGHT

The Southern Ramparts

With one exception – and that only because its combination of crowds, military presence, worn terrain and an openness that makes all these far too visible – I love the succession of hill-massifs strung out from east to west across the southern counties of Wales. From the grassy uplands nestling into the crook of the Wye below Builth, to the Black Mountains, the Carmarthen Van, Mynydd Preseli and little coxcomb Carn Ingli farthest west, this buzzard-mewed, wide-horizoned country shading down into The Valleys never fails to delight. I just wish I could bring myself to like the Brecon Beacons, but we all have some Achilles Heel of prejudice and this is mine.

A NIGHT ON THE BEGWNS

After a long day's traverse of that wonderful, wide-horizoned hill-country of Radnorshire contained within the arc of the River Wye as it spills down from Builth and slips east towards the soft shires of England, I drop down in late afternoon to Painscastle and climb beyond it to The Roundabout, highest point of the Begwns.

The Brecon Beacons are glowing westerly as I quarter round to the mawn pool hidden below. 'Mawn' is simply a version of a Welsh word for peat, and there are plenty such expanses of water in the folds of these hills. They're shallow, bulrushes around their margins, in a dry year many of them shrink or dry out entirely. This particular one I remember the farmer creating with a low earth and stone dyke over fifty years ago. The water spread through the hollow into a stand of Scots Pine, drowning them, and their dead forms give a stark and melancholic aspect to the scene.

It's offset by the industry of a tractor on the slope above, shaving the dry bracken and stacking it as great terracotta Euro-bundles. The work done, it groans and jounces away over the hill. I cut and lift a square of turf, make a fire with twigs and small branches from the old pines, and sit on the greensward with my back to a trunk, watching the water. A moorhen bobs into view, its call like a cold chisel glancing off rock. Sibilant goldcrests flit between rushes and pines. Opposite me a buzzard circles low with intent, suddenly floundering down in a scatter of wings. Clearly successful, it rips at whatever small prey it has pounced upon.

Dusk is filling the hollow with milky shadow, brightening the flames. I unroll my sleeping bag alongside them. A pair of mallard fly in. I think of Kilvert's description of the 'Wild Duck Pool' at Newbuilding nearby, to which people came 'on Easter morning, to see the sun dance and play in the water and the angels who were at the Resurrection playing backwards and forwards before the sun.' A breeze ripples the water, reflection of the pines sway, and darkness wraps itself round my fire.

(2013)

THE BLACK MOUNTAINS

From the top of The Twmpa on a clear evening in late July, I scan round a horizon which encompasses the greater part of upland Wales. Here, near at hand across the valley of the Wye, are The

Begwns, with the hidden pool surrounded by the drowned pines. I've lost count of the nights I've slept out there, my sleeping bag unrolled on the grass, a square cut and the close turf peeled back for a small fire that will, in the morning, have left no trace beyond an ash-flecked outline for the first rain to obliterate. Our largest landowner, the National Trust, has newly erected a squat and ugly sign on the pristine greensward nearby to order that I, and others so inclined, no longer may – or rather, because these growing prohibitions are terse, *must not*. Camp here, that is, since to sleep out under the stars is to make camp whether or not a tent is involved, so I'm told. Half-a-century of one of my life's chief pleasures dismissed by officialdom's edict or whim (and incurred, no doubt, because of my co-celebrants' irresponsibility and disregard). I take solace from memory of the moorhens' bobbing across that sky-reflecting plane of water, from the wind's breathing in from the west through the wind's breathing in from the west through the pines, and from the eternal necessity in our straitened society for retention of proper forms of disobedience: 'I please myself with imagining a State at last which can afford to be just to all men, and to treat the individual with respect as a neighbour; which even would not think it inconsistent with its own repose, if a few were to live aloof from it, not meddling with it, nor embraced by it, who fulfilled all the duties of neighbours…'

Looking out over this landscape from The Twmpa (still called – and you can formulate your own thoughts around masculinity, appropriation and possession here – 'Lord Hereford's Knob' on my 1996 edition of the Ordnance Survey map), I think about Thoreau's New England neighbourliness and the wishful application of it to these lovely uplands of Wales. Away to the east the Malvern Hills rise out of a haze across the Severn Plain, and in the same spirit of neighbourliness practised by successive Westminster governments on Wales, I imagine them cloaked with dark rectangles of spruce such as I can see from where I stand, choking the valley of Grwyne Fawr beyond Tarren yr Esgob to the south ('If conifers were common in Wales, the country would not be worth looking at. These lower mountains cannot overcome such blemishes.' The Reverend John Parker, 1831); or with the public excluded permanently from them by reason of military training and live firing, as on Mynydd Epynt to the north; or that lovely long rounded switchback Malvern crest from the Worcestershire to the Herefordshire Beacon 'decorated' with wind turbines, which has been the fate of hill after lonely hill in the northern Elenydd (a colonization which is now, I read, to be intensified, with even Friends of the Earth Cymru agitating for the lanes of Wales – with their resplendent summer hedgerows of dog rose and elder, their meadowsweet verges and ever-active pied flycatchers – to be 'improved' so that the new generation of 400-foot high turbines can be transported along them to the remote, high places of their installation. People who argue thus are no friends of Welsh earth.)

Would I, as a good Welsh neighbour, wish this fate upon one of the prime and hallowed hill-landscapes of the English shires? Of course not – and also, the Malvern Hills are personally dear to me. Their association with Langland's Middle English poem, 'The Vision of Piers Plowman', is part of my mental furniture. One of the sweetest seasons of my life was a Hardy-esque autumn in 1968 that I spent working from dawn to dusk driving tractor and trailer round the apple orchards at the hills' Herefordshire end, looking across the Wye and the townlands of Hereford to the Black Mountains beyond. Throughout the day I'd chug up and down the rows of trees, stacking on to the trailer the boxes of fruit the pickers had filled and taking them back to the farm store. In the mornings the hills would be islanded in a white mist-plain beneath the bluest of skies. In the evenings as I made my way back along Halfkey Lane, the Welsh hills westerly would be violet with shadow. That which is beautiful it is not proper to destroy, yet we allow it to be done – even endorse it at times by our ideologies. The impervious zealots of renewable energy will brook no objections to expansion of capacity in their cause, and refuse to consider how fundamentally important it is to our small and overcrowded nation's spiritual health that siting of their technology be appropriate and sensitive. In the last decade the proliferation of wind-factories across the Cambrian hills has been an environmental catastrophe to rank with the heedless and wilful afforestation of those same hills in the twenty years after the Second World War. Why Westminster and Edinburgh government and Cardiff Assembly have not as yet seen fit to implement a joint United Kingdom commission of enquiry into appropriate location for renewable energy installations, given the intense conflicts of interest here, beggars belief, and is utterly negligent and reprehensible. Up here on The Twmpa on a summer's evening, the sense comes to me that, as Raymond Williams wrote, 'this extraordinarily settled and that extraordinarily open wild country are very close to each other and intricately involved'. The sanity and stability of those of us who live in the crowded one is dependent on the accessibility and preservation of that space and freedom which exists in the other. Yet by so many means the space is being crowded out, these lungs of our nation becoming atrophied and diseased, our capacity and opportunity to breathe ever more diminished, and our governments and perhaps the majority of our electorates uncaring that it should have come to this.

Conscious of the sun's descent, I drop down from the Twmpa to the Gospel Pass and climb steeply again – a pair of ring ouzels dipping and scudding across the slope towards waterfalls in the valley down to my right – on to the ridge leading to Hay

Bluff, the violet-shadowed hill from those westward glances of fifty years ago. This is the northernmost point of the Black Mountains, and from it you gain some sense of their distinctive plan. It is one of my very favourite groups of Welsh hills, and there is something intensely appealing to the imagination about it. Raymond Williams wrote a rich and knowledgeable two-part historical novel, posthumously published, set here called *People of the Black Mountains*. More recently the young Welsh writer Owen Sheers brought out a work of fantasy, *Resistance*, which imagines the scenario of a remote valley – that of the Olchon – from which the men have gone to join a British Maquis after the D-Day landings were repulsed and Britain invaded. Both, in setting the scene, use the same topographical trope of the mountains as a hand, as here from *People of the Black Mountains*:

> See this layered sandstone in the short mountain grass. Place your right hand on it, palm downward. See where the summer sun rises and where it stands at noon. Direct your index finger midway between them. Spread your fingers, not widely. You now hold this place in your hand.

There is something primitive, animistic in this that captures perhaps the essence of the place. It is unique in British hill-areas, compactly defined, in the so-called Dark Ages was actually the separate kingdom of Ewyas, renowned for its lawlessness. Giraldus, writing in the twelfth century, commented that 'the natives of these parts are much given to implacable quarrels and never-ending disputes. They spend their time fighting each other and shed their blood freely in internecine feuds. I leave it to others to tell about the inhuman crimes which have been committed there in our own lifetime.' He was referring to the massacre of the Norman Marcher Baron Richard de Clare and attendants by the Grwyne Fawr in 1135. Something about these valleys and the bare-knuckled finger-ridges that separate them reeks of ancient secrecy and power. There are places here I have seen in the past and been unable ever to find again, as though they had disappeared from the land. Memory of the goose-quilled arrows still wuthers across centuries of twilights. It is the most secret place. Look across to it from the drowned-pine pool of the Begwns and that long northern scarp is so dark, devil's-heart black. But it is an illusion. Labour up to the Twmpa by the way I came, alongside the Afon Buwch, the cattle stream, and subtle tonalities of patched and mottled ground – the pale-green of bilberry, the summer purple of heather – everywhere delight. The bird cherry is white-blossomed across the lower slopes in spring and high along the stream the elegant rowans grow, that turn early to flamed leaf and bear the heavy red crops of berries on which the ouzels feast. In the stream itself, the exposed strata of this immensely thick deposit of old red sandstone is a dusky pink. The sun catches at the Darren, the huge landslip beyond Llanthony, and turns it to rose, which has me reciting Walter Savage Landor's perfect lyric of love and loss, 'Rose Aylmer', written at Llanthony. Beyond its black rampart, this is a landscape intensely colourful and various.

These valleys that hold the sense of seclusion and long history as clearly as their shadowed slopes hold the frosts of winter, these so-long and undulating spacious parallel ridges – nowhere else in Britain is quite like them. As I turn south at Hay Bluff and head down the ten-mile finger of Hatterall that is the finest section of the Offa's Dyke Path, past the Robber's Stone where a pair of long-maned hill-ponies watch me suspiciously, the Olchon valley opens up to the left, copsed and with its farms scattered along the spring-line above the valley floor. At a ruined cairn I veer away from the hog's-back and descend over spongy ground and by steep zigzags, darkness brimming in the valley now, to the farm called The Vision in the Vale of Ewyas. Its name puts me in mind of one of my favourite books, John Stewart Collis's *The Vision of Glory*:

> Today there is neither weeping nor rejoicing. We are not sorry, and we are not glad. We have no time, for we must keep pace with the machines. Even the gracious ceremony of grace before meals has been abandoned... We owe debts to no-one. We have nothing to fear.

...except for the loss of the land the spaciousness of which sustains us, and which, still, tenuously, is preserved in this place. And so, as if saying a grace, I give my most profound thanks for what the poet John Barnie called this 'open hand/Where the truth/Lies green and still.'

(2012)

MRS. MACNAMARA

All the way up from Hay I'd been scouring my brain for the names carved on two stones on a ridge of the Black Mountains that I'd seen for the first and last time nearly thirty years ago and the recollection of which, because of some conjectural romance, had inexactly stuck there:

> 'The first one,' I explained to Bill Bowker, 'was to an Irishwoman – Mrs O'Shea, Mrs O'Grady – something like that. And the second to a squire. And it's my belief that she was his mistress and they had natural children together and when she died he was so devoted to her that, because their relationship was illicit, he had her buried up there and himself close by her when his time came, in the wild, away from propriety and prying eyes.'
> 'That's just the sort of romantic gush you would believe, isn't it, Jim? Anyhow, I've never seen these stones, but I tell

you where they'll be. They'll be on the Rhos Dirion ridge, and I don't fancy our chances of finding them today, but we'll have a look. Or at least we'll go as far as The Twmpa and see how we get on.'

'I've got it! It was Mrs MacNamara,' I butted in, before Bill could launch into one of his lengthier tirades against my character and personal morality.

'What was Mrs MacNamara?'

'The name on the stone…'

'There you are, you see – obsessed by Irishwomen! What you need is a long, cold shower, and that's just what you're going to get.'

With that, Bill turned south into the gale and I – grateful for full waterproofs, feet sodden already – plashed alongside him, snapping and sniping and chaffing away in the full, friendly flow of old acquaintance. For two miles we tacked along the whaleback ridge at twenty degrees to the wind, surfing a solid wall of rain with nothing to be seen beyond it. Occasionally we passed forlorn groups of ponies, long manes hanging sodden and string-like across their withers. Sometimes we veered yards wide from the path to avoid trampled bog. We entered into a disquisition upon why we both liked the Black Mountains but felt no similar affection for the Brecon Beacons. And then we came upon the stone.

It's a small slab of the local sandstone, its top rounded like a gravestone, heavily encrusted with lichens, measuring perhaps eighteen inches wide by thirty tall. Mrs MacNamara's name is still legible upon it, and a date, which appears to be 1825, but is difficult to decipher and in this weather we were not inclined to study it for long. Thirty years ago, I remember the stone as being intact and firmly rooted in the greensward. Now, it has apparently been vandalized, a large corner of it broken away, and it lists, supported by a heap of stones, in a miry pool. I know nothing about it.[8] I wonder if Raymond Williams was constructing a story around it for the ambitious posthumous novel, *People of the Black Mountains* – a novel structured in part around a grandson's search for his grandfather in a storm along this actual ridge of Tarren yr Esgob? Was this stone part of his meaning in the last words he wrote for publication: 'Press your fingers close on this lichened sandstone. With this stone and this grass, with this red earth, this place was received and made and re-made. Its generations are distinct, but all suddenly present.'

That, I think, has something of the essence of this wonderful hill area's appeal. The long, high ridges and lovely valleys between are aesthetically appealing in themselves, but in their associative texture they pass beyond the merely recreational into a density of spiritual resonance. This is not just country of the geographical border – it is one of the rare places where time and historical moment shiver into concurrency. For our part we shivered too, and hastened along to Chwarel y Fan, too damp and dispirited to search for the partner to Mrs MacNamara's stone, before dropping off the ridge by the oddly-shaped stone called the Blacksmith's Anvil down a desperately steep and slippery hillside sentried with thorn, yew and whitebeam trees into the valley of the Honddu, or as Giraldus describes it, 'the deep vale of Ewias, which is shut in on all sides by a circle of lofty mountains and which is no more than three arrow-shots in width'. The aptness and reality of his image became even more strong as we turned north along the road and came to the tiny church of Capel y Ffin.

Kilvert, on his two visits here, describes this 'chapel of the

---

[8] Subsequently I've found out that Mrs MacNamara was the landowner, and this the boundary of her land. I prefer my version, this being too prosaic by half.

boundary' – the church of St Mary here is a chapel of ease for the church at Llanigon, over the scarp to the north-west – as 'squatting like a stout grey owl among its seven great black yews'. The trees and the raised, circular churchyard are obviously older than the church of 1762 that stands among them. It's easy to imagine the Welsh archers cutting their longbows here before departure for Crécy and Agincourt. And yet, despite so much of the association being of belligerence and war – the Third Crusade, border skirmishes, Sir John Oldcastle, Henry the Fifth, David Jones's masterpiece – the atmosphere is of simplicity and peace – an interior of whitewash and wood, without ornament apart from an east window that bears, in one of Eric Gill's elegant scripts, the text 'I will lift up mine eyes unto the hills, whence cometh my help'. It is a church that has about it not the expression of power and aspiration through stone – the sort of architecture, as at Tewkesbury, Exeter or Chartres, to which I thrilled in earlier years – but the yearning for oneness and harmony that in a more true and unsullied way is at the root of religious experience. In one of his late fragments, *The Roman Quarry*, set on the hillside above, David Jones wrote of the 'place of questioning where you must ask the/question and the answer questions you.' Capel y Ffin, with its simplicity and lack of pretension or guile, turns your own outlook and desire back upon you to reconcile you with the elemental world of which you are inescapably and most happily a part.

(1996)

A HOLY MOUNTAIN

Morning, and at last, briefly, the sun shines. To the south rises Ysgyryd Fawr, 'the Holy Mountain, the blue peak with the rockfall on its western scarp'. Wreathed in mist the previous evening, it had looked phantasmal, eerie, impossibly steep, the great landslip cleft on its weather-slope gothically accentuated and strange. In daylight, despite its summit's lowly altitude of 486 metres, it still has a striking and noble presence. I approach it by way of the gentle, grassy shoulder of Arwallt, zigzag up a steep bracken flank, and arrive on a twisting ridge leading to the top. Two squat pillars of sandstone give entry to the site of St. Michael's Chapel here, the Ordnance Survey pillar standing within confines of which only clear suggestion of a ground plan remains. As late as 1676 the Pope of the day, Clement X, decreed that plenary indulgences would be granted to pilgrims visiting the chapel at Michaelmas. I can remember a large wooden cross thirty years ago, but it has gone, along with much of the mountain-top earth. Several of the churches of Gwent were said to be built on mounds of this, taken particularly from within the chapel, where the soil was so holy that it was scattered on farms round about for good luck and on coffins at Catholic burials. Worm or slug could not live in it, according to some writers – and certainly the only worm I saw on the summit looked in poor shape, so I dug it into deep, moist soil lower down the hill. The superstitions all derived from the massive landslip to the west, that by tradition had occurred when the veil of the temple was rent at Christ's crucifixion. Who knows when it happened in fact? There are other huge landslips in the local sandstone – particularly by Cwmyoy in the Vale of Ewyas. What you can say with certainty is that the view from Ysgyryd Fawr must have thrilled and absorbed any pilgrim. Hills crowd in on every side. To the west, beyond the bracken whale's-back of Deri and the humped dome of the Sugar Loaf, is a hard, half-hidden land. Eastward lies a rich patchwork of hedged and copsed and tilled red fields with tidy farms and scattered cottages. South is the closing channel of Severn Sea, Somerset beyond it, and to the north and north-east hill upon hill: Herefordshire Beacon,

Abdon Burf, the Shropshire Hills, the Black Mountains, the distant Berwyn. They stressed that I was leaving the soft borderlands behind, moving into different terrain. I plunged on down, through Abergavenny, over the Sugar Loaf and into Crickhowell, eager to find what lay ahead.

(2002)

MYNYDD LLANGYNIDR

In Llangynidr the school pick-up run has begun, Shoguns and Fronteras and Discoverys driven by groomed women with blond highlights are packing into the cul-de-sacs. I head for the Red Lion. 'Are you open?' I ask the landlady.

'Well...' She looks me up and down, '... for another five minutes, maybe. What would you like?'

'You,' I feel like saying. She's tousled and funny and full of life. I glance along the bar. 'Pint of the Reverend James, please,' is what passes my lips, 'and do you have any sandwiches?'

'I'll make you one',' she smiles, and repeats again that devastating formula.

'Whatever's easiest.'

Two minutes later she's back with a stacked plate of good, clean food.

'Sit down here. It's alright. I won't shut. It's just that I got soaked in Abergavenny this morning, see, and I'll have to go upstairs and tidy myself up...'

She flicks the cascading curls.

'... and I need to take a shower before we open up for the evening. Would you like pickle?'

I shake my head, thank her, take my pint and food outside into the fading sun and the strengthening wind. Kind women are a gift in this life, to be treated kindly. She locks the door behind me. I sit at a table in the sheltered garden, the scent of honeysuckle all around me, and am ridiculously happy. A terracotta green man smiles down from under a laburnum tree on the pansies and the pinks, and a harassed-looking blonde woman walks across the lawn.

'Is the landlady in?'

'I think she'll be down in a few minutes.'

'Oh, I'll wait then. I'm new, see – first week covering this area – Castle Howell Foods, Carmarthen,' she explains. She's still waiting as I leave. By Sardis United Reformed Church ('formerly the Congregational Chapel') – services at 9.30 every Sunday with the Reverend Shem Morgan – I branch hillwards, but not before looking into the neat and flowery graveyard behind, with its view towards the Black Mountains from under the spreading yew, the UPVC windows looking down on it, the rows of Bevans and Watkins and Merediths, and the pinky-purple delaminating Silurian rocks of its wall. The lane I follow is bordered with wallflower and forget-me-not. *'Acaena mycrophilla'* reads the tag on one raised bed. The cottages are neat, empty, prosperous, expensively furnished, sun-terraced, devoid of books, and the coming gale is thrashing in the lilac and laburnum trees around them. I climb the lane, leaving this dormer village of rich rural dreams behind me. An uphill mile brings me to a path that forks south-west to follow the stream's course. From the last building standing at the old *tyddyn* of Blaen y Cwm, an elder grows from a windward wall and a corner has fallen away. The sheep bawl round it raucously, some already shedding across the rough pasture fleeces that once were a valued commodity. Heart-leaves of the celandine, so late in flower at this height, carpet the miry sunken way ahead, boulders of its walls downy with moss. Tiring now, the storm gathering around me and the traverse of the moor ahead, I catch at my own studied movement as I cross steps of a stile slick with algae, think that I have seen the old dance thus, carefully – but still, they dance. Behind me, a rainbow spans Llangynidr, rain drenches down on a whirling wind, and ring ouzels pipe and dip along the last pools of the stream before I broach the moor.

This moor – Llangynidr Mountain it's called – I have been to before, climbed on its rimming rocks in soft summer days, crawled far below the surface in labyrinthine underground passages, walked its heather, visited the Chartist Cave out of respect for those who sheltered there after the Merthyr Rising of 1831 – at the time of the martyrdom of Dic Penderyn who died with the single word 'Injustice!' on his lips – and at other times of foment and oppression in the industrial history of The Valleys. Today the cloud is down, and I look across the moor's high expanse with some anxiety. There are paths – two or three of them – marked on the map, but I know each of them to be discontinuous, conjectural, no more than the expression of legal license and cartographic hope. I have no compass to make this crossing. Out of the shelter of the valley the wind is blasting and wuthering and the ground is rough – knee-deep heather and bilberry over most of it, shake-holes where the underground caverns have collapsed, swallow-holes where the brief streams disappear, scatters of boulders, fields of slippery rocks. There is a sense about it that few now come this way, few make the crossing in either direction. By instinct, helped by occasional glimpses through scudding cloud of a veiled sun, I head south. The lash of rain pricks at my eyeballs. I feel the blast of wind – so strong at times as to bowl me into the heather – as almost a soft touch; but overlaid with cold points of pain. Sheep-paths through leads in the heather interlink, veer away in roughly the right quarter. The wind ever more violent, I have to blink into it to spy out the way, then thrust onwards. I think of the chambers and stream-passages underground into which the surface water, through cracks and crannies dissolved out of the rock, trickles and pours, its fierce, flooding rush down there like the power of our emotions, all swirl and confusion, devoid of light.

Two figures resolve out of the mist in front of me, one tall, with a massive head and the bulky shoulders and barrel chest of a miner, gesticulating, stopping momentarily to hammer points home with rock-like fists; the other darting, puckish, a will-o'-the-wisp. I hasten to catch them and as I draw close the big man fades into shreds of cloud as though he had never been, and the voice of the little one is murmuring behind the wind, 'He liked to run away from Bedlam. He liked to have all the harness taken off him.' A gap opens in the mist. Down there I see the straggling terraces of Beaufort, and catch a glimpse of the two of them again, toiling up here against the gale of the world, icy blasts of contempt at their back. '1929,' the wind hisses, 'that old unseated officialdom, the incumbents whose fire burns only in their self-importance, the ones with power to lose – no breath of mine was ever as cold as theirs':

> [After the miners' nomination] his first meeting was in Beaufort. It started in dead silence and ended in dead silence. He stammered badly, and, according to Archie Lush, made the worst speech of his life. That night the two friends went on one of their favourite walks across the Llangynidr Mountain, with Aneurin wondering whether it was wise to persist...

Michael Foot, in the two volumes of *Aneurin Bevan 1897-1960* that together constitute the most affectionate, lucid and generous-hearted political biography of the twentieth century, tells of 'the walks across the mountains, ten, fifteen or twenty miles in a day' of Bevan's youth. As I drop down towards the industrial estates along the Heads of the Valleys Road, I think of the potent cultural mix of that time: David Bevan's copy of *The Clarion* in the house every week, with its stress on egalitarianism, intellectual self-improvement and the open air; the musical and singing tradition of The Valleys; the library encounters with Thoreau's and Shelley's idealism; the novels of Conrad; the Hegelian philosophy of F.H. Bradley, whose father's sermons had rung out from under the silver bells of Glasbury-on-Wye beyond the moor and the Black Mountains to the north. With all that colour and texture of thought and rhetoric and art dancing in my head I plashed and skidded down the last mile of waterlogged ground to gain the old tramway running round from Trefil, a landscape opening up to the south bleakly and utterly different from those I had crossed on the other side of this harsh barrier.

The mines and quarries they once served long defunct, the engines that hauled along them gone for scrap, these level, high belvederes contouring the hill-scarps are green tracks now. With relief, I turned east and surfed with the gale at my back down to Nant y Croft. Seven burnt-out cars rusted in a gully beneath the tramway. Cases of used shotgun cartridges were littered around. A battered white Transit van parked outside the first houses carried the bird-brained-dog symbol of the British Association for Shooting and Conservation. I ignored a pub, crossed the bridge over the Heads of the Valleys Road, found marked public paths blocked off where the land they crossed had been acquired for more of the box-like, vast, subsidized factories, pylons that crackled in the mist crossing the grass and scrub towards them. The rain and wind slashed ever more savagely across a soured upland of waste and slag and industrial lagoons, lapwings careened and screamed on the turbulent air, a buffeted heron flapped slowly away from the tormented, gunmetal surface of one of the ponds: 'Now it is May in all the valleys,/Days of the cuckoo and the hawthorn,/Days for splashing in the mountain ponds...'

Idris Davies's lyrical description was unrecognizable on a day like this. Soaked to the skin, teeth chattering with cold, stopped in my tracks at times by the wind, I battled along the road and came to the exposed high promontory at Waun y Pound where the Aneurin Bevan memorial is to be found. Under a wooden shelter is a picture of the great orator, speaking to a crowd of men and women, their attention rapt, their faces excited, their dress meagre and poor. Beyond are the stones, big, rough-hewn, weathered limestone blocks, square and solid, four in number. There is one each for the major communities of his parliamentary constituency: Ebbw Vale, Tredegar, Rhymney. The central and largest one is for Nye himself, and bears this simple inscription: *From this point Aneurin Bevan spoke to the people of his constituency and the world.'* It's pocked by air-gun pellets, some letters illegible, and take-away cartons and Special Brew cans are strewn across the track from the car park.

There's a harsher tone to the voice in the wind now, and its disaffected burden runs thus: 'What the fuck are politicians to us? Any politicians? Even this politician..? Look what they done to us, mun, and look what they left us with...' I look around me, at these austere sheds of factories planted on the desolate moors and with all the signs around them of under-production and short-time; at the homes that were close to the industry, so there the people must live, clinging to the sides of valleys funnelling up every gale that blew from Severn Sea; and I think of the battles Nye Bevan fought: against militarism and the setting of working men of nations into conflict with each other; with the mine-owners who had, despite the Sankey recommendations, resumed so malevolently parsimonious a control over the mines after the Great War; with that 'new race of robbers', the Poor

Relief Commissioners, after the General Strike of 1926; with those who espoused non-intervention in the Spanish Civil War; with the Labour Party itself over its policies in the Second World War and on other occasions; with the despotic incompetence that lumbered behind the inflated and bellicose rhetoric of Winston Churchill, and with the rest of a Tory Party he regarded as 'lower than vermin' (God knows – pretty well by now, no doubt – what he would have thought of the cohorts of Thatcher and Blair); with the avarice and autocracy of the medical profession, particularly over nationalization of the hospitals and the sale of general practices (something that effectively crept in through the back door again during the 'reforms' of the 1980s), in the formulation, before its inception in 1948, of his greatest memorial, the National Health Service – modelled, he would always claim, on the Tredegar Medical Aid Society; for better workers' housing in the great programme of public building during the term of the Attlee Government; with the British press, that he regarded as 'most prostituted in the world'; with the Attlee Government itself over armaments expenditure in a time of social need. That any of these should have been battles!

Racked by fits of shivering, rain dripping from me, I turn again into the wind and head down a dismal twilight road, past a squalid pub with its gable end clad in corrugated iron, into Tredegar. And as I go, on to the wind I chant out the peroration from Bevan's last great speech, 'Why I am a Socialist', to the Blackpool Conference after the electoral defeat – any Conservative victory is a people's defeat – of 1959; with a sense of wonder as I do so at its prescience and continuing relevance, and a sad suspicion that no-one with this command of language and firmly principled selfless conviction is active in politics today.

'OH WHAT CAN YOU GIVE ME?/SAY THE SAD BELLS OF RHYMNEY.'
What I was given was the steep road out of Pontlottyn on to
Cefn y Brithdir, and I had come up here for a particular reason.
But first, there is the opportunity to look around, for this ridge
is as good a near viewpoint as any into The Valleys. In that
broken, falling ground away to the west, the industry that was
its ruin itself gone, are Merthyr Tydfil, Dowlais Top, Penywern
– the latter birthplace to The Valleys' most passionate modern
historian, Gwyn Alf Williams, who taught of human experience
and its meaning until the pain of all that witness gave way to
whisky's anaesthesia and – far too soon – he died: 'it was... a
place of warmth and fellowship and challenge; a centre of genuine
intellectual liveliness, of drama societies, readings, eisteddfodau,
above all a place dedicated to intellectual self-improvement as its
members conceived it, devoted to the readings of books (in any
language).'

Below me, running down to the south and east, is the
Rhymney Valley, the ridges beyond it enclosing Sirhowy and
Ebbw Vale and Blaina. Euro-millions have smoothed over the
industrial scarring, in collaboration with nature have brought
the land back to some semblance of its pre-industrial green. But
the evidence of these communities' dispossession, the erasure
of social hope here in the last two decades, is palpable. I look
across them and see concrete proof of the annual compound
Conservative disinvestment in – what Margaret Thatcher, in her
most chilling phrase, told us did not exist – society. I see clear
illustration of the statistic that in 1979, nine per cent of Britons
lived below the official poverty line, and in the year 2000 the
figure had leapt to a quarter of the population, the crossings of
the barriers out of that state had been made ever more difficult,
whilst at the other end of the spectrum the rich had grown ever
richer, and the social differentiations ever more stark. In the

bowl of the hill to the north, at an altitude of 1200 feet, the tailings of its former collieries all around them, are the terraces of Fochriw:

> Fuck you, fuck you, fuck you
> Snarl the bells of Fochriw.

I walk towards them, sense movement among the piles of refuse dumped, scattered and blown across the moor, see a man there, and a dog, both scavenging, an old child's push-chair nearby filled with broken pieces of laminate floorboards. I watch awhile, then call out a greeting. He looks up, straightens his back and walks over, dog trotting to heel, snickering its lip at the presence of a stranger, rangy and suspicious. The man's stocky, watchful, unshaven, his expression humorous and sidelong. I'd think him about 60:

> 'How's it going, mun? I thought you was the DSS for a minute. They'll dock your dole if they find you up here. Wouldn' make that much difference, mind – worth 'alf what it was. Firewood – burns well with the glue in it...'

He gestures towards the push-chair, reaches in the pocket of his torn ski-jacket, brings out a pouch of Golden Virginia, rolls a cigarette and offers me the pouch.

'You out walkin'..? Not the prettiest place, by 'ere.'

I tell him where I've been, where I'm going. We squat down in the heather out of the wind, smoking and talking. I take chocolate and bananas out of my rucksack, share them with him.

'I been out o' work eighteen years, and it's not for want of looking, but at my age they don' want you. I'm lucky, you know, children gone, but it's hard for the younger ones, what with wantin' everythin'. I don't blame them for takin' it sometimes, when they've 'ad so much taken from them. You read in the papers 'ow bad this place is, with the drugs and beatin' our wives and that, and then you see the people on telly all doing the same things, and you read the statistics. You know who's the worst for domestic violence, and that's the worst thing in my book, 'cos it's about trust, mun, isn'it?'

I look at him, shake my head.

'It's not us, up here in Fochriw or over in Merthyr or down in Rhymney. The women are the strength of these places – always 'ave been. It's the doctors and policemen. The women's groups'll tell you that. So what does that say about society, mun? That those on top and in charge are as big a set of fuckin' 'ypocrites as ever they were? Well, I'd better get these off 'ome. Been good talkin' to you, boy.'

He stands up, shakes my hand, collects the push-chair, whistles his dog and sets off along the road, 'endued with sense'. I feel strangely desolate at his going, turn south on the old Roman road that heads for Gelligaer. The wind tumbles a startling blue carton against my foot as I look at the map: 'Aries Ram – super satisfaction guaranteed,' it reads, 'soft and flexible, multi-speed. For more information on the use of this product contact www. sexcatalogue.co.uk.'

> Gimme that just to slot in,
> Shrill the belles of Pontlottyn.

Black plastic streams in the wind from barbed wire above all the moor's discarded objects of brief pride. Around the horizon spread the Sugar Loaf, the Black Mountains, the Brecon Beacons, Mynydd Llangynidr, Fforest Fawr, the Carmarthen Van. Larks are singing above me, and spring is bronzed across the remnant oakwoods above Rhymney. Lambs play among the detritus, ponies glance up in brief wariness, a bedraggled ram nibbles thin and waterlogged grass, nuzzles aside the plastic hand and arm of a child's doll. I find myself suddenly rehearsing the arguments of Marcuse, that I have not read in over thirty years, from his *Essay on Liberation*: on how capital stimulates and debases appetite and aspiration, to serve its own ends and keep the people in thrall. As I do so, an old car pulls up not far ahead. A woman steps from a rear door, smoothing down her skirt as she straightens up. She goes round to the other side, opens it, and helps out a frail, small, stumbling figure, his clothes hanging loosely upon him, a pair of thick-lensed wire-rimmed spectacles, twisting and askew, clinging uncertainly to his nose. He takes her arm and totters up the road. The driver and front-seat passenger remain, talk softly, concernedly. The walking pair have not gone many yards before it becomes too much for the man, and they turn again. Holding on to the woman's arm he slowly makes his way back along the road to the car, and gratefully enters it.

That was the saddest thing I saw during our friendship.

The vision fades, of Idris Davies and Morfydd, his fiancée, just before the poet's death, of cancer at the age of 48 in 1953. He came back here, the miner who'd studied during and after The Strike to become a qualified teacher, only to find the community he'd left irrevocably changed. His poems are why I have come to Rhymney, and why I'm taking this route along the ridgeway of Cefn y Brithdir, where he took his last walk.

> It is bitter to know that history
> Fails to teach the present to be better than the past.

(2002)

CRAIG TWRCH

Sleek streak of russet pelts down the field, making for a hen-run by the house below. Instead of expected cacophony, I hear dogs bark, plod on up-field to seven Scots Pines by a ruin. The old enclosure beyond is beech-ringed. This was drover-territory, cattle penned here for the night. One wall has collapsed in an explosion of white quartz, the quarry for which would have been a former cairn from the Bronze Age on the bluff close by. Every hill-top and ridge-end visible from here has one, white-cored with spirit-stone.

Up on Craig Twrch two are prominent. I drift off in that direction. Slant line of ascent from Ffordd Helen, most ancient of Welsh roads, is scored across the slope; Enclosure Acts stone wall and a barbed-wire fence of modern provenance prevent the use of what had been right-of-way through millennia. Casting about, a line of long marker-stones, laid low and turf-obscured, indicates another route by which to climb the ridge.

The cairns are atop its south-west gable, look down on a hillside pecked with pits of Roman metalworking all around the enormous prone megalith of Carreg y Bwci ('the Hobgoblin's Stone'). It's distance, though, that preoccupies the eye. On this clear day I can see Cader Idris and The Berwyn northerly; Preseli in the west; the long rimming southern scarps of Wales from Bannau Brycheiniog and the Brecon Beacons to the Black Mountains on the Herefordshire border, and floating beyond them the Malvern Hills.

Rough mountain pasture around this sentinel ridge is still winter-grey. Gravid ewes kneel to tug and chew at sparse fescues. Overhead a buzzard mews; from a fence-post a solitary raven observes, waits for her annual portion of afterbirth and eye of sickly lamb, to bring to red throats already agape in tree-top nest by the Long Wood. Spring, she knows, is coming to the hills.

(2012)

THE FAIRY LAKE

Narrow switchback lanes, bedraggled meadowsweet an astonishing December survival along sheltered verges, climb south toward the Black Mountain, dipping into quiet valleys of small farms, each new rise affording glimpses of dramatic hill-scenery ahead. The high tops of Bannau Sir Gaer and Fan Brycheiniog, between Afon Tywi's wide strath and the scarred gorges of Afon Tawe southward, mark a boundary between industrial valleys running down to Severn Sea and high grazing commons that stretch from here to Snowdonia. The northern sides of the two hills are elegant, ice-sculpted, streaked red in gullies where underlying sandstone's laid bare.

In the rare local glimmer of a fine afternoon, every peak but these cloud-hidden, I climbed the steep track above Llanddeusant that leads in a couple of miles to the dark corrie-pool of Llyn y Fan Fach. At this lake, deep and broad, lying close within the shadow of the scarp, locates one of the clearest recensions of a legend recurrent throughout Wales. It tells of a mortal and his encounter here with a fairy maiden who rises from the depths. He asks her to marry. She's dismissive at first ('Moist is your bread – I'll not have you!' is how her rejection of him translates from the Welsh); then relents, with the proviso that should he touch her three times with iron, she and her dowry of cattle will disappear back into the water.

The marriage prospers. Her skill in animal husbandry is remarkable. Three sons are born, who become in time famous physicians. But inadvertently, three times he touches her with iron, the last in tossing her a horse's bridle. The waters close around her. Fifty years ago I knew old people who claimed in all sincerity descent from the fairies. Some folklorists have argued that racial memory of intermarriage between aboriginal people and Iron Age invaders underlies these tales. I cast a final look across lake-water silvered by a rising moon and follow my shadow down – the story in its transfigured landscape no longer quite so incredible.

(2013)

TWO HEIGHTS ON PRESELI

1: Foel Drygarn

Green paths through heather, low sun picking out tints of its late flowering, led to the ramparts of Foel Drygarn. This easternmost top of Mynydd Preseli is a rewarding objective for short winter days. It only reaches 363 metres above sea level, but geographical and historical texture compensate for lack of height. Three huge, ruined, late-Bronze Age cairns lie within its defensive hilltop enclosure. The dragon-crest tor rising from moist haze westerly is Carn Goedog.

The Golden Road – an ancient ridgeway from Crymych to the Gwaun valley – faded into distant dove-grey, slipped across low ridges that terminate in successive fine headlands along the north Pembrokeshire coast. There's an atmosphere about Preseli that enchants. I offered prayers of thanksgiving to the Reverend Parri Roberts and the poet Waldo Williams, who successfully resisted post-war military designs on 16,000 acres of this prime landscape for more of the training areas that blight so much of Britain. 'We nurture souls in these areas,' Roberts wrote; and through his efforts Preseli does so still.

The sun dropped behind Foel Cwmcerwyn as I turned to the descent. A cold wind blustered against rocky outcrops. High above, wings outspread, long tail fanned and canted, a male kestrel, a flame-winged sky-jewel illuminated by the last light, hovered on the updraught. I sank into the heather before his presence, thought inevitably of what Gerard Manley Hopkins considered his own finest poem, 'The Windhover'. In recalling it, I marvelled too at the precise attention with which he rendered this exquisite little falcon's quality of movement, of being: '... how he rung upon the rein of a wimpling wing/In his ecstasy! Then off, off forth on swing,/As a skate's heel sweeps smooth on a bow bend...' The kestrel stooped into shadowed heather, missed his prey, rose to regain in a flurry of gold-vermilion the slant sun-rays, and at the last veered swiftly away over the moor to his dark forest roost. I followed on down, soul-nurtured and thankful.

(2016)

2: Foel Cwmcerwyn

Bwlch Gwynt – 'wind-pass' – lies between the two westernmost summits of Mynydd Preseli's moorland ridge. The name fits perfectly with this bleak saddle extensively marred by forestry clear-cut. Views distract attention from the ruined immediate landscape. They spread wide, take in Ramsey, the craggy crest of Ynys Bery off its southern tip, isolated rocks of the Bishops and Clerks in the sea beyond, and all the magnificent headlands – Dinas, Strumble, Penmaen Dewi – that ruckle the northern coast of Pembrokeshire.

Stonehenge's bluestone menhirs were dragged from Preseli millennia ago in a dumbfounding, still-incomprehensible feat of megalithic engineering. But the oriental end of Preseli's seven-mile whaleback whence they came (they've been identified as originating from the spikey outcrop of Carn Goedog) has a different character to its occidental heights. Here the ridge reaches its 536-metre highest point at Foel Cwmcerwyn, two miles distant from and 140 metres above the road that crosses through the *bwlch*.

On a June evening I set off from the latter, the ancient trackway of the Golden Road still miry from the winter rains, its surrounding vegetation typical of high moorland: cotton grass, sedge, heather, sphagnum moss, bilberry and the red moor grasses. My route to the summit branched off the trackway at the end of the old plantation. It veered away to zigzag gently up the shoulder of the hill. Swags of winter-bleached moorgrass gave the landscape a spectral feel, a very few wind-seeded spruce darkly punctuating it. On the topmost spike of one of them, a small and restless bird perched, making frequent forays down into the grass to probe around the roots before returning to his vantage point in a flurry of flicking tail and white-barred wing-beat. The still evening and the quiet place amplified the sweet staccato notes to which he gave voice from his perch. Too melodious for a stonechat, then? I focused my glass on him, saw clearly the broad eye-stripe of a whinchat – rare now, though these west Wales coastal heights seem a last stronghold for the species.

(2016)

Hill of the Angels

By west-leading footpaths I amble out of Trefdraeth to odd and ancient little stone bridge of Pont Ceunant, thence up to Carn Ingli common. From the fine Bronze Age standing stone of Bedd Morris, across which a rash of legends thin and tenuous as its lichens have spread, a long moorland mile curves past Carn Clust-y-Ci ('the Dog's Ear Cairn') and on expansively to the burial mound of Carn Briw. Above, along a path through the heather, is the summit crest of Carn Ingli itself – a jewel of a miniature mountain, commanding in its presence, expansive in its atmosphere, its rocks infused with western light. Angels kept the early Christian saint Brynach company here, and various New Age philosophers and guides insist that they hover around still. Lay down your head in the heather, enter your dreaming and they will come to you, say our modern sages. Perhaps they do still manifest; as a good thought or an intended sudden kindness, or the plumed featherings of high cirrus clouds – 'things/Extreme, and scatt'ring bright' – that look like angel wings and promise light and warmth after weeks of the dull, cold drench.

To rest within the hill fort ramparts or to bask on warm slabs of Preseli bluestone under an autumn sun is anyway in itself a version of heaven, particularly when a rare flock of curlews from the estuary wheel round and careen in across the moor on bubbling currents of song. Listening to their angelic effusions I dream-dozed contentedly on the ice-scoured summit slabs, whilst my sight rhapsodized and identified around the miraculous view. Ynys Enlli ('the Island of the Tide-race') was visible off the tip of the Llŷn Peninsula eighty miles to the north, Ireland's Wicklow Mountains away west of it, and all the redolent peaks of Wales were like glittering beads strung on the horizon in a great lunula around a north-easterly quadrant.

If heaven were ever to take a physical form, these hills of Wales would be an apt model for it.

Suggestions for further reading

George Borrow, *Wild Wales* (1862). Gomer Press published a fine edition in 1995, with an introduction by William Condry.

Keith Bowen. *Snowdon Shepherd* (Pavilion, 1991)

Jim Perrin (ed.), *A William Condry Reader* (Gomer, 2015).

John Davies, *A History of Wales* (Penguin, 1994).

Anthony Griffiths, *Elenydd: Ancient Heartland of the Cambrian Mountains* (Gwasg Carreg Gwalch, 2010).

Dewi Jones, *The Botanists and Mountain Guides of Snowdonia* (2nd Edition, Gwasg Carreg Gwalch, 2007).

R. Merfyn Jones, *The North Wales Quarrymen 1874-1922* (University of Wales Press, 1982).

The Mabinogion (Gwyn Jones' and Thomas Jones's translation of 1948, published by Everyman in 1949, is still the one that best reflects the landscapes in which these medieval stories take place).

Patrick Monkhouse, *On Foot in North Wales* (Alexander Maclehose, 1932).

Jan Morris, *The Matter of Wales: Epic Views of a Small Country* (Oxford, 1984)

T.H. Parry-Williams, *Detholiad o Gerddi* (Gomer, 1972)

Rob Piercy, *Mynyddoedd Eryri* (Gwasg Carreg Gwalch, 2008)

Ioan Bowen Rees (ed.), *The Mountains of Wales* (2nd edition, University of Wales Press, 1992).

The relevant volumes in the Welsh language series *Crwydro*, published in the 1960s and 1960s by Christopher Davies, Llandybie, are of a uniformly high standard, and invaluable.

For a more comprehensive list, see the bibliography in my *Snowdon: The Story of a Welsh Mountain* (Gomer, 2012).

*'For the whole of my outdoor life I've been under
the spell cast by this most beautiful and redolent of
British hills.'*

The life story of the British mainland's finest mountain is an
enchantment, parcelled in Jim Perrin's ribboned prose.

Possibly no other mountain has more story attached to it than Yr
Wyddfa, Snowdon. You can approach it from a surprising number of
directions: from the secrets within its fractured rocks, its shy flora, its
folk tales echoing an older race and its beliefs. Stone and hut circles,
forts and cairns, travellers' chronicles, industry, sport and an anthology
of literature – in two languages – work on one's mind, gradually revealing
the mountain's essence

ISBN 978 1 84323 574 3

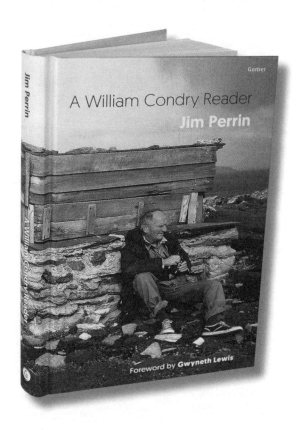

'As time passes I become ever more convinced that it is in the wild places that we have the best hope of finding such little sanity as survives in the world.'

So wrote William Condry, the pre-eminent writer on the natural history of Wales, whose Country Diary appeared in *The Guardian* for over forty years and whose influence on the present generation of nature writers continues to be felt. One of those is Jim Perrin, and this volume is his selection of some of William Condry's best published work, reminding us of the attentiveness, appreciation and concern for the land which underpinned so much of Condry's work in the field, its focus local and its perspective universal. A modest and affable man, he was, as Perrin concludes in his illuminating introduction, one of the twentieth-century masters of nature writing.

ISBN 978 1 84851 883 4